Praise for *Preserving the* Public *in Public Schools*

"Boyle and Burns have written a cogent and compelling book that takes us back to first principles. In a time when the education debate is reduced to student performance on standardized tests, they provide a powerful reminder of the broader public purpose of education—to preserve our democratic republic."

—**Richard D. Kahlenberg**, senior fellow, The Century Foundation, and author of *All Together Now: Creating Middle Class-Schools through Public School Choice*

"Boyle and Burns push us to a new level of thinking about our public schools and, more specifically, about public school governance. This is a must-read for all who truly care about the future of public education."

—**Paul Krohne**, executive director, South Carolina School Boards Association

"Our members believe strongly that public education is essential for a free, self-governing society and that local governance is vital for effective, efficient, and innovative public education. We have benefited from using the principles for solving policy problems and making policy choices described in this book."

—**Wayne Lueders, Ph.D.**, executive director, Associated School Boards of South Dakota

"It turns out there is a public for public schools and it's all of us. Boyle and Burns justify the continued existence of public education and provide the solution for restoring its essential purpose."

—**Mark C. Metzger**, past president, Illinois Association of School Boards, and former member, National School Boards Association board of directors

"This book is an urgently needed reminder of why we have public schools in this country and why our conversations at the board table are more important than we realize."

—**William P. Nemir**, director, leadership team services,
Texas Association of School Boards

"*Preserving the* Public *in Public Schools* addresses the complex choices that must be made concerning education in America today. It presents to educational decision-makers—who include legislators, school board members, and voters—a framework of values to guide them in their analyses and choices. Exploring how liberty, community, equality, and prosperity are intertwined in educational policy decisions, the authors challenge decision-makers to see beyond the need for students who can read, write, and compute, to the need for citizens and community members who can actively and intelligently participate in our messy but wonderful democracy."

—**Jane Wettach**, education law professor,
Duke University Law School

"This book provoked me to think about the cross-currents shaping public education. Few things are as important as preparing the next generation for the future."

—**Stan Norwalk**, member,
Wake County board of commissioners,
North Carolina

Preserving the *Public* in Public Schools

Preserving the *Public* in Public Schools

Visions, Values, Conflicts and Choices

Phil Boyle and Del Burns

ROWMAN & LITTLEFIELD EDUCATION
A division of
ROWMAN & LITTLEFIELD PUBLISHERS, INC.
Lanham • New York • Toronto • Plymouth, UK

Published by Rowman & Littlefield Education
A division of Rowman & Littlefield Publishers, Inc.
A wholly owned subsidiary of The Rowman & Littlefield Publishing Group, Inc.
4501 Forbes Boulevard, Suite 200, Lanham, Maryland 20706
http://www.rowmaneducation.com

Estover Road, Plymouth PL6 7PY, United Kingdom

British Library Cataloguing in Publication Information Available

Library of Congress Cataloging-in-Publication Data

Boyle, Phil, 1953–
Preserving the public in public schools : visions, values, conflicts, and choices / Phil Boyle and Del Burns.
p. cm.
ISBN 978-1-61048-542-5 (cloth: alk paper) — ISBN 978-1-61048-543-2 (pbk: alk. paper) — ISBN 978-1-61048-544-9 (electronic)
1. Public schools—United States. 2. Education—Aims and objectives—United States. I. Burns, Del, 1935– II. Title.
LA217.2.B695 2011
371.010973—dc23 2011023705

™ The paper used in this publication meets the minimum requirements of American National Standard for Information Sciences—Permanence of Paper for Printed Library Materials, ANSI/NISO Z39.48-1992.

Printed in the United States of America

Dedication

Dedicated with love to our wives and best friends: from Del Burns to Vickie Morgan Burns, for her unwavering faith, her enthusiastic encouragement and support, and her limitless patience, extending not only to the work of writing this book but to our entire family; and from Phil Boyle to Scottie Seawell, without whose unremitting encouragement this book would not have been written, and whose good judgment and gentle way through this world evidences itself daily in our three daughters, Erin, Rachel and Lauren.

Contents

Acknowledgments

We'd like to thank the following people for their review and comments on drafts of this book: Ramey Beavers, Maurice Boswell, Jackie Cole, Fenwick English, Christopher Gergen, Grant Godwin, Alan Gottlieb, Dorothy Graham, Richard Kahlenberg, Paul Krohne, Tom Koerner, Wayne Lueders, Catherine McCoy, Tom McCoy, Mark Metzger, William P. Nemir, Stan Norwalk, Susan Parry, Diane Ravitch, Lawrence Rouse, Richard Schwartz, Buie Seawell, Terrell Tracy, Karen Weeks, Jane Wettach, and Jonibel Willis.

Preface

What's *public* about public schools? What is *public* about public education other than its funding? For what purpose, and towards what ends, do we invest in educating the next generation of Americans? Let us state our thesis quite bluntly. We procreate for a variety of reasons, but ultimately to preserve the human race. Similarly, we educate children for a number of reasons, but ultimately to preserve our democratic republic.

We welcome you to this exploration of the *public* in public schools with three statements so outrageous and preposterous that you might be tempted to put this book down right now. But don't! Because you won't find out what those statements are. And when you do find out, you'll want to read more. Because if even the slightest part of these statements is true, your future and the future of every citizen, every community and of the republic itself may depend on what you do after reading this book. In the spirit of Socrates, we don't ask you to agree, and we don't expect to teach you or persuade you. But we do expect you to think.

Statement #1: Public schools have little to do with children. Public schools are political and ideological institutions in which each generation of adults battles among itself for supremacy in determining the purposes, goals and direction of public education. The *public* in public schools is many things, but to help us get started, it's about four big things.

First, it's about how we preserve liberty, personal freedom and individual differences yet still maintain a *United* States of America. Second, it's about how we forge a sense of "we" and of connection and belonging in a nation of individuals predicated on the principle of self-interest. Third, it's about how we grapple with issues of justice, fairness and equality in a nation less homogenous than any other. And fourth, it's about the role we expect a market economy to play in our lives, an economy central to the nation's founding as a commercial republic.

When asked why they ran for election, the vast majority of school board members reply that "it's about the children." Children are seldom considered during these battles, and rarely invited. Consider for a moment the school board that rejects a student request for a non-voting student representative on the board. If public education is truly " about the children," why are students routinely excluded from being part of policy discussions and decisions? And what group of children do you know who would debate the merits of recess?

Statement #2: There are no new arguments or solutions in the battles over the direction and future of public schools. Generations, technology, and politicians change, but the arguments about public education do not. These arguments are as old as our republic. They have been articulated in the words and writings of the founders and framers. From battles over school lunch to school dress to school prayer, each generation reinterprets and recapitulates the political and ideological arguments that date back to the founding of our nation.

Nor are there any permanent solutions. More than two centuries after the American Revolution, public schools continue to serve as political battlefields for debates about religious freedom and whether students should be allowed to wear U.S. flag t-shirts. Everyone knows the right answers, but few of us stop to ask why we are still having such arguments.

Statement #3: The governing processes we use to decide how to educate the next generation, what to teach them, how to distribute educational opportunity, who should go to school where and with whom, and how to pay for public schools reflect the social, political, and economic character of America. The sheer volume of school reform efforts over the past century should have produced more tangible results, something both supporters and critics of public schools can agree upon.[1] But trying to change schools is really about trying to change America, a process which the Founders made very difficult on purpose.

As a short-term, results-oriented people, American governance—public, corporate and non-profit—is constantly seeking the quick fix, the magic bullet, the one-size-fits all solution that will solve our problems once and for all. We will never stop searching for our version of the Holy Grail. But we won't find it, either.

What is this book about? Every society educates its children. But why, how, and towards what ends? Why, in educating children, do public schools give rise to so many controversial issues? What is it that drives our common purpose in educating children and at the same time divides us so passionately about how to educate them? This book is about the purposes of public schools, the competing visions of public education, and the values of the public good that comprise the *public* in public schools.

This is not a book about what's wrong with public education, how to reform public schools, how to restructure classrooms, how to improve teaching, or how best to teach children. There is no shortage of such books, each offering the one right prescription for what ails America's public schools. Our purpose is not to offer one right answer, but rather to help identify the right questions that will preserve public schools.

We invite you to join us in exploring the *public* in public schools; the issues and choices facing parents, communities and public school leaders; why so many choices in public schools are political rather than technical or educational; who should govern public schools; how school boards, administrators, educators, and citizens can resolve difficult choices in public schools; and what's at stake for every American in preserving the public in public schools.

Why write a book about the public in public schools when there is such strong popular and political sentiment that we should get on with the business of fixing public schools? Our answer is simple. Because as even ardent reformers acknowledge, public schools are about more than just curriculum, teaching methods, and testing. "What interests should education serve? What is public in public education other than its funding? If education does not serve a community of interests beyond the economic interests of the individual, is the common good defined as the aggregation of individual interests?"[2]

These are philosophical questions. They require reflection, an act that does not come easily to us as a people. As Alexis de Tocqueville noted in the early 1830s, Americans seemed to pay less attention to philosophy than in any other country of the civilized world.[3] Philosophy may not be our favorite pursuit, but as founder George Mason wrote, "No free government, nor the blessings of liberty, can be reserved to any people, but by...a frequent recurrence to fundamental principles."[4]

Tocqueville observed that the knowledge Americans seemed to value most was knowledge that was practical and useful. To this day we are fond of saying things like "get to the point, cut to the chase, to make a long story short, and what's the bottom line?" While admiring our practical nature, Tocqueville cautioned us against confining ourselves to practice, lest we lose sight of basic principles. Should we forget these principles, he warned, ". . . we may apply the methods derived from them badly. We might be left without the capacity to invent new methods, and only able to make a clumsy and an unintelligent use of wise procedures no longer understood."[5]

To avoid this dilemma, Tocqueville suggested that we ". . . keep people interested in theory. . . ," and that "They will look after the practical side of things for themselves."[6] We have tried to follow Tocqueville's advice and focus on the theory and principles underlying the *public* in public schools. We trust you, our fellow citizens, to look after the practical implications yourselves.

We have organized this book into five parts. Part I explores the fundamental question of what's *public* about public schools? We begin with a prologue in the form of a visit to Crestwich, a fictional school district. Last fall, citizens, interest groups and political parties prepared for a school board election that would garner national attention and serve as a referendum on the district's policy direction during the past quarter-century. Following this prologue we step back from Crestwich to explore the broader meaning of *public*, the normative or value-based questions the meaning of *public* suggests, how this *public* has become lost or diminished in public schools, and how we might rediscover it.

Part II explores the visions and values of public education in our democratic republic. Chapter 1 explores how the value of liberty helped shape the origins of public schools, and how liberty and its many dimensions and meanings are represented in public education and public schools today. Chapter 2 looks at how public schools acquired a socialization role, and how today's public schools are asked to satisfy the value of community. Chapter 3 looks at the role of public schools in helping realize the egalitarian promise of the American Revolution. Chapter 4 looks at ways we have used public education to address challenges of economic prosperity, and how schools are asked to mediate the interests of markets and the public good. These are parallel chapters, each looking at public schools through a different value lens.

Part III explores how these visions and values have shaped our fictional Crestwich Public School District, focusing on three big issues. In Chapter 5 we look at efforts in Crestwich to provide educational opportunity to school-age children, to distribute educational opportunity equitably, and to level the social and economic playing field of public schools. Themes such as merger, magnet programs, integration and desegregation play a prominent role.

In Chapter 6 we explore who goes to school where, with whom, and why. We look at efforts to assign students to classrooms efficiently, to use school facilities cost-effectively, and to create communities of students within each school that represent the social, economic, racial and ethnic diversity of the community. Themes such as student assignment, parental choice, reassignment, transfers, stability, and socioeconomic balance play a prominent role.

In Chapter 7 we look at taxation and funding, the relationship between Crestwich public schools and other units of local government, factors that influence whether the public sees public schools as a cost or as an investment, and some of the ways in which the school system pursued greater economy and efficiency. Themes such as taxation, spending, cost-cutting, audits, return-on-investment and running schools more like a business play a prominent role.

Part IV examines the context of public leadership in public schools and the governance challenges involved in preserving the public. Chapter 8 explores the kinds of policy problems that public values give rise to in public schools, and the choices these create for citizens, students, parents and public school leaders. Chapter 9 explores how public school leaders can use these values to create a shared understanding of policy problems with the public and craft solutions from among competing choices consistent with democratic principles. Chapter 10 explores contemporary challenges to school board governance, the timeless question of "who shall rule?" as it applies to public schools, and the role of elected boards of education in a democratic society.

Part V brings us full circle to the *public* in public schools. We explore what a vision of public education for the public good might look like. We identify principles for preserving the public in public schools. Whether we choose to preserve this public, and how we preserve it matters. As Abraham Lincoln observed, "The philosophy of the school room in one generation will be the philosophy of government in the next." We end the book by revisiting Crestwich to see what changes have occurred and to suggest what the future holds for preserving the public in Crestwich Public Schools and throughout the nation.[7]

This book is intended for several audiences. It is for school boards and administrators who share responsibility for governing public schools. It is for new board members who may have received a great deal of information and training on what boards can and cannot do, but less on why boards exist and their purpose. It is for experienced board members who understand that differences and conflict are an integral part of board life, but would like a better way to express conflict and address these differences. It is for school administrators who appreciate and support representative democracy with its system of shared power between elected and appointed officials, and who want to help their boards govern rather than manage.

It is for public school leaders and professionals and their associations—principals, teachers, schools of education, principal and superintendent associations, professional development programs, school board associations, university programs in public administration and public policy, and university-based and independent institutes and centers—who are interested in the relationship between democratic ideals and public schools, in improving governance education for public school officials, in better understanding the normative context of public school governance, and in understanding the broader role of public values in representative democracy.

And it is for the community at-large—citizens, parents, PTAs, school study circle programs, school governance committees, chambers of commerce, community associations, faith-based institutions and civic groups—who are concerned about the health and vitality of public schools in their communities.

In sum, this book is for anyone involved in or affected by public schools and public education. It is for anyone who is interested and willing to take time out from the manic rush to reform public schools and reflect for a moment on the purposes, goals and aspirations of public schools. We believe that these purposes, goals and aspirations are at the core of not only public schools, but also at the core of ourselves as a people and as a republic. Education is a progressive discovery of our own ignorance, remarked historian Will Durant. And in that process of discovery, of enlightenment, there can be only participants.[8] If you agree, this book is for you.

NOTES

1. Ravitch, D. (2000). *Left behind: A century of failed school reforms.* New York, NY: Simon and Schuster.
2. Education Commission of the States. (1999c, p. vii). *The invisible hand of ideology: Perspectives from the history of school governance.* Denver, CO: Author.
3. Tocqueville, A. de. (1969.) *Democracy in America.* Mayer, J. P. (Ed.), and Lawrence, G. (Trans.). New York, NY: HarperPerennial. (Original work published 1835).
4. George Mason in 1776.
5. Tocqueville, p. 464.
6. Ibid., p. 464.
7. While the Crestwich school district is fictional, all of the issues, choices and policy dilemmas described in this book are real. If any part of this book bears resemblance to your school district, the resemblance is completely intentional.
8. Jurgen Habermas.

Part I

What's *Public* about Public Schools?

As a nation, we invest heavily in public education. According to the National Center for Education Statistics, in 2008 we spent an estimated $584 billion to educate 49 million K-12 students, an average of nearly $12,000 per child.[1] Given such a massive public investment, its reasonable to think we are quite clear about our goals for public education and our reasons for investing public dollars in public schools. We are not. If we were, public school supporters and reformers would not disagree so vehemently about whether the public education glass is half-empty or half-full.[2]

This lack of consensus makes policy discussions about public schools often difficult, proposed policy solutions often contentious and political elections for local school boards often acrimonious. Consider the titles of this briefest of samples of recent publications about public schools and public education: *The Battle Over School Prayer; Left Back: A Century of Battles Over School Reform; Voucher Wars: Waging the Legal Battle Over School Choice; The War for Children's Minds, and The Evolution Wars.*[3]

These publications reflect more than just a lack of consensus. They reflect fundamental differences in American society that are rooted in deeply-held beliefs linked to the religious, ideological, and world views we hold. If democracy has become America's public religion, the public school, according to philosopher and social critic Ivan Illich, has become the established church of secular society. Conflicts over the primacy of each core policy value are America's version of a holy war. How else do we explain the prominent use of military metaphors in the titles mentioned above?

We agree with Abraham Lincoln when he said, "Upon the subject of education, not presuming to dictate any plan or system respecting it, I can only say that I view it as the most important subject which we as a people may be engaged in." Along with Lincoln, we also cannot say which is the most important goal of American public education. There are multiple goals, and at any given time, some people perceive some goals as more important than others.

For some it may be student achievement. For some, it may be ensuring equal educational opportunity. And for some, it may be developing responsible citizens and adults. For others it may be developing a competitive work force. And for still others, it may be ensuring social and moral order. We can say that in public schools, all of these goals matter, all of the time, although not every goal matters equally all of the time.

We suggest, however, that while these are all goals of public schooling, they are also means to a much larger goal and to a much broader purpose of public education. That broader goal and purpose is to preserve our pursuit of the good life that is only possible in a democratic republic. "Educate and inform the whole mass of the people," Thomas Jefferson wrote to James Madison in 1787. "Enable them to see that it is their interest to preserve peace and order, and they will preserve them. And it requires no very high degree of education to convince them of this. They are the only sure reliance for the preservation of our liberty." In this context, the most important purpose of public education is to preserve and perpetuate our democratic republic within which all of these other goals are possible.

Public schools carry out a public role in socializing children into society, for preparing the next generation to take their place as Americans in what is today the oldest republic in the world. All other socialization is a private responsibility – carried out by and through parents, families, and sacred and community institutions. Public schools serve as the public institution by which we transmit our collective knowledge and shared values of the good life to each succeeding generation.

If we are serious about tasking public schools with such a purpose, then we must be willing to engage in an equally serious conversation about the meaning of 'public' and the public purposes of public schools. In this part we explore the meaning of *public,* first within our fictional school district of Crestwich, and then within our larger national context. We recognize that it's not easy for many Americans to have this conversation. "The fact is that Americans are not a thoughtful people; they are too busy to stop and question their values."[3] All the more reason to proceed.

NOTES

1. National Center for Education Statistics. (2009). *Revenues and expenditures for public elementary and secondary education: School year 2007–08.* Washington, DC: U.S. Department of Education.

2. Dierenfield, B. J. (2007). *The battle over school prayer.* Lawrence, KS: University Press of Kansas; Ravitch, D. (2000). *Left back: A century of battles over school reform.* New York, NY: Touchstone; Bolick, C. (2003). *Voucher wars: Waging the legal battle over school choice.* Washington, DC: Cato Institute; Law, S. (2007). *The war for children's minds.* New York, NY: Routledge; Wallis, C. (2005). *The evolution wars.* TIME, August 7. Retrieved Oct. 25, 2010 from http://www.time.com/time/magazine/article/0,9171,1090909,00.html.

3. *Newsweek* (2010). "The key to saving American education." March 15.

4. William Ralph Inge.

Prologue

Crestwich Faces a Public Test

A standing room only crowd gathered for the nine-member Crestwich Board of Education's first meeting since the fall election. Supporters of four newly-elected members of the board filled the room and spilled into the hallway. The election campaign had pitted supporters of a district-wide policy promoting socioeconomic diversity in all schools against supporters of a return to neighborhood schools. The swearing-in ceremony marked the beginning of a new era in the history of the Crestwich Public School System. Thomas Jefferson's declaration "That government is the strongest of which every man feels himself a part" would soon be tested.

The four board members-elect were seated in the audience, awaiting their turn to come to the dais to take the oath of office required as the last official step before beginning their service as a member of the board of education. Seated at the board table for the last time were four outgoing board members who were about to be replaced. Three of these members had served a single four-year term, while the fourth had served two terms. Only one of the four had chosen to run for re-election—and was defeated.

One by one the board members-elect were called forward. Each stood in front of a judge selected to administer the oath of office. Each placed a hand on a Bible, and solemnly repeated the oath they swore to uphold. In turn, each outgoing board member left the table, shook the hand of their replacement and took a seat in the audience, no longer members of the board of education. Each new board member marked this occasion by speaking to the audience. When finished speaking, each new member took their seat at the board table.

Their inaugural speeches were heartfelt. They thanked family and friends, supporters, God, Jesus Christ, and the political action committees and political party that had endorsed their candidacies and supported their campaigns financially. This swearing-in ceremony illustrated, in both subtle and not so subtle ways, that not only had four new board members taken office, but a different board of education had come to power in Crestwich.

THE UNDERSEA EARTHQUAKE OCCURS

The board chair welcomed the new board members and challenged them to serve in the best interest of all of the children in the Crestwich Public School System. The chair then called a recess, signaling the conclusion of the swearing-in ceremony and the start of a reception honoring the new board members.

Hundreds of supporters had arrived to see and hear the swearing-in ceremony. Many had never been in the board room before. Now they had the opportunity to congratulate those members they had helped to elect and to talk with fellow supporters. Elected officials, political party leaders, parents, citizens, business leaders, district staff and representatives from television, radio, and print media formed the largest crowd in recent memory to witness a board of education meeting.

Everyone in attendance realized that the four new members joined the now-longest serving member of the nine-member board to form a new five-member majority. Most everyone in attendance anticipated that the new majority would use this first meeting to plant its flag in the boardroom. But few of those in attendance—not the chair, not the four minority board members, not the superintendent, not the staff and certainly not the public at large—had any inkling that the swearing-in ceremony and reception were only a prelude to a seismic shift about to unfold when the board meeting resumed.

Some tension around the board table, to be expected with so many new members, was palpable as the meeting resumed. The meeting progressed first with routine comments by the chair and the superintendent and followed by what appeared to observers as routine board business. The board's code of ethics was distributed and signed by all members, in accord with a recently adopted board policy. Because one of the departing board members had served as vice-chair, the printed board agenda included the election of a new vice-chair. A newly-elected member was nominated and quickly elected, foreshadowing events to come.

Never suspecting the tsunami of change about to sweep over the board, following the completion of routine business the board chair called for approval of the meeting agenda. The first wave of change would culminate with being ousted as chair.

The formerly lone minority member of the board, now the de facto leader of the majority, made a motion to amend the agenda. The motion proposed adding eight items to the agenda, listed in priority order, and to precede all other agenda items. All public comment would be delayed until after board action was taken on all eight new items. None of the items was listed on the public agenda distributed prior to the meeting, and no materials were provided in advance to the board, staff or public.

The newly-introduced agenda items were not surprising in themselves, as adamant criticism of the previous board and its policies dominated the election campaign. Nonetheless, the speed with which they were announced and the manner in which the new majority took control shocked many in the audience. The new items listed on the amended agenda were:

- Election of a new chair of the board of education.
- A resolution to appoint an interim special legal counsel.
- A motion to change the district's student assignment policy.
- A resolution to ensure parental choice for students attending year-round schools.
- A resolution to end all efforts and expenditures on a site selected for a new high school by the previous board and to seek an alternate site.
- A resolution to immediately reduce system-wide spending and costs.
- A resolution to end early release Wednesdays that had been approved by the previous board to aid teacher planning and coordination.
- A motion to schedule a new regular board meeting in two weeks.

Under existing board policy, meetings for the purpose of electing board officers were typically held at the last regular board meeting each June. But with the newly-elected majority in control, the four former majority board members had little choice but to watch as a motion was made, seconded and approved 5-4 to elect a new board chair.

Following the rules of order, the gavel was passed to the superintendent to preside over this special meeting. In a swift, second 5-4 vote, the current board chair was replaced by the senior member of the new majority. When the gavel was handed to the new chair, the seven remaining new items were added to the agenda and presented one by one by a new board member. Each of the seven motions and resolutions was adopted by a 5-4 vote.

The audience soon realized that this was more than the planting of a new majority flag. In a matter of mere moments, the new board had ousted the chair, swept away a policy of socioeconomic balance that had been nurtured by board members and district staff for over three decades, and made good on several campaign promises. What had led to this tsunami of change?

WATER RECEDES FROM THE SHORE

All nine seats on the Crestwich board of education are elected by district. With no at-large seats, citizens may vote only for a candidate from their district. During this most recent election cycle, a bloc of four candidates emerged, with each of the candidates running together on a single platform. Several other candidates, campaigning individually, also filed for a board of education seat. The bloc of four received funding and endorsements from political action committees. Though board of education elections are officially non-partisan, a major political party provided endorsements and financial support to the bloc of four.

Technically independent, the political action committees supporting the four-member bloc leaned toward the same political party. In addition to PAC and party support, several prominent wealthy individuals with similar ties also provided endorsements and financial support. Unified in their opposition to having more students reassigned and bused to new, different schools, a concerted effort was undertaken to find, encourage and promote candidates backing a 'local school' option. For practical purposes, the school board election had become a partisan campaign.

Campaigning began in earnest after Labor Day and quickly picked up steam. The bloc of four employed a consistent message opposing the "status quo," as they referred to the actions of the previous board. Their loudest message, and the one that received the greatest media attention, was a call for a system-wide move to neighborhood or community schools, and away from the existing policy of student assignment adopted to achieve, among other goals, socioeconomic diversity in each of the district's schools.

In an off-year election, voter turnout was even lower than predicted. And with only four of the nine districts involved in the election, many voters were unable to weigh in on the change in direction at stake in this election. The four new board members were elected by seven percent of the total registered voters in their four districts. "The tyranny of a prince is not so dangerous to the public welfare as the apathy of a citizen in a democracy" wrote Montesquieu.

Touting the majority of votes they received from a minority of voters, each newly-elected member declared they had won a mandate from the people. Like water receding from the shore, the first signs of the imminent arrival of the tsunami were revealed.

A TSUNAMI OF CHANGE ARRIVES

Earthquakes occurring under the sea generate tsunamis. Geologists tell us that pressures over time result in the sudden shift of tectonic plates, causing earthquakes. Sometimes there are multiple shifts along fault lines, and sometimes one shift causes a shift somewhere else. Giant waves are created, causing water to recede from the shore as the wave approaches. This certain indicator that a tsunami will soon arrive is also a sign that it's too late. The seismic event has already occurred. The wave just keeps rolling, sweeping away all in its path, until its energy is depleted.

Pressures leading to the outcome of the election had built up over time. During the preceding decade, growth in Crestwich occurred at a breakneck pace. In some recent years, Crestwich added nearly 100 new residents each day, and two entire classes of kindergarten students were born each day.

Political responses to this growth were counter-intuitive. The property tax rate was reduced which also reduced the available capital and operating funding for the school system. A bond referendum proposed to address school construction needs failed. A subsequent scaled-back bond referendum did pass the following year, but district funding and school construction continued to lag behind student growth. Even though some new schools were built, seats were often scarce. The district was forced to reassign students to use existing seats efficiently.

Because of its visible effects, strategies for addressing growth dominated much of the district's attention. But the board of education and district staff struggled to meet other challenges as well, including maintaining educational quality, reducing teacher turnover, maintaining high parental satisfaction with schools and creating safer and more attractive school environments. The district expanded magnet programs to protect diversity and draw students from more to less crowded schools. It implemented some use of a multi-track year-round calendar to increase student capacity. Ironically, the magnet program became so successful that demand for seats in highly desirable magnet schools outstripped the available supply.

Even though only a small percentage of reassignments were made to maintain socioeconomically diverse school populations, the message about why students were being reassigned got lost among the media attention paid to projections of how many new students the district would add each year, who would be reassigned and how.

Compounded by growth, student reassignment became increasingly contentious. Parents, neighborhoods and whole communities became increasingly frustrated with too-frequent reassignments, prompting calls for more stability and less disruption. Parental choice and neighborhood schools became rallying cries in response to the inconvenience of reassignment, much of which was perceived to result from busing for diversity.

With the population of many individual schools and of the district as a whole in a state of flux, the board adopted and strengthened policies to buffer families from the consequences of constant change. The board limited the frequency of reassignments, adopted grandfathering privileges for students at existing schools, increased public access to student enrollment data and publicized plans designed to implement less frequent reassignments.

Mere months before the school board election, the board of education implemented early student release on Wednesdays to provide teachers with additional planning and collaboration time to address student learning needs. Adopted by the board with the best of intentions as a strategy to improve instruction in the face of inadequate funding, it became the proverbial straw that broke the camel's back.

These measures, designed as positive responses to significant change and disruption, became disruptive in their own right. The board was portrayed as out of touch with its constituents. Public dissatisfaction with the governance of Crestwich Public Schools began to grow and mushroomed in the media. As Thomas Jefferson observed, "When the government fears the people there is liberty, but when the people fear the government there is tyranny." The tectonic plates began to shift. The inevitable earthquake occurred, the water receded from the shore and the tsunami arrived.

The passions that surfaced during the campaign did not subside after the election, but instead became more inflamed. Protests, arrests at public hearings and demonstrations marked the early meetings of the new board. What, some residents of Crestwich began to wonder, do people want from their public schools? "What the people want," U.S. Representative Barbara Jordan once remarked, "is very simple. They want an America as good as its promise."

What might we learn from this election about public schools that is relevant beyond the boundaries of Crestwich? As in every election, there were winners and losers. But what about the community as a whole? Determining winners and losers in Crestwich would not be as simple as determining who won the election. Looking at Crestwich as a microcosm of America, what might we discover about the role and importance of public schools in our democratic republic? To answer these and other questions, we invite you to join us in an exploration of the *public* in public schools.

Introduction

The *Public* in Public Schools

Residents of Crestwich disagree whether their public schools glass is half-empty or half-full. Some like the direction taken during the past quarter century. Some like the overall direction, but would like to see some course corrections. Others oppose the direction altogether, and want nothing less than a complete reversal.

Supporters of district-wide student assignment recite a narrative of progress made by the school system. Supporters of greater parental choice and neighborhood schools recite a narrative of lack of progress made by the school system. How can the same school system be seen as making progress and as not making progress at the very same time? Why are supporters and opponents of the current policy direction so passionate about their respective narratives? What can these conflicting perceptions tell us about the *public* in Crestwich public schools?

The world of public policy, writes Deborah Stone, is a world of stories. Public policy stories are often characterized by two broad story lines, one of progress and the other one of decline.[1]

One story of public school progress goes like this. Taken as a whole, the news about public education is largely good news. Most parents, while skeptical of public education in general, look quite favorably on the public schools their children attend. A little more than a decade ago, a federal government analysis showing that the state of American public education was considerably less gloomy than the prevailing national rhetoric was not released because administration officials viewed it as "dead wrong."[2]

Those who recite a story of progress point out that we are educating more citizens and educating them more than at any time in our nation's history. By any measure, the current adult population is the most highly educated generation of Americans ever. Author and journalist Nicholas Lemann recited a story of progress during the making of *School: The Story of American Public Education.* "I am not excusing problems. I am not saying 'please don't evaluate public education.' But I think that the honest starting premise has to be that, on the whole, public education has been a big success in America. We have more people under the roofs of public schools learning than any of the advanced industrial democracies."[3]

The story of decline dates back a half century to *Sputnik*. Sometime in the past generation or so, probably because of the 1960s, the educational system began to fall apart under a siege of social promotion, loss of discipline, grade inflation, multicultural education and social engineering resulting in an inefficient, out-of-control government-run monopoly that wastes huge amounts of money and has allowed foreign countries to leave America behind.[4] Governed by career bureaucrats and local politicians who do not understand that their foremost goal is student achievement, public schools are doing a poor job of preparing students for global economic competition.

In this story of decline, public schools are neither responsive nor accountable to the public. Local boards of education (and unions, in states that permit collective bargaining) are to blame for much of what is wrong with public schools and should go the way of the one-room schoolhouse. To stem and reverse this decline, public schools should be managed more like a business. They should spend less time addressing wasteful social issues such as student assignment and spend more time preparing students for economic success.

DECLINING PUBLIC SCHOOLS OR A DECLINING PUBLIC?

Rather than debating the supremacy of either of these stories, we suggest that it's likely that there are elements of truth in both. How can this be? Public education is a paradox. Education is both a means to an end and an end in itself. The content of education is both positive or fact-based and normative or belief-based. Public school issues are technical, involving questions that we need experts—legal, administrative, and scientific—to answer. But they are also political, involving questions that only citizens can answer.

Generally speaking, Americans are uncomfortable with paradox, with the notion that something can be two different things at once, or that two contradictory interpretations can both be true.[5] Yet, political life is full of them.

We pay much more attention to enhancing children's performance within the classroom than we do to enhancing their lives outside. Surely we know that both are important. We readily criticize public schools for failing to equip students with critical thinking skills and then demonstrate precisely the lack of those skills in supporting candidates who offer us simplistic solutions to complex problems. The idea of a flat tax, for example, is appealing precisely because it's simple. It's only when we stop to think about the consequences do we realize it's not so simple after all. "What the American public doesn't know," says a character in the movie *Tommy Boy,* "is what makes them the American public."

As our Crestwich story suggests, public schools face many challenges. Many of these reside within the classroom. Developing appropriate curricula, preparing teachers, selecting and organizing what to teach in a world where information and knowledge expand exponentially, deciding what constitutes appropriate student progress, and developing valid and reliable means of evaluating student learning are no small tasks.

The public cannot address these challenges directly. We require experts to frame solutions, and citizens to weigh in on how well these solutions meet our values. For example, learning and curriculum specialists can design a state-of-the-art program of homework for fifth grade students. But parents, as citizens, must decide how to weigh the good they expect from homework with the good they expect from family, leisure and employment opportunities.

This is the essential democratic task of the public in relation to public schools—to decide how much of the public good public schools should address. This was the key question in Crestwich's election test. The election ballots offered solutions represented by Candidate A or Candidate B. But the question citizens were being asked to decide, even though it wasn't printed on their ballots, was to what degree individual families and neighborhoods should be responsible for their children's education compared to what degree all families and neighborhoods as represented by the district should be responsible for the education of all children. We know the good, wrote the Greek playwright Euripides, but we do not practice it.

There were two clear results from that test. First, even though the test date and testing centers were announced on television, radio and in all the local newspapers, only a very small proportion of citizens took the test. Second, most of those who did voted to reduce the scope of the public in Crestwich Public Schools by reducing the responsibility of the district and increasing the degree of individual family and neighborhood responsibility.

Our Crestwich example illustrates how in our efforts to make public schools more accountable to the public we have lost sight of the notion that the public should be responsible to public schools and accountable to the ideals that public schools represent. The narrow, technical kind of accountability prevalent in schools today might benefit citizens as taxpayers and as consumers of school services, but not the communities in which schools are located and in which those citizens reside.[6] This may help explain why many Americans report feeling torn between their sense of duty to support public schools and their sense of responsibility to their children.[7] A democratic republic should not force such a choice upon its citizens.

In campaign politics, keeping most voters on the sidelines and mobilizing more supporters for change than for the status quo is a strategy for electoral victory. Consequently, Crestwich has a different board of education. But is the community as a whole better off, or just different?

We can get to the good we seek by asking questions. In Crestwich, the question in front of the public is how should the district balance the collective responsibility for educating all children with the rights and responsibilities of individual families and neighborhoods for educating their children? It's not a very big leap to conclude that most citizens would answer that the district should keep some elements of its current policy of being responsible for the education of all children and adopt the best of the new policy for increasing individual family and neighborhood responsibility.

That's not what happened. Instead the new board majority struck the word "diversity" from its policy documents. For all intents and purposes, such a policy never existed. Virtually every public high school student reads a book about a society in which words and history are being constantly revised in accord with the current political philosophy. Fortunately for the residents of Crestwich, that book is only fiction.

The citizens of Crestwich will only create the public schools they want when they reclaim them and take responsibility for them.[8] Having called upon public schools in Crestwich and across the nation to serve as a panacea for nearly every social and economic challenge we face, it should not be surprising that we often scapegoat public schools for much of what we believe ails society. Is it any wonder that the public's support for the *public* in public education is waning?

PUBLIC, REPUBLIC, *RES PUBLICA*

What do we mean by the *public* in public schools? Earlier we provided a brief description of what we mean by the public in public schools. *Res publica,* a Latin phrase, means public thing or public matter. The origin of the word republic, it is often used to refer to the general public good or welfare. To fully understand the public thing in public schools we need to explore the particular American beliefs and ideals upon which public schools were founded.

The essence of what it means to be American is a creed, a set of beliefs, an ideal. As Teddy Roosevelt defined it, "Americanism is a question of principles, of idealism, of character; it is not a matter of birthplace or [religion] or line of descent." Woodrow Wilson deflected criticism of himself as an idealist saying, "Well, that is the way I know I am an American. America is the only idealistic nation in the world." "My favorite thing about the United States? Lots of Americans, one America," remarked Val Saintsbury.

American journalist John Gunther remarked that "Ours is the only country deliberately founded on a good idea." Former U.S. Representative and Speaker of the House James G. Blaine pointed out that "The United States is the only country with a known birthday." Marshall McLuhan, Canadian philosopher and writer on media and communication, observed that "America is the only country ever founded on the printed word." English author G. K. Chesterton observed that "America is the only nation in the world that is founded on a creed . . ."

Sweden's Gunnar Myrdal wrote extensively about this creed in the 1940s, characterizing the emerging civil rights movement as the gradual realization of the American Creed that emphasized ideals of liberty, equality, justice, and fair treatment of all people.[9] Myrdal believed it is these ideals that keep the diverse melting pot of America together, enabling so many different people to co-exist as one nation.

Myrdal was not the only foreign observer to take note of this creed. In the 1930s *The Atlantic Monthly* published a series of articles by the French author Raoul de Roussy de Sales on politics, courtship, and identity in American life. In a 1939 article titled "What Makes an American," he wrote that "To become an American is a process which resembles a conversion. It is not so much a new country that one adopts as a new creed."[10] German political theorist Carl Friedrich put it another way when he wrote in 1935, "To be an American is an ideal, while to be a Frenchman is a fact." Friedrich observed that the French knew who and what they were, but Americans were constantly searching for their identity and reinventing themselves in the process.

Taken together, these beliefs and ideals constitute the American Creed, the American Dream, and our distinctly American view of the good life and the good society. Neither government nor public schools can exist separately from these ideals. And neither can we, who in holding a shared public office known as citizen, constitute the polis, our political community.

While differing on the specifics, political philosophers generally agree that the fundamental purpose of any legitimate government is to help create the good life, the good society.[11] To some American philosophers, the good society is ". . . a widening of democratic participation and the accountability of institutions; an interdependent prosperity . . . that enables everyone to participate in the goods of society."[12] As public administration scholar Dwight Waldo pointed out, anyone who writes political philosophy has an idea of the good life, otherwise he or she would not write political philosophy.[13]

As part of government, public schools are also part of *res publica,* the public thing. Their fundamental purpose is to help create this good life and good society, to help the next generation realize the American Dream, and to do so in accordance with the norms and values of the American Creed.

When we speak of the good life or the good society we are referring to a set of values that reflect what's most important to us as a nation, as a society, and as a people. Political philosophers identify things such as community, efficiency, egalitarianism, equality, fairness, freedom, individualism, justice, liberty, pluralism, responsibilities, rights, safety, security, social equity, utilitarianism and volunteerism.[14] A sampling of these political writers and philosophers reveals a convergence of ideas and concepts, with three fundamental themes emerging.

The first theme addresses the relationship between individual liberty and the interests of the community and the common good. Although in tension with one another, neither liberty nor community is sustainable without the other.[15] Many different and independent organizations and associations, from chambers of commerce to churches, make up the Crestwich school district. A sense of commonality, of community and place, can encourage cooperation among self-reliant individuals and autonomous organizations and institutions.[18]

Concepts of liberty and individuality help us define when and under what circumstances society should have authority over individuals and the limits of that authority.[16] For example, how much authority should a school district have to assign students to schools? And tensions between individual liberty and the common good help us think about how we should balance rights with responsibilities.[17] For example, it's more difficult to exercise our right to a trial by a jury of our peers if our peers are unwilling to serve on a jury.

The second theme addresses the relationship between liberty and equality. In general, greater liberty leads to greater inequality, while efforts to create more equality limit liberty. Therefore no universal balance between the two is possible or desirable.[19] For centuries, societies have used elements of equality such as justice and fairness to protect liberty by countering inequality and discrimination.[20] Justice, a dimension of equality, depends not upon eliminating differences among people but on ensuring that we live in a society free from domination.[21]

The third theme addresses the relationship between economic prosperity and equality. Tensions between these values exist because the political sphere emphasizes equal rights and equal opportunity while the economic sphere creates few rights and produces less equal opportunity.[22] Free markets are fairly effective at creating material well-being and economic prosperity, but less effective in enhancing social justice.[23] However, a just economy can use mechanisms of economic distribution to reduce economic inequality.[24]

Because these are the values of our society, they are also the values of our institutions, including public schools. These values and the tensions between them have much to tell us about the purposes and goals of public schools.

ONE VALUE, TWO VALUES, THREE VALUES, FOUR

These values of the good life, the good society, the American Creed and the American Dream are reflected in our founding documents, such as the Declaration of Independence, the Constitution, and the Bill of Rights. We express these values in a myriad of ways, for example, when we refer to America as the land of opportunity or as the cradle of liberty, and when we pledge "liberty and justice for all." They represent a set of ideals that we share as Americans and define what we mean by the concept of "American." These ideals unite and connect us in ways which no other features of being American can.

For our purposes we have grouped these many elements of the good life and good society into four core values of the public good—liberty, equality, community and prosperity. We call these values *public* values because they arise in the context of our public or political relationships with each other. The definition of politics as the total complex of relations between people in a society is the least used definition of politics but the most important one for our purposes.

Each core public value has multiple dimensions, which give rise to a variety of policy conflicts and choices. Take liberty and freedom, for example. Liberty implies independence, autonomy and separation, while freedom, from an Indo-European root shared with "friend," connotes the right of belonging within a community of free people.[25] We will discuss these values and their relationship to public schools in greater detail in Part II. For now, a brief synopsis of each core value will suffice.

Liberty

Liberty is the value of the individual, of the "I." Liberty is about rights, personal freedom, choice and individuality. Other dimensions of liberty can include independence, access, autonomy, mobility, openness, transparency, voluntary, opportunity, privacy, accountability, personal responsibility, self-determination, self-sufficiency, self-help, and self-rule.

Liberty means being free and able to enjoy social, political, and economic rights and privileges. We express liberty in terms of our support for lower taxes, less government, less regulation, open access to state and national parks, taxpayers' bill of rights, sales tax holidays and property rights.

We often think of rights in terms of the political liberties contained in the Bill of Rights. The First Amendment, for instance, guarantees freedom of speech. This freedom allows citizens to speak publicly without fear of reprisal about laws passed by Congress, new courses required for high school students, and plans to build a new road through an existing neighborhood.

Should individual liberties like freedom of speech be absolute? What happens when individual liberties clash with larger social rights and obligations? The answer lies in understanding that liberty cannot be made absolute without causing harm. As Thomas Jefferson explained, what we should seek is rightful liberty, not absolute liberty. "Rightful liberty," Jefferson wrote, "is unobstructed action, according to our will, within limits drawn around us by the equal rights of others."

Within these limits, liberty should and must be protected, not just for ourselves, but for others also. To Thomas Paine, a loss of liberty by another could easily become our loss as well. Liberty is not just something I enjoy, but something you must enjoy also, or the day may come when I no longer enjoy my liberty. In other words, there is a certain element of equality to be found in our liberty.

Equality

Equality is the value of the group. In order to realize our individual aspirations we sometimes address issues as a group, e.g., equal access, equal rights, and equal opportunity. Theodore Roosevelt expressed the value of equality when he remarked, "This country will not be a good place for any of us to live in unless we make it a good place for all of us to live in." Other dimensions of equality include fairness, justice, tolerance, acceptance, diversity, difference, equity, comparable, equivalent, inclusion, representation, compensation, redistribution, equal treatment, equal results, and a level playing field.

We express the value of equality by offering bilingual public information, applying motorcycle helmet laws to everyone, ensuring gender equity in public facilities and services, and providing equal access to public goods and resources such as parks, schools and courts.

Equality is critical to any society. As Aristotle observed, "The only stable state is the one in which all men are equal before the law." Philosopher Bertrand Russell observed that Americans have a particular sense of equality, in that we admit no superiors, and only begrudgingly acknowledge equals.

Some equality issues are very apparent, such as the equal right to vote. Other equality issues are more subtle, like differences in wealth, health, and how some public policies may affect different groups differently. Being for equality in no way guarantees that we will have equality. "There is all the difference in the world between treating people equally and attempting to make them equal."[26]

Tocqueville supported the former but expressed concerns about the latter, writing that "Americans are so enamored of equality that they would rather be equal in slavery than unequal in freedom." We need only to reflect on George Orwell's *1984*, Aldous Huxley's *Brave New World* or Kurt Vonnegut's "Harrison Bergeron" to see the undesirable consequences of too readily subjugating freedom and individuality to equality.

Most Americans believe that everyone should share some basic equalities, such as access to education and to employment, but such equalities don't always occur naturally. Should public schools, acting on behalf of the public, try to correct inequalities? Which inequalities should schools seek to remedy, what should schools do to achieve greater equality, and how do we decide when equality has been reached? Is equality perceived equality achieved? Not to Langston Hughes who wrote in *The Black Man Speaks*: "I swear to the Lord, I still can't see, Why Democracy means, Everybody but me."

Liberty and equality enjoy a certain tension in their relationship with one another. Greater freedom tends to accentuate inequality, while attempts to create truly equal societies require freedom to be restricted. Historian Will Durant explains this paradox: "Nature smiles at the union of freedom and equality in our utopias. For freedom and equality are sworn and everlasting enemies, and when one prevails the other dies. Leave men free, and their natural inequalities will multiply almost geometrically ... To check the growth of inequality, liberty must be sacrificed."

What can be done about this dilemma? Tocqueville offers this solution. "Democracy and socialism have nothing in common but one word: equality. But notice the difference: while democracy seeks equality in liberty, socialism seeks equality in restraint and servitude." Tocqueville is suggesting that if democracy is based on freedom, we must seek equality through liberty, rather than in lieu of liberty. If Paine and Jefferson suggest there should be a certain equality in our liberty, Tocqueville suggests there should be a certain liberty in our equality.

Community

If liberty is the value of the "I," community is the value of the "we." Community means having a sense of connection and belonging to people and places where we live, work, learn and play. "We cannot live only for ourselves," wrote Herman Melville. "A thousand fibers connect us with our fellow men and women; and among those fibers, as sympathetic threads, our actions run as causes, and they come back to us as effects."

We express community in terms of holidays, traditions, ceremonies and celebrations, in support for public art, in concern for health, safety and quality of life, the appearance of our neighborhoods, and in debates about what should be legal and illegal. We invoke the meaning of community when we consider the boundaries between public and private, such as public displays of religion. And we invoke a sense of "we" when we call for conservation, preservation, and restoration, and when we join together to take collective action on behalf of all of us.

A tension exists between community and our sense of individuality and personal freedom, as we must decide how to balance what is best for the individual with what is best for everyone. "We can take a first, crucial step away from romance about community by recognizing that it is a value in conflict with other values we hold—and that in our decisions, community usually loses out . . . We must begin by recognizing that our verbal homage to community is only one side of a deep ambivalence that runs through the American character—the other side of which is a celebration of unfettered individualism."[27]

Prior to the closing of the American frontier, both individualism and community seemed possible. The settlers of the frontier had to possess both the strength of individuality and the capacity for building community. "They needed to both stand alone and to stand together. And there seemed to be no contradiction between the two."[28] Community and individuality were less conflicting because with so much open space, community was a choice freely made.

We value community for the security and comfort it gives us. Belonging is based on members having a sense of shared values. We should note that community can mean different things in American political thought, sometimes a place or a thing, and other times a calling or a journey.[29] As communities become more diverse, whose values should be the values of the community? How can we develop communities among so many different peoples?

Prosperity

Prosperity is the value of capitalism and utilitarianism. Prosperity maintains a close relationship with liberty, as it values the freedom of the market and of individual actors and decision makers, so-called rational actors, to make their own choices and decisions. As characterized by Ayn Rand, "In a capitalist society, all human relationships are voluntary. Men are free to cooperate or not, to deal with one another or not, as their own individual judgments, convictions and interests dictate."

Other dimensions of prosperity can include economy, efficiency, growth, profit, productivity, return on investment, development, competition, centralization, standardization, specialization, performance measurement, benchmarking, standard of living, commercialization, incentives, privatization, merger and consolidation, quantity of life, and using market rules and principles to make decisions.

We express prosperity in terms of reducing costs and waste, measuring performance, establishing standards, promoting performance-based pay for teachers, consolidating smaller school districts to increase efficiency, and managing school districts more like a business. Liberty and prosperity are often closely allied. When we invoke the "free market," for example, we are joining liberty and prosperity.

Sometimes when we think of good government, or good public schools, we think of what's good for business. We expect government and public schools to be aligned with economic interests. In his first Inaugural Address in 1801 Thomas Jefferson defined good government this way: "A wise and frugal government, which shall restrain men from injuring one another, which shall leave them otherwise free to regulate their own pursuits of industry and improvement, and shall not take from the mouth of labor the bread it has earned. This is the sum of good government."

But is the right to prosper absolute? Should there be limitations on the means by which prosperity is achieved? Do those who achieve more prosperity have any responsibility to those who achieve less? Should states, for example, redistribute some of the wealth of more prosperous school districts to less prosperous districts?

THE *PUBLIC* IN PUBLIC SCHOOLS— NOT ONE THING, BUT MANY THINGS

Ask Americans about the meaning of the good life and the public good and you will hear references to all of these values. Ask those same Americans about the public good involved in a specific issue, and you will hear distinct preferences for some values over others. Even though we share these values that comprise the public good, we differ greatly in our preference for a particular value in a given situation. To illustrate this, consider the following news about public schools:

1. A first-grader was so excited about joining the Cub Scouts that he brought a camping utensil that can serve as a knife, fork and spoon to school to use at lunch. School officials decided he violated the district's zero-tolerance policy on weapons and sentenced him to 45 days in the district's reform school. After its 80-page code of conduct received national attention, the district rescinded the sentence.
2. A mayor announced that the city-run school system will begin using student test scores as a factor in deciding which teachers earn tenure.
3. A nationwide study by the Fordham University Center on Law and Information Policy found that states often collect far more information about students than necessary and fail to take adequate steps to protect their privacy.
4. A school district reported that a majority of its students speak a language other than English at home.
5. A state legislature passed a bill that permits local school districts to promote "critical thinking" and "objective discussion" about evolution, the origins of life, and global warming by allowing teachers to use supplementary materials to critique the standard textbook.
6. Because of the attention garnered by the books involved in book banning efforts announced each year by the American Library Association, one superintendent banned the list of banned books.
7. Football cheerleaders at a public high school, wanting to make the Bible a bigger part of Friday night games, painted messages like "Commit to the Lord" on giant paper banners that the players charged through onto the field. After the school was cautioned about the risk of a constitutional challenge due to an insufficient separation of church and state in school-sponsored activities, the school board struck down the 8-year old tradition.
8. Selling candy didn't raise much money, so a middle school parent advisory council recommended that a $20 donation should get a student 20 test points—10 extra points on two tests of the student's choosing. The principal endorsed this idea.

These vignettes illustrate issues of privacy and tensions between individual freedoms and rights and the common good. They describe efforts to distinguish personal responsibility from collective responsibility, and present arguments about the proper role and scope of government, how much government we should have, and when government should act. They highlight issues of safety and security, social and moral order, fairness, equity and justice. And they suggest ways in which we should use markets to deliver public education, govern public schools, and run public schools more like a business.

But more than this, these examples illustrate how public education is a political and moral practice that presupposes a vision of society and of the future.[30] We believe the best way to engage citizens in a genuinely democratic discussion of the purpose and place of public schools in America is by acknowledging several key questions that lie at the heart of the idea of a *public* in public schools.

1. What purposes do public schools serve, why do we educate children, towards what ends, and what do we want and expect from public schools?
2. What should we teach children and what is the best way to educate the next generation of Americans?
3. Who should educate children, and how?
4. What role should public schools play in our children's lives, how do our communities benefit from public schools, and how might our communities be different without public schools?
5. Why do public schools give rise to so many controversial issues, and what should public school leaders do about these issues?

These questions are about the *public* in public schools. They involve our visions of the good life and our understanding of the public good. They are not technical or expert questions about how we teach arithmetic or about whether state history should precede U.S. history in the curriculum or vice versa. They are value-based questions about the social and political context of public schools and about our vision for the future—what kind of society we wish to create and perpetuate. Public values are the values of public education, because public schools comprise the public institution by which we prepare each generation of Americans to become Americans.

One great truth about our political beliefs is that the aspirations of the American Creed and American Dream unite us, but our interpretations of those aspirations and how best to achieve them divide us.[31] As playwright Eugene Ionesco wrote, "Ideologies separate us. Dreams and anguish bring us together."

The great paradox of the American polis is that if not for the values we hold in common, there would be far less to disagree about. Yet our tolerance for and appreciation of genuine political discourse and difference seem to erode daily. As an institution of political socialization and cultural transmission, how should public schools come to grips with their responsibility for cultivating the public life of our communities? What good is education if it does not inculcate any sense of political, ethical and moral responsibility in its citizens?[32] Should we lose the capacity to develop these virtues in our citizens our republic will edge ever closer to the precipice of political extinction. If public schools serve no other purpose, they should serve this one.

NOTES

1. Stone, D. (2002). *Policy paradox: The art of political decision making* (rev. ed). New York, NY: W. W. Norton.

2. Mondale, S., and Patton, S. B. (Eds.). (2001). *School: The story of American public education.* Boston, MA: Beacon Press.

3. Schrag, P. (1997). "The near-myth of our failing schools." *The Atlantic Monthly,* 280, 4, 72–80.

4. Ibid.

5. Stone, 2002.

6. Mathews, D. (2006). *Reclaiming public education by reclaiming our democracy.* Dayton, OH: Kettering Foundation Press.

7. The Harwood Group. (1995). *Halfway out the door: Citizens talk about their mandate for public schools.* Dayton, OH: Kettering Foundation.

8. Mathews, D. (1996). *Is there a public for public schools?* Dayton, OH: Kettering Foundation Press.

9. Myrdal, G. (1944). *An American dilemma: The Negro problem and modern democracy.* New York, NY: Harper & Row.

10. de Roussy de Sales, R. (1939). "What makes an American?" *The Atlantic Monthly,* 163, 3, p. 295.

11. O'Toole, J. (1993). *The executive's compass: Business and the good society.* New York: Oxford University Press.

12. Bellah, R. N., Madsen, R., Sullivan, W. M., Swidler, A., and Tipton, S. M. (1991). *The Good Society.* New York, NY: Vintage, p. 9.

13. Waldo, D. (1984). *The administrative state* (2nd edition). New York, NY: Holmes & Meier.

14. Bellah et al., 1991; O'Connell, B. (1999). Civil Society: The underpinnings of American democracy. Hanover, NH: University Press of New England; O'Toole, 1993; Richardson, W. D., Martinez, J. M., and Stewart, K. R. (1998). *Ethics and character: The pursuit of democratic virtues.* Durham, NC: Carolina Academic Press; Saul, J. R. (1995). *The unconscious civilization.* Concord, ON: Anansi Press; Stone, 2002.

15. Brinkley, A, Polsby, N. W., and Sullivan, K. M. (1997). *New federalist papers: Essays in defense of the constitution.* New York, NY: W. W. Norton.

16. Mill, J. S. (1859). *On liberty.* Currin V. Shields (Ed.) (1956). Indianapolis, IN: Bobbs-Merrill.

17. Etzioni, A. (1993). *The spirit of community: The reinvention of American society.* New York, NY: Touchstone.

18. Kemmis, D. (1990). *Community and the politics of place.* Norman, OK: University of Oklahoma Press.

19. Stone, 2002.

20. Haar, C. M., and Fessler, D. W. (1986). *Fairness and justice: Law in the service of equality.* New York, NY: Simon & Schuster.

21. Walzer, M. (1983). *Spheres of justice: A defense of pluralism and equality.* New York, NY: Basic Books.

22. Okun, A. (1965). *Equality and efficiency: The big trade-off.* Washington, DC: The Brookings Institution.

23. Stiles, P. (2005). *Is the American dream killing you? How the market rules our lives.* New York, NY: HarperCollins Publishers.

24. Thurow, L. C. (1975). *Generating inequality: Mechanisms of distribution in the U.S. economy.* New York, NY: Basic Books.

25. Fischer, D. H. (2005). *Liberty and freedom: A visual history of America's founding ideas.* New York, NY: Oxford University Press.

26. Economist Friedrich August von Hayek.

27. Palmer, P. J. (1977). "A place called community." *Christian Century,* March 16, 1977, p. 8.

28. Ibid.

29. Fowler, R. B. (1991). *The dance with community: The contemporary debate in American political thought.* Lawrence, KS: University of Kansas Press.

30. Giroux, H. A., and Saltman, K. (2008). Obama's betrayal of public education? Arne Duncan and the corporate model of schooling. Retrieved December 19, 2008 from http://www.truthout.org/121708R, p.1.

31. Stone (2002).

32. Giroux and Saltman (2008).

Part II

Visions and Values of Public Education in Our Democratic Republic

Public education has always been shaped by the values of our republic. From colonial and revolutionary times, to the settling of the west and the closing of the frontier, to urbanization and industrialization, and onward to internationalization and globalization, public schools and the republic have proceeded apace. As we will see, contemporary public schools recapitulate the ideological arguments of the republic, albeit in more modern form.

Early forms of public education, which took root in colonial America, were voluntary and locally funded.[1] In relatively homogenous communities, early public schooling focused mostly on civic and religious education. Schools had limited authority and responsibility. Families and churches had principal responsibility for raising and socializing children. Much of what children learned came through the family, church and workplace.

An influx of new Americans seeking religious freedom made early communities more diverse, and opposition to learning only in English and having clergy in teaching roles undermined early public education. By the time of the American Revolution much of education had become private. Consequently, much of early education was not free, secular or equal.

As the new American states wrote their own constitutions after independence, many of them included provisions for education. A public role in education was often linked to preserving liberty and the ideals of the American Revolution. "There is but one method of rendering a republican form of government durable," wrote Benjamin Rush, a signer of the Declaration of Independence, "and that is by disseminating the seeds of virtue and knowledge through every part of the state by means of proper places and modes of education and this can be done effectively only by the aid of the legislature."

To ensure that education was universal and free from religious biases, Jefferson proposed government control. Other founders and framers also advocated for public education, but the changing political, demographic and economic landscape of early America made it difficult to translate such an abstract concept into practice. Schooling continued to be primarily the province of private, charitable and religious interests for most of America's first century.

The common school reform movement of the mid-nineteenth century transformed public education. Horace Mann and others argued that common schooling could create good citizens, unite society and prevent crime and poverty. Public acceptance of state school systems grew over time, encouraged by popular commitment to republican government, trust in Protestant values, and the development of capitalism.

The founders' civic and moral vision of republican government made education in government, law and ethics important. The earliest public schools sought to prepare citizens for a moral and civic life. Moral education and training would produce virtuous citizens who practiced punctuality, honesty, and industriousness.

Capitalism made education in commerce, finance, geography, science and language important. In conducting commerce, citizens would reflect Alexander Hamilton's notion of acquisitiveness rather than avarice. They would exhibit virtues of frugality, economy, moderation, labor and prudence, excellences that Montesquieu believed were encouraged in a democracy founded on commerce.[2]

In the 1850s, Massachusetts and New York, two original colonies, adopted compulsory school attendance laws. Free elementary public education was available for nearly all American children by the end of the 19th century. By 1918, during the peak of the Progressive Era, all states had passed laws requiring children to attend at least elementary school.

Native American children were excluded from common schools. Native American children were educated in "Indian" schools. At one point the U.S. Congress forbid teaching Indian children in their native languages. African-American children were also excluded from common schools. impelling them to create their own schools, the forerunners of what we refer to today as historically black universities and colleges. And Catholics, in response to religious and cultural discrimination, created a separate educational system of parochial schools. Their right to determine their own education was supported by the Supreme Court in 1925, which ruled that states could not compel children to attend public schools, and that parents could send their children to private schools instead.

As America entered its second century, the nation saw the closing of the frontier and a shift from an agrarian society to a more urban one. Waves of immigration led to reforms aimed at creating Americans from the raw material of other nations, preparing future workers for an industrial economy, and maintaining the existing social and economic order. The early twentieth century saw business models applied to education—centralized and professional administration, corporate organizational structures, and efforts to improve the efficiency and productivity of education.

The mid-twentieth century saw continuing progress on equality as a result of World War II and the U.S. Supreme Court's *Brown vs. Board of Education of Topeka* decision. It also saw the adoption of aptitude tracking, achievement testing and the first of numerous efforts to reinvigorate math and science to ensure global military and economic superiority.

The latter part of the twentieth century saw a backlash against government. Efforts to sustain racial and economic integration were curtailed and in some cases, reversed. Opting out of public schools became more acceptable and a central piece of education policy. Some states imposed term limits on elected school board members. Some critics saw the problem with public education as too much democracy, and called for reforming schools along the lines of markets or for replacing democratic politics in schools with markets.[3]

From 19th century battles over social order, inclusion and discrimination to 20th century battles over segregation, market-based education, and economic competitiveness, public schools provide a window to America's past and a door into its future. The historian Joseph Ellis helps us understand this through his discussion of the key political challenges that shaped our ideological heritage at the founding of the nation. Ellis does not address public education, but the challenges and beliefs he identifies remain with us today, and clearly manifest themselves in public schools. These include:

1. The unprecedented task the Founders faced of establishing a republican government on the scale and scope of the United States.
2. The dominant intellectual legacy of the Revolution that rejected centralized political power and repudiated any energetic expression of governmental authority.
3. No common history or experience as a nation in working together and taking collective action, other than uniting against the British.
4. According to the first census in 1790, the nearly 700,000 black slaves who inhabited the new republic as a kind of demographic defiance of republican rhetoric uttered since 1776.

5. Ideological tension between Jefferson's republicanism, emphasizing freedom and individual interests and Hamilton's federalism, emphasizing social order and collective interests.[4]

With this backdrop, public schools became a stage upon which the American experiment would play out and upon which competing visions and values of America were scripted. The early civic and moral vision of the role of public education would crumble under the weight of the numerous social and educational responsibilities we would later assign to public schools.

These responsibilities included parenting, health, nutrition, after-school programs, anti-smoking, athletics, bicycle and gun safety, business and careers, character, child abuse monitoring, consumer, death, driving, drug and alcohol abuse, early childhood, ESL and bilingual, environmental, foreign languages, global, Head Start, HIV/AIDS, immunization, keyboarding, computer and Internet, kindergarten, leisure and recreation, mental health, multicultural, music and art, peace, physical, school breakfast and lunch, sex and sexual abuse prevention, special, speech and drama, stranger/danger, technical/vocational, and Title IX.[5]

Today we have multiple and competing visions of public education, but no national consensus about the fundamental purposes and roles of public schools. The Education Commission of the States concludes as much in its monograph on the history of school governance. "Currently, there is no evidence of a national consensus regarding the institutional framework in which public schooling operates or the larger social and cultural purposes a system of public schools ought to serve."[6]

Why we created public schools, what we expect of them, and the beliefs that frame public education are all shaped by the "invisible hand of ideology."[7] In debates about who should be educated, what they should learn, how they should be taught, who should govern public schools, and how schools should be funded, ideology, values and beliefs matter.

The history of public education and the future of public schools are connected by each generation's attempt to translate the philosophical ideals of our democratic republic into an institutional mechanism for educating and socializing the next generation of Americans. Each generation wages a "war for children's minds," battling among itself to define the purposes and goals of public schools.[8]

As we will see, these struggles and debates are more about a philosophy of politics than a philosophy of education. All the more important that we explore these normative visions and tensions, and look at how they frame the public context of public schools today.

NOTES

1. Kaestle, C. F. (1983). *Pillars of the republic: Common schools and American society, 1780–1860.* New York, NY: Hill & Wang.

2. Richardson, W. D., Martinez, J. M., and Stewart, K. R. (1998). *Ethics and character: The pursuit of democratic virtues.* Durham, NC: Carolina Academic Press.

3. Chubb, J. E., and Moe, T. M. (1990). *Politics, markets, and America's schools.* Washington, DC: The Brookings Institution.

4. Ellis, J. J. (2000). *Founding brothers: The revolutionary generation.* New York, NY: Vintage Books.

5. Vollmer, J. (2001). "Schools cannot do this alone." Retrieved Nov. 27, 2004 from www.jamievollmer.com/burden.doc.

6. Education Commission of the States. (1999c). *The invisible hand of ideology: Perspectives from the history of school governance.* Denver, CO: Author, p. 20.

7. Ibid., p. 2.

8. Law, S. (2007). *The war for children's minds.* New York, NY: Routledge.

Chapter 1

Liberty and Public Schools

Freedom, Choice, Opportunity

The American Revolution established the colonies' independence from England, and the right of new Americans to political and religious freedom. Having won the war, Americans were faced with the daunting challenge of transforming thirteen independent colonies into a united republic strong enough to withstand attacks from without and rebellion from within. This was no small challenge, as many of the colonies were as distant from one another politically as they were geographically from England.

Some new Americans, including many of the founders and framers, believed that public education held the key to both preserving independence and creating a united America among very independent states. "Knowledge will forever govern ignorance, and a people who mean to be their own Governors must arm themselves with the power knowledge gives," wrote James Madison. "Liberty cannot be preserved without a general knowledge among the people, who have a right...and a desire to know," wrote John Adams.

If education was to become the means by which the ideals of the Revolution might be realized, it had a long way to go. Wealth, race, and gender largely determined who became educated. Since the nation's founding Americans have struggled to turn the ideals of equal opportunity and equal treatment into reality. More than two centuries later, issues of race, ethnicity, wealth, religion, and to a lesser degree gender, still play a significant role in public schools.

Liberty requires some constraints if it is not to become anarchy. To preserve liberty and prevent the newly united states from fragmenting into independent states, a balance between freedom and independence on the one hand and unity and social order on the other needed to be struck. Here lies the origin of one of the great democratic responsibilities of public schools, articulated by a number of founders, framers and progressive reformers across America's early eras. Their vision was a system of tax-supported schools that would mix people of different backgrounds and reinforce the bonds that tie Americans together. The common public school would become a means of political socialization in which the competing forces of individual freedom and social order might be reconciled.

LIBERTY AND THE THREE R'S: REVOLUTION, RELIGION, AND THE REPUBLIC

There are numerous examples of challenges to this vision of liberty through commonality in American history. One of the most important is the role of religion in public life, and the role of public schools in educating citizens about religious freedom.

In a nation founded in part on religious freedom, public policy and religion are bound to intersect frequently. From its very beginning, the national government believed strongly that the public prosperity of the nation depended on the vitality of its religion. Several Founders made frequent use of religious symbols and biblical references to communicate the ideals and goals of the Revolution to the inhabitants of colonial America.

How would the first generation of Americans balance the ideals of social and moral order promised through religion with the quest for religious freedom? Carefully, and continuously, would be the answer. "The American Revolution was a beginning, not a consummation," observed Woodrow Wilson. We would soon learn that while the war for independence had been won, the battle to preserve the ideals of the Revolution would be never-ending.

1785—The Revolution Faces an Early Public Test

The question of public funding for religion was one such challenge to the new nation's ideal of liberty. As early as 1785, Congress debated setting aside part of each newly established township in the West for the support of schools and for the support of religion. Support for schools passed. The proposal to establish religion by granting state financial support to a church to be controlled by one denomination was considered but voted down. And in Virginia, Madison and Jefferson joined Baptists and Presbyterians to defeat a campaign for state financial involvement in religion.

Far from being anti-religion, Congress strongly supported a religious nation but not state support for religion. In the famous Northwest Ordinance of 1787, Congress affirmed that "Religion, morality, and knowledge being necessary to good government and the happiness of mankind, schools and the means of education shall be forever encouraged."[1] In retrospect, 1785 marked one of the nation's earliest tests of liberty. It would not be the last.

2008—The Republic Faces the Same Public Test!

When the U.S. Constitution was signed in 1787, it did not contain the essential freedoms now outlined in the Bill of Rights, because many of the Framers viewed their inclusion as unnecessary.[2] It wasn't until 1791 when the Bill of Rights, the first 10 amendments to the Constitution, went into effect. In crafting the exquisitely simple language of the First Amendment, "Congress shall make no law respecting an establishment of religion, or prohibiting the free exercise thereof; . . ." the Founders forged a blend of liberty and equality so artful that it has afforded us the opportunity to continue debating the boundaries of religion in the public sphere to the present day.

This briefest of histories is important, as we are destined to play out these issues and arguments as long as the republic survives. Here's one example. In July 2008, the state of Maine's highest court rejected an appeal by a couple who wanted their municipality to pay for their children's education at a religious school. The couple argued that since the subsidy to send their children to a religious school would come from town funds, not state funds, it was exempt from state law banning the use of public money for religious education. In a unanimous opinion, the Maine Supreme Judicial Court ruled that the law applies to all public funds.

Implications of Religious Freedom for Public Schools

Our choice and practice of religion is a private matter. Where and how we learn our religion is also a private matter. But how we treat each other's religions is a public matter. Public education has an important role to play in preparing citizens to understand the interdependence between freedom of religion and equality of religion. Freedom of religion can exist only among a free people, and education is critical to that freedom. "Education makes people easy to lead, but difficult to drive; easy to govern, but impossible to enslave."[3]

If education should enhance knowledge, tolerance and understanding, how do we explain the all too frequent dismissal of religious equality by adult citizens, including many elected officials, who have presumably benefitted from a public education? Tocqueville observed that many elected officials seemed to talk about religion much more than they practiced it.

If we look closely at the establishment and free exercise clauses of the First Amendment in the context of public values, what leaps out at us is that religious liberty depends upon religious equality. If we truly value religious freedom, then we are obligated to accept other religions as equal to our own. If we treat another religion as less equal, then we will have curtailed the freedom of those who practice that religion.

In other words, we cannot have freedom of religion without equality of religion, and vice versa. When we promote religious freedom without a corresponding obligation to religious equality, we violate this principle of reciprocity and invite rebellion and revolution. To paraphrase Voltaire, a nation with a single religion has oppression, a nation with two religions has civil war, but a nation with a thousand religions has peace.

Most Americans profess religious liberty and tolerance, but sometimes balk when different religious practices or beliefs conflict with their own. They support some degree of separation of church and state, but disagree with banning school-sponsored prayer and removing the Ten Commandments from public buildings. Different religious practices, observances and holidays; school prayer, religious clubs, and Bible education; evolution, creationism and intelligent design; and the Pledge of Allegiance are just some of the ways in which public schools play a part in continuing the arguments and debates of the Founders and Framers regarding the proper role and scope of religion in the public sphere.

The Constitution and Bill of Rights are more than historical documents. They are living documents, as vital to our lives today as they were to the founding of the nation. Public schools should be in the vanguard of educating future citizens about this linchpin of democracy. They are arguably the only institution positioned to take on this task. If we think it's important to ask how well students score on standardized tests, shouldn't we also ask how well students are prepared to protect religious freedom and uphold the standards of the Constitution?

Public education, a revolutionary idea in itself, is the key to keeping alive the ideals of the revolution. As the 2008 Maine court case illustrates, public schools have a dual task—to educate young Americans and to help preserve the foundations of our liberty.

A LIBERTY-CENTERED VISION OF PUBLIC EDUCATION AND PUBLIC SCHOOLS

Many Americans take public education for granted, assuming that we have always had a nationwide system of public schools. Students are often surprised to find no specific reference to education in the Federalist Papers, the Declaration of Independence or the Constitution. Consistent with a nation created by revolution, the value of liberty plays a powerful role in public debate about education. Numerous national and state-wide organizations promote individual rights, personal freedom, choice, personal responsibility, limited government, lower taxes, less regulation, and free enterprise in public schools.

Examples of liberty-based organizations with a focus on public education and public schools include the Alliance for School Choice and the Center for Education Reform in Washington DC, Oregon's Cascade Policy Institute, Maryland's Free State Foundation, the Great Plains Public Policy Institute in South Dakota, the Heartland Institute in Illinois, the Josiah Bartlett Center for Public Policy in New Hampshire, Parents for Educational Freedom in North Carolina, Parents Challenge in Colorado, and School Choice Wisconsin.

Based on the mission of these and similar organizations that espouse greater liberty in public education and on the dimensions of liberty we described earlier, what might a liberty-centered vision of public schools look like that emphasizes such things as freedom, rights, individuality, personal responsibility, freedom of speech, freedom of expression, religious liberty, and privacy? Following is a composite liberty-centered vision of public schools, drawn from a wide variety of liberty-centered organizations across the country.

Free education from government laws and subsidies. Break away from entrenched education bureaucracies. Deconsolidate centralized school districts to restore power and control to local communities. Offer tax credits for public, private or home school education providers. Take advantage of vouchers. Control teacher pay and per student spending. Discourage government interference with home schooling, Repeal compulsory attendance laws.

Promote alternative schooling approaches, including charter schools, private schools, home schooling, magnet programs, cyber schools, accelerated programs, differentiated instruction, and individualized learning. Adopt privately managed alternatives to existing public schools and educational programs. Give schools the opportunity to innovate, teachers the independence to customize curricula, and administrators the freedom to make school management decisions.

Maximize parental choice because children have unique needs, because parents should have the freedom to choose the best education to meet those needs, and because education, training, and discipline of children are properly placed in the domain of parents. Allow parents to send their children to the school of their choice regardless of address or income. Allow open enrollment and transfers. Put parents in charge of approving books and reading assignments, and make parents responsible for values and sex education. Provide information to parents as consumers of education, and let families control how their education dollars are spent.

This isn't a single vision, but a composite of the visions of many organizations and groups that believe liberty is central to public schools and public education. As this description illustrates, a liberty-centered vision of public education sits upon a tripod of individual freedom, choice and personal responsibility. American journalist and historian Henry Brooks Adams expressed the essence of a liberty-centered vision this way: "Absolute liberty is absence of restraint; responsibility is restraint; therefore, the ideally free individual is responsible to himself."

LIBERTY AND PUBLIC SCHOOLS TODAY: FREEDOM OF OR FREEDOM FROM?

Freedoms of are things we want, for example, freedom of speech. Freedoms from are things we don't want or want less of, for example, government. The essence of America is "finding and maintaining that perfect, delicate balance between freedom of and freedom from."[4] Following are three examples that address parental choice, home schooling, and ways of financing choice. They illustrate some of the ways in which liberty affects public schools, sometimes as freedom of and sometimes as freedom from.

Parental Choice

"Choice is one of those words to look out for. It means different things to different people."[5] School choice can mean something as simple as offering more choices within and among existing public schools. Or it can mean something more complex, such as providing vouchers and tuition tax credits for parents to use at the schools of their choice.

Supporters of school choice cite a variety of benefits, including autonomy, privatization, deregulation, cost reduction, parental rights, freedom from bureaucracy, and greater individuality and creativity. Proponents believe they should be able to decide which school their children attend, regardless of economic or geographic factors. In some cases parents have created choice options within their school district. In other cases the district has extended choice options beyond the district's boundaries. And in some cases choice includes public or private vouchers to attend private schools.

Supporters believe that free market competition will improve student and school performance. They argue that if public schools have to compete for funding, then schools will be motivated to improve. They see schools as an education marketplace, where parents and students are education consumers who can sift through information to determine the best choice of schools for their particular needs and interests. Other supporters view vouchers as a "life-boat" for low-income students currently trapped in ineffective and mismanaged schools.

A common argument against greater school choice is that it leads to equity problems.[6] Critics point out that to be a truly educated consumer in an education marketplace requires parents to be able to access information and evaluate it, and have the time, ability and resources to do so. If not all parents can exercise choice equally, and if access, ability and resources are distributed unequally within a community, then not all families have equal choices. In general, families with greater resources and access to information have greater choice.

Opponents fear that choice programs will drain much-needed support away from the schools that are in most need of public funds. Low-income families will not be able to use vouchers because they cover only a fraction of the tuition costs. Choice will therefore be exercised by a limited number of parents, leaving "under-chosen" schools under-funded and charged with educating even more needy students. In addition, opponents point out that tax-funded vouchers for religious schools violate the First Amendment separation of church and state.

Some states offer no choice options. Others limit choice options in law, for example, a legislative cap on the number of authorized charter schools. State policies that limit choice can mask the level of demand for alternatives. In Colorado, for example, traditional public school enrollment (excluding charter schools) declined from 88 percent of all school students to 86 percent between 2004 and 2008. Looked at another way, total traditional public school enrollment grew in Colorado by four percent during that same time, while alternative enrollment (charters + home schools + non-public) grew by 24 percent.

Home Schooling

Parents who home school are often seeking freedom from government-sponsored education and from certain social and political influences. The right of parents to raise their children as they see fit can create conflict with the emphasis of states on student standards and teacher certification. In response, some state legislatures and courts have ruled that parents can home-school their children even if they lack a teaching certificate.

One liberty issue that home schooling can present for school districts is whether or not to allow home-schooled students to participate in extracurricular school activities. Some districts lean towards barring non-enrolled students from joining district sports teams, academic competitions, and district-led field trips. They argue, for example, that allowing a non-enrolled student to participate on a sports team could deny the same opportunity to an enrolled student.

But parents of home-schooled students often see it differently. They argue that their children should be privy to the school services their taxes help pay for. They are not asking for special treatment compared to enrolled students, but just for the opportunity to try out. As more families choose home schooling, public schools will continue to get requests for participation in school-sponsored extra-curricular activities from non-enrolled students.

Financing School Choice

States have explored several ways of using taxation and public financing to create greater choice. In one state, for example, legislators proposed income and property tax credits for tuition paid to nonpublic schools. Supporters claim this would provide access to better educational opportunities for poorer families, improve the public schools by increasing competition and save millions of dollars in state funding to support public schools. Opponents argue that it would drain public money away from public schools, particularly those public schools most in need of additional funding.

In another state, a group of citizens launched a ballot initiative for a constitutional amendment to create a new system of school governance in which state money could go directly to parental advisory councils at each school. Most money would be earmarked by the state for teacher salaries, but parents could spend the rest on programs and activities of their choice, such as athletics, art or after school tutoring.

In yet another state, legislation was introduced to allow school districts to use tax revenue from slot machines installed at racetracks and casinos to lower local property taxes. School districts would have to increase their tax rate by a minimum amount to qualify for matching gambling dollars.

Not all proposals to finance greater choice aim for reducing the role of public schools or reducing public taxation. Some states, for example, allow voters in school districts to adopt special district taxes in addition to normal local school funding. Voters can choose to increase their taxes on behalf of their public schools. Of course, in response to decisions by some school districts to raise taxes, some states have proposed capping local property taxes for schools.

HOW MUCH LIBERTY SHOULD WE HAVE IN PUBLIC SCHOOLS?

Can we have too much liberty, too much individual freedom? How much liberty should students have in public schools? At times we ask government, including public schools, to decide how much freedom individuals should be allowed or how much constraint should be placed on individual freedom.

Following are three examples that address student transfers, privacy, and freedom of association and speech. In each example public schools must decide how much liberty to allow students, when to restrict student freedom, and when to balance concerns for liberty with concerns for the other core public values of equality, community and prosperity.

Student Transfers

If individual liberty was the only factor considered in the decision, then districts would approve all student transfer requests. But if a district were to include the freedom of the district and of the requested school in its decision criteria, it might only approve requests provided there was sufficient free space at the requested school and provided students or their families accept responsibility for providing transportation. This would minimize the cost to the school to accommodate the student and to the district in terms of providing additional transportation.

A district might also decide that diversity should be a factor. In this case, a district might take into account the racial, ethnic and socioeconomic characteristics of the transferring student. Districts seeking greater diversity in a particular school might give priority approval to students who diversify the population of the requested school.

A district might also decide that a sense of community should be a factor. In this case, the district might be less likely to approve transfers that disrupted an existing school community or neighborhood. The district might give priority approval to students based on how close they lived to the requested school. Regardless of how district officials resolve this issue, it requires them to strike some sort of balance between liberty, equality and community, and in some cases, also with prosperity.

Surveillance Cameras and Locker Searches

Some districts have installed or have considered installing surveillance cameras in classrooms, on buses and in cafeterias to monitor student behavior. Some schools search the contents of student lockers, while others allow police to search student lockers. These actions clearly have implications for student privacy and anonymity. If individual liberty was the only factor a district considered, then cameras and searches would not be condoned.

Why might a district install cameras or search lockers? The most apparent answer is because of concerns about safety, legality and theft. A district might do so because of concerns about social and moral order, which are dimensions of the public value of community. Surveillance cameras and locker searches are means by which the district could address concerns about safe, legal and moral behavior by students. But implementing these requires sacrificing some degree of liberty.

Some district officials, parents and students might raise concerns about how much liberty should be sacrificed. They could suggest, for example, that officials should be required to obtain consent from some students, particularly older students, before searching their lockers. They could also argue that students might learn to behave safely, legally and morally only when they know they are being watched.

They might suggest that if schools want to teach students safe, legal and moral behavior, they should emphasize personal responsibility more than external monitoring. Regardless of how school officials resolve this issue, it requires them to strike some sort of balance between liberty and community.

Freedom of Speech and Association

Schools and districts must sometimes decide whether to allow groups with controversial purposes or messages to meet in school facilities during the school day or after hours. They must sometimes also decide whether to allow or prohibit speech that is potentially hateful or harmful toward a particular individual or group to be printed in a school newspaper. Again, if personal liberty and freedom of speech and association were the only factors considered, schools would not constrain either of these student activities.

Why might a school or district constrain student speech or association? In this instance, we might answer with concerns about fairness, equal treatment, inclusion, and discrimination. In other words, this example of student freedom raises concerns for the public value of equality. Schools might protect a student's freedom of speech and of association as long as that speech or association was not harming another.

Using the advice of Jefferson and John Stuart Mill, we are not justified in constraining a student from saying things or associating with other students that might not be in his or her best interest. But we are justified in constraining a student from saying things or associating with other students when that speech or association causes harm to another person. Regardless of how school officials resolve this issue, it requires them to strike some sort of balance between liberty and equality.

A ROLE FOR PUBLIC SCHOOLS IN PRESERVING LIBERTY

If we are to thrive in our third century, we will do so only by continuing to build a nation in which Americans of vastly different backgrounds can work together to build the next iteration of America. In this context, democracy and public education are less about government and government schools and more about how we live. As John Dewey observed, "A democracy is more than a form of government; it is primarily a mode of associated living, of conjoint communicated experience."[7]

Public education has a critical role to play in preserving liberty and the republic, but perhaps not the one most people think. When asked why public education matters in a democratic society, most Americans suggest that a government resting upon popular suffrage cannot be successful unless those who elect their governors are educated.

Dewey suggested a deeper reason. A democratic society, he wrote, one that is self-governing, repudiates the principle of external authority. It must therefore "find a substitute in voluntary disposition and interest; these can be created only by education."[8] For Dewey, a fundamental purpose of education is to help prepare individuals to be self-governing, the ultimate expression of personal liberty.

Individuals, Dewey argued, don't acquire the self-governing skills and virtues of citizenship that a democratic society requires simply because they procure diplomas and degrees. Rather it is through the process of education, particularly civic and democratic education that requires them to make room for different people and different views, that individuals become self-governing citizens.

America is a work in progress, because developing self-governing individuals in each generation requires constant attention to nation and public building. Republics, historians tell us, fall mostly from within. As Abraham Lincoln remarked a century and a half ago, "America will never be destroyed from the outside. If we falter and lose our freedoms, it will be because we destroyed ourselves."

Within the context of the founders' "grand experiment," the public purpose of public schools is not to produce the same results or to make us the same. It is to provide us with a common socializing experience that preserves the energy and vitality of our individual and cultural differences and yet allows us to recognize and accept each other as fellow citizens and Americans. "We dare not forget, cautioned John F. Kennedy, "that we are the heirs of that first revolution." Developing self-governing individuals within the context of a shared and common heritage is the critical task of public schools in preserving liberty.

NOTES

1. Frohnen, B. (Ed.) (2002). *The American republic: Primary sources.* Indianapolis, IN: Liberty Fund, p. 227.
2. Buchanan, B. J. (2009). "About the First Amendment." Washington, DC: First Amendment Center. Retrieved Dec. 30, 2009 from http://www.firstamendmentcenter.org/about.aspx?item=aboutfirstamd.
3. British statesman Henry Peter Broughan.
4. Marilyn vos Savant.
5. Medige, B. (2003). "Privatization of public education: Segregation, desegregation, resegregation." Retrieved from http://buffaloreport.com/articles/030502medige.html, p.1.
6. Moe, T. M. (2002). "The structure of school choice". In Hill, P. T. (Ed.). *Choice with equity.* Stanford, CA: Hoover Institution Press, Ch. 7, 179–212.
7. Dewey, J. (1916). *Democracy and education: An introduction to the philosophy of education.* New York, NY: Macmillan, p. 101.
8. Ibid.

Chapter 2

Community and Public Schools

Connection, Belonging, Social Order

In 1890 the U.S. Census Bureau proclaimed the American frontier closed. In 1893 historian Frederick Jackson Turner delivered his famous address in Chicago on the frontier's special role in shaping American society and the character of Americans. In 1896, William Jennings Bryan and his frontier and agrarian populism came up short in the presidential election against William McKinley and the urban commerce of Wall Street and the advertising of Madison Avenue. If the open frontier helped shape our sense of individualism, the closing of the frontier helped shape our sense of community, and heralded the ushering in of a new chapter in the American story.

While some observers saw the closing of the frontier as the end of an era, others saw it as a beginning. Only once the frontier closed could America develop a real republic and a true civil society that would be forced to grapple with the challenges of its unique and diverse population, history, and cultural values.[1] We could no longer rely solely upon open territory, unlimited individual freedom and great natural wealth to achieve the American Dream.

The closing of the frontier meant that to a significantly greater degree than was true when the frontier was open, future social and economic progress would depend on government. Restrictions on markets and individual freedom emerged as the nation built a civil society to replace the self-regulating mechanism of the frontier. Railroads, a cornerstone of the original *Monopoly* board game and a revolutionary way to move people and goods to the less-settled west, led to the nation's first regulatory institution. The unfettered individual freedom of frontier America would give way to a social compact between citizens, business and government.

The closing of the frontier was more than a geographic and physical closing. It was also a political and psychological closing, heralding the end of a way of life that had shaped the very essence of the American character.[2] John F. Kennedy sought to tap into this frontier spirit in his inauguration address. "We stand today on the edge of a new frontier—the frontier of the 1960s, a frontier of unknown opportunities and perils—a frontier of unfulfilled hopes and threats. . . . The New Frontier I speak of is not a set of promises - it is a set of challenges."

What kind of America would develop after the frontier had closed? An urban America, characterized by the transformation from rural agrarian communities to cities and metropolitan areas. An immigrant America, with nearly four million new residents arriving during the last decade of the nineteenth century and bringing with them new languages, cultures and customs. An industrial America, characterized by technological change, belief in progress, science, and reason, and new concentrations of private power in the form of business corporations. And a professional America characterized by government, bureaucracy, technical experts, professional managers and a quest to make the most efficient use of labor, resources and machines.[3]

The closing of the frontier created changes in American society that extend to the present day. During the late 1800s and early 1900s, a number of national movements would emerge. These included a management movement to ensure that the growing enterprises of both business and government were efficient, e.g., scientific management; a conservation movement to save and preserve natural resources, e.g., national parks ; a labor movement to address the new social and economic relationships between workers and owners, e.g., unions; a human resources movement to save human beings, e.g., vocational rehabilitation; and a political reform movement to separate electoral and legislative politics from professional administration, e.g., the adoption of the city manager plan.

Not everyone saw these changes as positive. Many of these changes would leave future generations nostalgic for the past. As government became more pervasive, many Americans began to feel that a part of America might be lost forever. This sense of loss would help fuel future efforts to revive the republicanism, populism and civic culture of the frontier. More than two centuries after the Constitution was debated and adopted, and more than a century after the frontier closed, "more and more people are speaking of the need for a renewal of civic culture, often couching their call in explicitly republican terms."[4]

Despite these changes, we remain emotionally and ideologically attached to the agrarian individualism, self-reliance and personal responsibility of frontier America. We continue to value self-help over public help. "Pull yourself up by your bootstraps" is a phrase virtually every American understands today, even if they've never seen or worn bootstraps. Most Americans understood the concept of self-sufficiency long before politicians made it a centerpiece of national welfare reform in the 1990s.

The frontier values of individual freedom, self-help and personal responsibility would now be joined by values of social order, collective action, and social responsibility. Settling America would give way to socializing Americans. As American journalist Walter Lippman observed, "The great social adventure of America is no longer the conquest of the wilderness but the absorption of fifty different peoples."

FROM EDUCATION FOR NATION-BUILDING TO EDUCATION FOR COMMUNITY-BUILDING

Concerned about the potential threat to social and economic stability from urbanization, industrialization and immigration, an alliance of business leaders and progressive reformers sought ways to preserve social and economic order. Common schools, soon to be known as public schools, would become a primary vehicle for preserving the American way of life. In its second century the republic would begin to realize founder George Mason's vision that "Every society, all government, and every kind of civil compact therefore, is or ought to be, calculated for the general good and safety of the community."

If the founders saw a relationship between public education and political freedom, progressives saw a relationship between public education and social and economic progress. John Dewey saw the good society as one "which makes provision for participation in its good of all its members on equal terms...Such a society must have a type of education which gives individuals a personal interest in social relationships and control, and the habits of mind which secure social changes without introducing disorder."[5]

Teaching the 3 R's was no longer sufficient for this new good society. Public schools would be asked to address issues of assimilation and socialization in order to preserve the American way of life. Americanization would become a responsibility of public schools. To socialize immigrant students, schools began to teach life skills, such as the 3 H's—health, hygiene, and home economics. "Officially, the idea was to get us out of the barbarism of our immigrant background. But the idea was to 'Americanize' us, as they say, and it did."[6]

Teaching became more feminized as schools assumed greater responsibility for socializing children. American women had long been seen as the keepers of morals and the builders of community in early American and frontier culture. Tocqueville attributed the bulk of America's social progress to its women despite their subordinated political and economic status. The role of women as teachers was seen as a natural extension of women as homemakers, and classrooms became a social and moral extension of the home.

Addressing large-scale social change and administering a rapidly growing school system also required new ways of organizing and managing the education enterprise. Specialization, centralization, hierarchical authority, expert administration, and standardized curricula came to characterize the modern public school. The increasing size, cost and complexity of school districts led them, as well as many state and federal government organizations, to turn to business corporations for management principles and administrative processes.

A COMMUNITY-CENTERED VISION OF PUBLIC EDUCATION AND PUBLIC SCHOOLS

Tocqueville noted that Americans have made better use of the power of association and for more purposes than anywhere else in the world. Numerous national and state-wide organizations promote connection and belonging, quality of life, social responsibility, collective action, social and moral order, safety and security, and seek to preserve place, heritage and identity.

Examples of community-based organizations that focus on public education and public schools include the Coalition for Community Schools and the National Coalition for Parent Involvement in Education in Washington DC, Action for Children and the Center for the Prevention of School Violence in North Carolina, the Chicago Campaign to Extend Community Schools in Illinois, Colorado's Statewide Parent Coalition, Virginia's Communities in Schools, Eat Smart Maryland, Iowa's Safe Schools, South Dakota's Connect, the Whole Schooling Consortium in Michigan, the National Center for Family and Community Connections with Schools based in Texas, and the Forum for Education and Democracy based in Ohio and Washington, DC.

Based on the mission of these and other organizations that espouse greater community-building in public schools and on the dimensions of community we described earlier, what might a community-centered vision of public schools look like that emphasizes meeting the physical, social and emotional needs of students to provide a critical foundation for learning? Following is a composite community-centered vision of public schools, drawn from a wide variety of community-centered organizations across the country.

Encourage one-on-one relationships with caring adults. Build mutual support within the classroom, school, and community. Use the community as a learning resource to engage students in work that makes a difference in their community as well as inviting the community to make a difference in the lives of children. Connect schools with community services and resources, including after school care, health care, nutrition, and out-of-school time programs to help children and families. Create a culture in which young people successfully learn, stay in school and prepare for life.

Create school environments that are supportive and welcoming. Every student will attend a school that is safe and secure, one that is free of fear and conducive to learning. Schools would be places to learn and grow, and to foster a healthy start and a healthy future. Students would have adequate time to eat lunch.

Organize schools to be small and personalized enough so all children and adults are well known to each other. Schools would avoid becoming places of competition, social sorting, and ranking. Emphasize the importance of schools as social centers, not only for students but for parents and families—dances, social clubs, competitions, performances, trips, outings are only marginally curriculum-related. It would organize networks of parent volunteers. Promote raising children, not just teaching children.

Emphasize a sustained commitment to strengthening schools, families and communities so that children and youth succeed. Promote high-quality early educational experiences to improve school readiness, reduce the need for special education and social services, reduce drop-outs and teen pregnancy, and help launch children toward successful adulthood. Help communities address the complex relationships between students, families, and their school experience. Adolescents drop out of school for a variety of reasons related to their experiences at home and their educational experiences in school. Develop teachers' knowledge in the cultures of the students they teach and mentor.

Help students learn to function as effective citizens in a democracy. Design school experiences to nurture in all children the habits of judgment that democratic life requires. Ensure that all children learn together across culture, ethnicity, age, language, ability, and gender. Make room for art, music, civics, character education, service learning, and recess.

This isn't a single vision, but a composite of the visions of many organizations and groups that believe community is central to public schools and public education. As this description illustrates, a community-centered vision of public education is built upon a strong sense of connection and belonging, on mutual support and collective responsibility, and on meeting the needs of the whole child. It is built upon a sense of how schools can help create a sense of "we" out of so many different individuals.

COMMUNITY AND PUBLIC SCHOOLS TODAY: ORDER, CONNECTION, AND BELONGING

The following examples address religion and culture, staying in school and zero tolerance. They illustrate some of the ways in which we expect public schools to satisfy the value of community, and some of the tensions that efforts to build community can create with other public values.

Religious Education and Cultural Celebration

Students often recognize religious and cultural celebrations in school by wearing special clothes or adopting a specific diet. Deciding which celebrations to recognize or accommodate can create issues of fairness and equal treatment for other students.

A number of school districts, concerned about students wearing costumes portraying scary or violent characters, have adopted strict guidelines regarding what clothing and costumes students can wear to school at Halloween. Some districts have banned Halloween all together. Decisions to allow, limit or ban Halloween can create tensions with parents over religious issues, freedom of expression issues, and whether the school is part of or separate from the community.

Several states have approved high school elective courses aimed at using the Bible to understand literature, history and more. State legislators say they are responding to communities' desire to teach biblical literature and history. State boards of education and school districts that choose to adopt Bible course curriculum standards face the challenge of how to teach the course without running afoul of the freedom of religion clause of the U.S. Constitution. To meet legal standards, course material must be presented in a neutral manner without proselytizing. Both supporters and opponents acknowledge that it can be very hard to teach religion without preaching.

Staying in School

We may encourage students to stay in school for economic reasons, but dimensions of the value of community have much to do with why students drop out. Students and their families may not value education, may have low expectations, or may not see the long-term value of a high school diploma. Students may be bored, increased class size may lead to a lack of personal attention, and too many requirements for non-college bound students may encourage some of them to give up.

There also may be discipline issues, family problems at home, drugs and alcohol, pregnancy, a perception that school is not cool, or gang involvement.

There may not be enough alternatives for higher-risk students. Some students may feel that no one cares whether they succeed, and they may not be engaged early and often enough to build positive adult and mentoring relationships. Some students and their families may have economic needs that make working as important as attending school.

Smaller schools and classes have been proposed as one way in which to strengthen student connection to school. To some people, smaller schools and classes nurture a sense of place, heritage and identity. They cite the 1999 Columbine High School shooting as an example of what can happen when these connections fray and alienation sets in. But fostering greater connection and belonging must compete with pressures of cost, standardization, and educating students to participate in a global economy.

Proponents acknowledge that smaller schools have limitations, but suggest that we have gone too far in creating huge schools with fine facilities but no sense of belonging, and that small schools offer important lessons about not just teaching children, but raising them.[8] They see smaller schools as extensions of the family which encourage parental involvement. And keeping younger children with the same teachers for several years, mixing students of different ages, engaging older students in teaching and helping younger students, and breaking larger schools into several smaller school neighborhoods are some other ways in which schools seek to recreate a sense of community, connection and belonging.

Zero Tolerance

Zero tolerance policies, intended to remove dangerous children from classrooms, spread throughout the country over the last two decades, giving school officials wide latitude to impose discipline.[9] Zero tolerance policies became popular as a way to address issues of social and moral order, maintain discipline and safety, and reduce incidents of violence. As tolerance declined, suspensions rose. Historically, the most common reasons students receive long-term suspensions are possession of an illegal substance, minor assault and possession of a weapon that's not a firearm.

Many zero tolerance policies require students to be suspended for the rest of the school year for a wide range of offenses, including drug possession and fights that cause serious injuries. In addition, many schools issue short-term suspensions for non-compliance, in which students are disciplined for not following directions.

But critics argue such policies are used too readily and can have a disparate impact on children of color. Recently, more and more school districts are beginning to rethink their student safety and discipline policies. Some public school leaders fear that long-term suspensions steer students toward drug and gang involvement, create a school-to-prison pipeline in which African-American students are most likely to be suspended or expelled, and create a one-size-fits-all approach to dealing with children and teens who need to be treated more individually. In addition, they argue such policies deprive children of opportunities to learn the skills they are attending school to learn in the first place.

Changing zero tolerance policies involves more than just shifting priorities among existing values. It may also introduce other values. Moving away from zero tolerance may mean giving principals greater flexibility and more freedom to exercise discretion. In turn, that may increase pressure on districts to ensure fairness by being consistent and standardizing suspension procedures. And keeping suspended students in an educational setting rather than at home requires spending more on alternative education and may result in a greater cost per student than regular classroom seats.

HOW MUCH COMMUNITY SHOULD WE HAVE IN PUBLIC SCHOOLS?

Can we have too much community, too much focus on the common good? Many Americans tend to be wary of communitarian efforts to balance rights and individual freedom with a greater emphasis on social responsibility and obligation to the common good. Voting is one example. While most Americans may agree in principle that citizens should vote, many are likely to resist any effort that would compel citizens to vote.

How much community should we try to create in public schools? Following are three examples that address health and nutrition, recess and the pledge of allegiance. In each example public schools must decide how much community to emphasize, and when to balance concerns for community with concerns for the other core public values of liberty, equality and prosperity.

Health, Nutrition and Edible Education

Once upon a time, students brought their lunch to school or went home for lunch. Today most students eat lunch in a staffed cafeteria that serves hot lunches. Some students still bring their lunch to school in a lunch box or bag. Since nutrition is considered basic to childhood development and readiness to learn, the nutritional responsibilities of schools have expanded. Schools offer federally-funded school lunch and breakfast programs for needy children. In an effort to encourage healthier eating, high schools have begun to feature more grown-up items. Better nutrition is one way in which schools can counter poor health and obesity.

Some healthy eating advocates lobby for edible education, not just school lunch reform. Edible education is an approach to teaching that integrates classroom instruction, school lunch, cooking and gardening into the studies of math, science, history and reading. It involves not only teaching children about where food comes from and how it is produced but giving them responsibilities in the school garden and kitchen. Proponents argue that this approach teaches not just nutrition, but citizenship and civic responsibility.

Most school districts have very specific procedures and requirements for conducting background checks on employees, but when it comes to food safety, far fewer conduct inspections of their cafeterias, even though students are at greater risk from disease and illness than they are from employee threats or violence. Schools that receive food as part of the National School Lunch Program are required by law to have kitchens inspected twice a year. Virtually all school districts post students test scores on the internet for the public to access, but few post the results of food inspections. Should schools also post kitchen and cafeteria inspection scores?

Choices about what food to serve to students create policy problems in public schools. Because schools tend to break even or lose money on subsidized meals, many schools rely upon higher profit margins from premium a la carte foods, single-serve packaged foods, and fast food from well-known retailers like Pepsi, Pizza Hut and McDonald's to cover expenses, generate revenue, or reduce the local tax burden.

But growing awareness about junk food, nutritional quality, and increases in obesity and Type 2 diabetes have forced schools to respond to public health concerns. Faced with both funding and health concerns, schools must weigh the economic benefits of retail sales against the health consequences for students. Should districts accept a commercial contract guaranteeing new revenue in exchange for allowing a company to sell its products in schools?

Recess and Playtime

Many schools do not regard recess and leisure time as essential to education. Recent research suggests that play, leisure and rest time may be as important to a child's academic development as reading, science and math, and that regular recess, fitness or nature time can improve behavior, concentration and even grades. Several studies have found that between 30 and 40 percent of children have little or no daily recess, that nearly half of all elementary schools have reduced recess time, and that teachers often punish children by taking recess away.

Children are rarely punished by having math class taken away. Should schools value recess and play time as much as academic time? Should schools make more recess and play time available, or should they consider play and leisure time to be the responsibility of parents and students during non-school hours?

Pledge of Allegiance

In recent years a number of states have codified a practice many parents never knew had faded away—reciting the Pledge of Allegiance. According to the National Conference of State Legislatures, 37 states require schools to include the pledge in their daily schedules. Six other states have made the practice optional.

Legislators, school officials and students disagree on the merits of such legislation. Some see it as a civic duty and argue that it creates a sense of common identity and connectedness. Some raise issues of fairness for children of different faiths and cultures. Some see it as a waste of time and resources, citing pressures for increasing student achievement that have reduced the amount of non-curriculum time available.

Some argue that when a class of students recites the pledge it puts pressure on all students to go along, putting a damper on students thinking for themselves and being willing to ask questions about the nation's values. Others embrace the pledge but not the requirement, arguing that daily recitation diminishes the pledge's meaning rather than deepening a sense of citizenship.

The history of the pledge shows how public values remain constant even though our allegiance to specific values may shift. In 1892, socialist utopian and Baptist minister Francis Bellamy wrote and published the pledge in a leading family publication, citing allegiance to the republic. In the 1920s, the American Legion and Daughters of the American Revolution added the phrase "United States of America" to the pledge. In 1942, Congress adopted the pledge as part of the nation's flag code. In 1954, the Knights of Columbus persuaded Congress to add the phrase "under God."

A number of states have passed laws requiring schools to set aside time for students to recite the pledge voluntarily. A few other states have tried to require students to recite the pledge. In 1943, the U.S. Supreme Court ruled that schools cannot require students to recite the pledge. Note that this occurred during a time in our nation's history when many Americans might have found it quite reasonable to require students to recite the Pledge of Allegiance in public schools.

A ROLE FOR PUBLIC SCHOOLS IN BUILDING COMMUNITY

Populism may have lost out to commercialism in the 1896 presidential election, but the romantic notions of frontier community and civil society live on. Much of our dissatisfaction with modern life can be traced to the populism and republicanism of our early heritage. From William Jennings Bryan to John Anderson to Ross Perot to Steve Forbes to Sarah Palin, populist candidates have evoked images and memories of frontier values, and of how we have lost our sense of self-reliance, community and civic virtue. Many Americans are nostalgic for the small town life prevalent at the time of Tocqueville's visit to America in the early 1830s.

The values and mores of the American frontier are ingrained in us as a sort of collective political consciousness, rising to the surface whenever our revolutionary passions are fanned. This historical and cultural consciousness helps explain why land use planning, zoning and development are among our most contentious local public issues. We are quick to proclaim "not in my backyard" and "it's my property and I'll do with it what I want" as if we were the only inhabitants for hundreds of square miles. We can include school choice and student assignment in this group, as land use and school use are ideological offspring of the same frontier heritage.

We cannot help but invest our romantic notions of frontier independence and agrarian community in public schools. Our increasingly complex society requires an expanded and extended socialization period and process. While parents continue to fill the primary socialization role, public schools have served this role for decades.

Some citizens, as well as some parents, teachers, administrators and school board members, think public schools would be better off if they could rid themselves of social issues and focus on the business of education within the classroom. This seems unlikely to happen, given the continuing social, cultural and economic transformations taking place in American society.

While student achievement and state and national standards garner most of the headlines, curriculum and standards are not what concern parents and the public most about public schools. In a survey about the most pressing problem facing local high schools, 63 percent of parents and 56 percent of the general public cited "social problems and kids who misbehave," while only about three in 10 cited "low academic standards and outdated curricula."[10] And while proponents of greater parental freedom, school choice, and treating education as a marketplace may view the government "monopoly" on education as paternalistic, the unfortunate truth is that for some children, school is the best parenting they will ever get.[11]

Public schools did not make socialization a public schooling responsibility. Social and economic forces changed America in ways that strained the social fabric and capacity of traditional families, neighborhoods, communities and economies. To maintain the American way of life in the face of these changes we enlisted public schools in the process of Americanization and socialization. In doing so we made public schools into an institution of social and moral order.

Enlisting public schools in the effort to preserve social and economic order and sustain the American way of life did not come without a cost. As we saw in our Crestwich story, and as we will see again, a growing sense of loss of control over the impacts of bureaucratic processes is a key factor in the deteriorating relationship between citizens and their public schools.

Preserving our American way of life in the face of social, economic, and demographic transformations requires us to sometimes change how we live in order to preserve what we live. If we are to preserve our ideals of liberty, equality, community, and prosperity as the face and fabric of our nation changes daily, public schools must accept some public responsibility for socializing children and young adults. In carrying out this role, public schools help maintain social and economic stability, social and moral order, and preserve democracy. For public schools, the socialization die is cast. There is no turning back.

NOTES

1. Kemmis, D. (1990). *Community and the politics of place.* Norman, OK: University of Oklahoma Press.
2. Ibid.
3. Waldo, 1984.
4. Kemmis, D., 1990, p. 33.
5. Dewey, 1916, p. 115.
6. Author Alfred Kazin in Mondale, S., and Patton, S. B. (Eds.) (2001). *School: The story of American public education.* Boston, MA: Beacon Press.
7. Kristof, N. D. (2003). "4 teacher's pets." *The New York Times,* November 1.
8. Eckholm, E. (2010). "Ruling limits state's power in school suspensions." *The New York Times,* October 8.
9. Johnson, J., Rochkind, J., and Ott, A. (2010). *Public and parents buy into the need to ramp up math and science education but most still think their local schools are doing fine.* New York, NY: Public Agenda, June.
10. Medige, B. (2003). "Privatization of public education: Segregation, desegregation, resegregation." Retrieved December 18, 2003 from http://buffaloreport.com/articles/030502medige.html.

Chapter 3

Equality and Public Schools

Difference, Diversity, Equal Opportunity

As immigration, industrialization and urbanization transformed America, education became more and more important as a means of achieving the American Dream. By the beginning of the twentieth century, the United States was schooling more children than any other nation.

But despite being the "cradle of liberty" and the "land of opportunity" to much of the world, millions of Americans were excluded from full participation in the American Dream. The realities of discrimination, segregation, and exclusion meant that not all children could attend public schools together. Horace Mann's once radical notion of common schools for all children had given way to separate schools for different children.

Special government schools were created for Native American children. African-Americans, freed from slavery but excluded from public schools, founded their own schools and gave rise to what we now term "historically black colleges and universities." Religious and ethnic discrimination against Irish Catholics spurred the creation of our parochial school system. The lesson is clear—deny people access to the American Dream, and they will create their own.

Like liberty and community, equality is an ideal that inspires tremendous faith and passion. And also like liberty and community, equality has multiple dimensions and means different things to different people. Equal and equitable, for example, are both dimensions of equality, but have different meanings. Equal refers to the quality or condition of being exactly the same as something else. Equity refers to the state, action or principle of treating people in accordance with differing needs. This distinction bears repeating, as we sometimes confuse equal opportunity with equal outcomes or equal results.

Equality can take many forms, including equal access, equal rights and equal opportunity. We may agree that equality matters, but we don't agree on who or what should be equal, when, or how much. Like the other public values, we want as much equality as we can have. But we also understand that like the other public values, too much equality can create harm as well as good. Philosophers since Aristotle have warned against seeking to make everything equal, as attempts to make unequal things equal are often the worst form of inequality.

Total equality is neither achievable nor desirable. The right to vote is one of our most universal rights. But even universal suffrage does not guarantee political equality, because not everyone exercises this right equally. A society founded on freedom cannot make citizens equal. But it can, and should, as Jefferson advised, treat them equally. "The most sacred of the duties of a government is to do equal and impartial justice to all its citizens."

EDUCATION FOR ALL: DIFFERENCE, DIVERSITY AND DISCRIMINATION

Our pursuit of liberty and the nation's founding went hand in hand. But it would take nearly a century for the ideal of equality to overcome slavery. As Abraham Lincoln astutely noted, "The assertion that 'all men are created equal' was of no practical use in effecting our separation from Great Britain, and it was placed in the Declaration not for that, but for future use."

In our second century, that future use would take place in public schools. The ideal of equality in public education would fracture along two key fault lines—one based on race and ethnicity, the other based on language and culture. When the dream of common schools for all faded to uncommon schools for some, visionaries of equality would march with raised banners. They would make their stand on the field of public education.

From Segregation to Desegregation to Resegregation

In 1896, the U.S. Supreme Court ruled in *Plessy v. Ferguson* that racial segregation was permissible as long as facilities were equal. This decision and its separate but equal doctrine would remain the law of the land for more than a half-century.

In 1938 the Carnegie Corporation commissioned Gunnar Myrdal, a Swedish economist, to conduct a study of what was referred to as the "Negro question," the chasm between the American principle of equality and the reality of African-American lives.[1] Myrdal concluded that discrimination in the South was due less to prejudice on the part of whites than to the failure of public authorities to enforce the Constitution. Myrdal criticized the separate but equal doctrine and predicted that the democratic principles of the American Creed would eventually prevail.

In the fall of 1950, a half century after *Plessy,* the Rev. Oliver Brown walked his eight-year-old daughter Linda to school. The rest, as they say is history. But it would take nearly four more years before the U.S. Supreme Court cited Myrdal's critique of "separate but equal" in refuting *Plessy.* The court ruled unanimously in *Brown v. Board of Education of Topeka, Kansas* that, "It is doubtful that any child may reasonably be expected to succeed in life if he is denied the opportunity of an education. Such an opportunity . . . is a right which must be available to all on equal terms. Separate educational facilities are inherently unequal."

The history of desegregation in public schools is accounted for elsewhere. Suffice it to say that many observers describe the crusade for equality in public schools as a journey from segregation to desegregation to resegregation. Some argue that today desegregation is turning into resegregation, while others argue that desegregation never became integration. Regardless of whether the desegregation glass is half full or half empty, critics of efforts to fully achieve desegregation have characterized a number of court cases in the 1980s and 1990s as resegregation decisions.[2]

By the 1990s, resegregation had become a national trend.[3] Researchers acknowledge that there may be some confusion about the status of desegregation law, but the basic trend is "toward dissolution of desegregation orders and return to patterns of more serious segregation."[4] A number of studies, articles and reports document the dismantling of desegregation and the resegregation of public schools a half-century after the *Brown* decision.[5]

Fueled by white flight from cities to suburbs, the dissolution of desegregation court orders, parental choice advocates pushing for a return to neighborhood schools and voter backlash, many school districts are returning to a two-tiered system that is increasingly divided by race, class and student performance. Equality may well be the great unfinished task of American democracy.

Language, Culture, and Bilingual Education

Language has always been central to the identity of Americans. The uniformity of community and the diversity of equality create a perennial tension between those who view America as a great melting pot with a common national identity and those who view it as a mosaic of peoples with their own customs and culture.[6]

These competing views are reflected in statements by two different presidents. Theodore Roosevelt expressed the melting pot view of America: "We have room for but one language here, and that is the English language; for we intend to see that the crucible turns our people out as Americans, of American nationality." The mosaic view of America was expressed by Jimmy Carter: "We have become not a melting pot but a beautiful mosaic. Different people, different beliefs, different yearnings, different dreams."

New languages and cultures posed challenges to the ideal of common schools, pitting equality and community against each other. The constant demand to assimilate new Americans raised questions about how much difference we can have and still have something in common. As a Chicano civil rights leader remarked, "In the American school, they want to make Anglos out of all of us. They want to take our Spanish away and teach us English. Well, you don't make anybody greater by making them less."[7]

Public schools have been embroiled in the debate over language and identity since the nineteenth century. Congress legislated the right of Mexican citizens to speak Spanish in the United States, passed prohibitions against Native Americans being taught in their own languages, and passed the first federal English-only law in 1906. Some public schools adopted German language instruction in response to the growth of German immigrants in the mid-nineteenth century, only to witness a national backlash against German and Germany during World War I. By the 1920s a national backlash against foreigners had virtually eradicated bilingual education.

Bilingual education experienced a resurgence in the civil rights climate of the 1960s and 1970s, only to be curtailed once again by a backlash against new waves of immigration in the 1980s. State English-only laws proliferated in the 1990s. In 2001, the *No Child Left Behind Act* brought an official end to national endorsement of bilingual education. In Ohio, which adopted the nation's first bilingual education law in 1839, things came full circle with the introduction of the Ohio English Unity Act in 2006. Melting pot or mosaic, public schools cannot separate themselves from public debates about language and identity.

AN EQUALITY-CENTERED VISION OF PUBLIC EDUCATION AND PUBLIC SCHOOLS

Many different national and state-wide organizations exist to promote equity, fairness and justice, equal opportunity and access, equal treatment and results, and a level playing field. Examples of equality-based organizations that focus on public education and public schools include All Children Matter in Michigan, the Campaign for Fiscal Equity in New York, the Colorado Children's Campaign, New Hampshire's Communities Actively United for Social Equality (CAUSE), the Consortium for Adequate School Funding in Georgia, Equality Texas, Oregon's Equity Foundation, the Mid-Atlantic Equity Consortium based in Maryland, the National Association for Single Sex Public Education based in Pennsylvania, the National Center for Fair and Open Testing based in Massachusetts, New Jersey's Institute for Social Justice, Progress Now Colorado, the North Carolina Justice Center, and Rethinking Schools Wisconsin.

Based on the mission of these organizations and other organizations like them that espouse greater equality in public education and on the dimensions of equality we described earlier, what might an equality-centered vision of public schools look like that would emphasize educational opportunity for all children, equal treatment and fair and adequate funding? Following is a composite equality-centered vision of public schools, drawn from a wide variety of equality-centered organizations across the country.

Inequalities of wealth and privilege, not teaching and curriculum, are the critical challenges in public schools. Refocus public debate on reducing inequality rather than on increasing choice. Address the underlying causes of social and economic disparities and barriers that constrain communities, residents and students from achieving their full potential.

Promote equal educational opportunity for all students regardless of the per capita property wealth of individual school districts. Ensure that educational funding in poorer urban districts is substantially equal to that of wealthy suburban districts and not dependent on budgeting and taxing decisions of local school districts. Education spending and the quality of educational opportunity are positively related, and opportunity should not be tied to local resources or limited by the amount of state revenues.

Reverse resegregation and close achievement gaps. Assign students to schools to achieve socioeconomic balance. Support tax-credit and tuition credit laws to help equalize school opportunities for families. Do not support the use of vouchers because vouchers would privatize schools and remove them from public responsibility.

Level the playing field by supporting increased access to quality child care and early education opportunities, programs to reduce dropout rates, alternative, special, and bilingual education programs, and free and reduced breakfast/lunch programs. Increase opportunities through public education, community organizing and community action for individuals with disabilities and others who experience a diminished quality of life due to social injustice. Support adequate and equitable funding for the education of disadvantaged students.

Promote fair, open and valid evaluations of students, teachers and schools. Support fairness in high-stakes testing and in suspension and expulsion policies. Create learning environments free of race, gender, class, ethnic and cultural biases so that students of all backgrounds have equal opportunities to flourish. Adopt non-discrimination facility use policies. Teach all history and cultures, and make all courses and sports available to all students. Support Title IX.

Make schools places that are physically and psychologically safe, where what students feel has value, where they are entitled to respect, and where they are not alone. Every student is able to obtain an education free from physical and mental harm. Prohibit any form of harassment or bullying in schools, including but not limited to harassment or bullying based on race, color, disability, religion, sex, national origin, age, sexual orientation, gender identity, or physical appearance of the student or the student's parents. Provide teachers with the training they need to address and stop acts of harassment and bullying in order to protect students.

This isn't a single vision, but a composite of the visions of many organizations and groups that believe equality is central to public schools and public education. As this description illustrates, an equality-centered vision of public education is built upon equal opportunity, equal treatment and a strong sense of fairness and justice. It is built upon an adequate and equitable distribution of public goods, although not necessarily an equal one. And it is built upon a level playing field, in which differences become assets and not disadvantages.

Horace Mann expressed an equality-centered vision of public schools and public education this way: "It is a free school system. It knows no distinction of rich and poor . . . it throws open its doors and spreads the table of its bounty for all the children of the state. . . . Education then, beyond all other devices of human origin, is the equalizer of the conditions of men, the great balance wheel of the social machinery."

EQUALITY AND PUBLIC SCHOOLS TODAY: LEVELING THE PLAYING FIELD

Public schools serve as a great equalizer in American society, distributing educational opportunity and mitigating socioeconomic inequality. Public schools cannot guarantee equal outcomes, but they can do a great deal to equalize opportunity. As Voltaire observed, "All the citizens of a state cannot be equally powerful, but they may be equally free." The following examples address school readiness, health and wealth, and diversity. They illustrate some of the ways in which equality matters in public schools.

Ready, Set, Go: School Readiness

Where children start matters, both in life and in school. Virtually every school system has collected data showing that schools with lower numbers of free and reduced lunch eligible students tend to have higher graduation rates and higher reading, writing and math scores.

Our belief that we have achieved at least relative equality can lead us to assume that all children start on an equal footing. A recent study of American children says otherwise. Some 10,000 U.S. children were tracked starting at age 9 months, with language, literacy and math skill tests at ages 3, 4 or 5. Lower-income children were less prepared to begin school than higher-income children.

The poorest fifth of the children tracked scored at the 34th percentile for literacy, compared to the 69th percentile for the wealthiest fifth. Significant factors included fewer financial resources, lower parental levels of education, and negative impacts of economic stress. The single most influential factor was differences in parenting, which accounted for between one-third and one-half of the readiness gap between lower and middle-income children.[8]

Health, Wealth and Opportunity

Our belief in the heroic power of the individual is so strong that we are sometimes tempted to think that money doesn't matter. But it does. Compared to children from lower income families, children from moderate and higher income families have better overall physical and dental health. They are also more likely to have stories read to them, more likely to participate in organized activities after school or on weekends, and are less likely to repeat a grade in school.[9]

Looking at the relationship between family income and SAT scores, North Carolina Policy Watch reported the following average 2009 SAT scores for North Carolina high school students: 930 for students from families with incomes of less than $40,000 a year; 1082 for students in families with incomes of at least $120,000; and 1141 for students in families with incomes of more than $200,000.[10]

Over the past few decades, the federal government and most states have increased their funding for K-12 public education. Most states have adopted school funding formulas that allocate more resources to districts with lower local property values. But nearly half of public school funding today is still provided through local taxes, and despite the efforts of state governments, significant per-student funding disparities within and between states persist.

Most Americans believe that public education should provide a level playing field for all students. But efforts to redistribute funding between higher and lower wealth districts within states have been met with considerable resistance. Despite some claims that funding isn't important and that more dollars won't improve education, dollars do make a difference. Research and experience show that districts need additional revenue to pay for more teachers and smaller classes in lower-performing schools.

When the economic advantage of higher-wealth homes is combined with greater school funding, achievement scores from school districts where funding is substantial and student poverty is minimal are similar to those earned by the highest-scoring countries in international comparative studies.[11] Scores from districts where funding is inadequate and poverty levels are higher are similar to those of the lowest-scoring foreign countries.

Minority, Majority, Diversity

Between 1972 and 2006, the proportion of minority students in public schools nearly doubled from barely 20 percent to 38 percent. If this trend continues, minority students are likely to outnumber white students within a decade or so. In at least six states—California, Hawaii, Louisiana, Mississippi, New Mexico and Texas—they already do.

Despite the projected browning of our public schools, the majority of black and Hispanic children in the United States attend majority-minority schools.[12] At the peak of desegregation, nearly half of all black students attended predominantly white schools. By the mid-1980s, this trend had begun to reverse. Today, 70 percent of black students attend predominantly minority schools, with more than one-third attending schools that are at least 90 percent minority.[13] The figures are similar for Hispanic students. Less than a third of white students go to school with black or Hispanic students.

Majority-minority schools are more likely to be lower-performing, at least as measured by standardized test scores, and they are more likely to have inexperienced staff, higher teacher turnover and more special needs students. Research shows that children in majority-minority schools perform poorly in reading, regardless of the quality of their teachers.[14]

With both the diversity and classroom segregation of public schools increasing, school districts adopted a continuum of approaches to diversify classrooms over the past few decades. These included race-based assignment, socioeconomic-based student assignment, and most recently, assignment based on student achievement. Regardless of what we call it, the goal remains the same—diversifying classrooms. And the goal remains the goal because our citizens and communities experience significant differences in their standard of living and in their quality of life. In public schools, these differences matter.

How much should schools resemble the demographic makeup of the workplaces and living spaces of tomorrow? Some citizens want to avoid social engineering and restricting school choice. Some citizens prefer to reallocate resources and use market-based incentives to help parents choose diversity. And some parents value a sense of community more than classroom diversity. For example, relatively strong support among African-American families for neighborhood schools and charter schools that are more caring, more supportive, and more connected to them and their communities suggests that for some minority families, the loss of community is too high a price to pay for the presumed benefits of integration.[15]

HOW MUCH EQUALITY SHOULD WE HAVE IN PUBLIC SCHOOLS?

Can we have too much equality, too much focus on leveling the playing field? Treat everyone the same all the time and you will hear cries of "that's not fair." But treat everyone differently all the time and you will hear cries of "that's not fair." Freedom isn't always free, and equality isn't always equal.

How much equality should we try to create in public schools? The following examples address gender diversity and sexual orientation, equity in classrooms and equal access and equal opportunity in higher education. These examples illustrate some of the tensions that efforts to achieve greater equality can create with other public values.

Gender Diversity and Sexual Orientation

Most school districts have vision statements or policies that pledge they will ensure that students achieve at their highest potential regardless of race, gender or socio-economic status. Including gender diversity and sexual orientation is more problematic.

Districts may be hesitant to recognize gender diversity because some people will view recognition as endorsement. Board members and administrators may have personal views that conflict with including sexual orientation as a protected category. There was a time when school districts would not have included references to race or ethnicity. Today, it's unacceptable not to include racial and ethnic characteristics as part of a district's policy regarding equal treatment, regardless of whether all board members and administrators agree.

Proponents of recognizing gender diversity argue that recognition is important for students in order for them to feel included, to receive equal treatment, to prevent or at least discourage discrimination and to be accepted as equal members of the school community. Opponents argue that recognition violates community norms and encourages greater social and moral disorder.

Excluding gender diversity and sexual orientation is often done on grounds that organizational performance will be impaired. But exclusion may also have a performance and economic cost. The U.S. Senate, the Center for the Study of Sexual Minorities in the Military and the U.S. General Accountability Office each cited the loss of some of the nation's best and brightest as a result of the recently repealed "don't ask, don't tell" policy approved by Congress in 1994.

Equalizing Classrooms

In public schools, equality principally takes the form of equal treatment and equal outcomes. Schools devote a great deal of attention to equalizing treatment of different groups and equalizing results within and across groups. Here are two recent efforts to create greater equality, both of which stirred up controversy.

One school district's decision to adopt classroom differentiation—classes containing students of varying ability and socioeconomic backgrounds—was criticized by a local newspaper columnist, who wrote that the "elusive quest for equality gets in the way of meaningful progress for minorities."[16] The columnist went on to say that differentiation sounds great in theory, but in practice it has a dark side that impedes achievement and limits opportunity.

A handful of schools have set off an emotional national debate by giving minimum scores of 50 rather than 0 for students who receive a grade of F. Proponents argue that it is more fair to assign a point range (e.g., 50–59) to a grade of F equal to that assigned to other grades (e.g., D = 60–69, B = 80–89) than to have points for a grade of F range from 59 to 0. Opponents argue that doing this will lessen the distinctive value of other grades.

Equal Access and Equal Opportunity in Higher Education

Universities are both expanding and contracting access by minority students. Part of a growing national movement, a top 30 national university in the *U.S. News & World Report* rankings announced it would make SAT and

ACT college entrance exams optional for admission beginning with the 2009-10 academic year. University officials say they changed their policy after reviewing extensive research that shows that standardized tests favor wealthier students, tend to exhibit racial and socioeconomic biases, and aren't the best predictors of college success. University officials said that this is the fair and right thing to do.

The Education Trust reports that the nation's public flagship universities are becoming whiter and richer than residents of states they serve, and that they are enrolling disproportionately fewer low-income and minority students than in the past.[17] Students at these schools look less and less like the state populations those universities were created to serve. Financial aid choices made by prestigious public universities also result in higher barriers to college enrollment and less success among low-income students and students of color.

A ROLE FOR PUBLIC SCHOOLS IN ACHIEVING EQUALITY

A nation committed to the ideals of democracy cannot impose a condition of inequality without risking harm to democracy itself. It cannot claim equality as a virtue if it exists only by fiat of the law. For without ideals, even the law may be tempted to respond to lesser virtues. The *Brown* decision is important to all Americans as an affirmation of the moral basis of democracy and the fundamental values of the American Creed. It is both a culmination of decades of effort to achieve greater equality and a reminder that the pursuit of the ideals represented by public values is never ending.

Efforts to maintain integrated and equal public schools have largely ignored issues of racial, class and economic segregation, choosing instead to attempt to equalize outcomes within the existing structure of segregated schools.[18] The irony of school resegregation is that white students, who are most in need of knowing and learning about America's increasing diversity, are the most segregated students of all. They are far more likely to attend public schools that are less racially diverse than any other demographic group.

Most Americans acknowledge the value of diversity, but equality's fundamental tensions with the personal freedom and choice of liberty and the sameness and belonging of community pose serious obstacles to actually achieving diversity. One way a democratic society resolves this dilemma is through institutions that amplify our national values, such as the church, the state and the school. This is one reason why public schools are public. Teaching in and of itself is not a public function, but amplifying and discussing national values is.

The school, like the sermon in church, is likely to be somewhat more broadminded than local opinion, and legislation, on the whole, is likely to be more equitable than legislators are themselves as private individuals.[19] We place in these institutions our "ideals of how the world rightly ought to be."[20] Public schools matter in our quest for equality precisely because they are public and are therefore repositories for and conservatories of our ideals. Public schools matter because it is in schools where we teach children the lessons that democracy teaches us about the tensions between individual opportunity and equal opportunity.

Today the United States has the most diverse population of public school students in its history. Public schools are poised to become the first major nonwhite institution in America. How we treat public school integration and segregation will influence American society for generations to come.

NOTES

1. Myrdal, G. (1944). *An American dilemma: The Negro problem and modern democracy.* New York, NY: Harper & Row.
2. Orfield, G. (2001). "School more separate: Consequences of a decade of resegregation." *Rethinking Schools Online, 16, 1.* Retrieved December 18, 2003 from http://www.rethinkingschools.org/archive/16_01/Seg161.shtml.
3. Orfield, G. (1999). "The resegregation of our nation's schools: A troubling trend." Retrieved December 18, 2003 from *Civil Rights Journal* at http://www.findarticles.com/cf_dls/m0HSP/1_4/66678562/print/jhtml.
4. Orfield, G., and Eaton, S. E. (1996). *Dismantling desegregation: The quiet reversal of Brown v. Board of Education.* New York, NY: New Press.
5. See, for example, Medige, B. (2003); Orfield, G., and Eaton, S. E. (1996); Orfield (2001); and Simmons, T., and Ebbs, S. (2001). "Separate and unequal, again." *The News & Observer,* February 18.
6. For a more complete account of the challenge of language in public education, see Mondale, S., and Patton, S. B. (Eds.) (2001). *School: The story of American public education.* Boston, MA: Beacon Press.
7. José Angel Gutierrez, a Chicano civil rights leader, in Mondale and Patton (2001).
8. Washbrook, E., and Waldfogel, J. (2008). "Family income and children's readiness for school." *Research in Public Policy,* Bulletin of the Centre for Market and Public Organisation, 7, 3-5.
9. Action for Children North Carolina (2006). *North Carolina Children's Index.* Raleigh, NC: Author.
10. Fitzsimon, C. (2009). "The weekly numbers." *N.C. Policy Watch,* September 8.

11. Biddle, B. J., and Berliner, D. C. (2003). "What research says about unequal funding for schools in America: Retrieved from *Policy Perspectives* at http://ed policyreports.org.

12. National Center for Education Statistics. (2009). *Revenues and expenditures for public elementary and secondary education: School year 2007-08.* Washington, DC: U.S. Department of Education.

13. Fitzsimon, C. (2005). "The education poverty gap." *NC Policy Watch.* Retrieved Oct. 10, 2006 from http://www.ncpolicywatch.com/cms/2005/10/10/the-education-poverty-gap.

14. Research conducted by Frank Porter Graham Child Institute at the University of North Carolina at Chapel Hill as reported in Astigarraga, C. (2007). "Study links poor reading with minority schools." *The News & Observer,* June 22.

15. Simmons, T. (2001). "Where do we go from here?" *The News & Observer,* February 25.

16. Martinez, R. (2004). "Facing challenges at school." *The News & Observer,* January 29.

17. Gerald, D., and Haycock, K. (2006). *Engines of inequality: Diminishing equity in the nation's premier public universities.* Washington, DC: The Education Trust.

18. Orfield, 2001.

19. Myrdal.

20. Ibid., p. 80.

Chapter 4

Prosperity and Public Schools

Economy, Efficiency, Competitiveness

For much of the twentieth century it seemed that only parents with children paid much attention to public schools. Teachers were seen as extensions of parents and other forms of authority. School board service was a civic obligation more than a political platform. For much of that same period American business had served us well. Peter Drucker attributed much of our victory in World War II to superior American management and production.

By the 1980s, that superiority had seemingly disappeared as "made in Japan," once a derogatory term, came to symbolize a quality that Americans feared they could no longer create. Government, considered by the public to be the most capable institution in post-World War II America, fell to record levels of citizen distrust and loss of confidence.

President Jimmy Carter spoke a few years earlier of a national malaise. But the public wasn't in any mood to hear that the problem was with "we the people." It was easier to blame "them." "Them" was government bureaucrats, career politicians, all those receiving welfare (other than homeowners, corporations, and the vast majority of Americans who considered themselves to be middle class) and anyone who didn't produce wealth.

Outsiders (Reagan), populists (Perot), and libertarians (Forbes) capitalized upon an environment of bureaucrat-bashing, term limits, tax revolts, taxpayers' bill of rights, property tax relief, tax caps, and no tax pledges. Campaigning against government became, and still is, the best way to get into government. Less government, lower taxes, and higher test scores became the political mantra of the decade, bringing to life Woodrow Wilson's observation that "Prosperity is necessarily the first theme of a political campaign."

This loss of faith in our economy and in government trickled down to public schools. The National Commission on Excellence in Education (1983) noted this sense of fear and loss of confidence in its landmark report, *A Nation at Risk* (1983). "What lies behind this emerging national sense of frustration can be described as both a dimming of personal expectations and the fear of losing a shared vision for America."[1]

If public schools in the 1880s were shaped by a perfect storm of urbanization, industrialization and immigration, public schools in the 1980s were shaped by a perfect storm of declining economic superiority, a national perception of educational decline, and rising anti-government sentiment. Our exploration of public schools so far has shown that public schools are shaped by the times that produce them, and in turn help shape how we respond to those times. Public schools in the 1980s were no exception.

PUBLIC EDUCATION FOR THE BOTTOM LINE

With much of American business buffeted by global economic competition, public schools served as a rallying cry for a renewed national emphasis on the economic outcomes of education. The National Commission on Excellence in Education (1983) echoed this call when it wrote that "Our society and its educational institutions seem to have lost sight of the basic purposes of schooling, and of the high expectations and disciplined effort needed to attain them."[2]

Calls for reform gave rise to a back-to-basics movement, minimum competency tests, standardized and publicly reported testing, increased instructional time and graduation requirements, a core knowledge curriculum emphasizing sequential and structured instruction, expansion of formal accountability mechanisms, competency testing for teachers and students, and adoption by several states of national education goals and student assessment aimed at making American students "first in the world" in math and science.[3]

This renewed emphasis on performance and assessment was not new. The early 20th century saw the development of the standard unit, standardized IQ tests, achievement tests, the use of IQ tests for tracking by most major urban school districts, the widespread adoption of the Life Adjustment curriculum, and the founding of the Educational Testing Service.

In the 1950s the Soviet Union's launch of the *Sputnik* satellite led to calls for more science, math, and foreign language instruction amid criticism of low standards for American students. It also led to recommendations for intelligence testing, grouping, and tracking spurred by concerns for national security and competition with the Soviets. This metaphor was resurrected in the 1980s by the National Commission on Excellence in Education when it concluded that "We have, in effect, been committing an act of unthinking, unilateral educational disarmament."[4]

A number of national reports since *Sputnik* have identified weaknesses in public education and recommended strategies for improvement. Several notable reports are described briefly to illustrate how the value of prosperity frames our visions and expectations for public education.

The National Commission on Excellence in Education

Created in 1981, it issued its report, *A Nation at Risk: The Imperative for Educational Reform* in 1983. The Commission was charged with examining the state of education in America, including:

- Assessing the quality of teaching and learning;
- Comparing American schools and colleges with those of other advanced nations;
- Studying the relationship between college admissions requirements and student achievement in high school;
- Identifying educational programs which result in notable student success in college; and
- Assessing the degree to which major social and educational changes in the last quarter century have affected student achievement.

The commission's recommendations addressed improving educational delivery and performance and included:

- Strengthen high school graduation requirements and adopt more rigorous and measurable standards and higher expectations for academic performance at all levels of education;
- Devote significantly more time to learning the new basics, including more effective use of the existing school day, a longer school day, or a lengthened school year;
- Adopt competency standards, performance-based pay and a career ladder model for teachers (i.e., beginner, experienced, master);
- Tie teacher employment decisions to student performance and use market incentives to address teacher shortages; and
- Hold educators and elected officials responsible for providing the leadership and citizens responsible for providing the fiscal support required to bring about these reforms.

In addition to improving educational outcomes, the commission noted that education serves a purpose larger than that of just commerce and industry. "A high level of shared education is essential to a free, democratic society and to the fostering of a common culture, especially in a country that prides itself on pluralism and individual freedom. For our country to function, citizens must be able to reach some common understandings on complex issues, often on short notice and on the basis of conflicting or incomplete evidence. . . ."[5]

Rising Above the Gathering Storm: Energizing and Employing America for a Brighter Economic Future

In 2005, the National Academy of Sciences, the National Academy of Engineering and the Institute of Medicine undertook a study of America's competitiveness in the global economy in response to a request by Congress who asked the National Academies to respond to the following question: What are the top 10 actions, in priority order, that federal policy makers could take to enhance science and technology so that the United States can successfully compete, prosper, and be secure in the global community of the 21st century?[6]

This study, usually referred to as the "Gathering Storm" report, focused upon the ability of Americans to compete for employment in a job market that increasingly knows no geographic boundaries. *Gathering Storm* described a vision of America clearly dependent upon its economic and educational systems. "The United States takes deserved pride in the vitality of its economy, which forms the foundation of our high quality of life, our national security, and our hope that our children and grandchildren will inherit ever-greater opportunities."[7]

Gathering Storm, released as a report in 2005, published in book form in 2007, and revisited in 2010, cited a wide range of facts, indicators and studies suggesting existing and pending economic decline. Key education-related findings included:

- The World Economic Forum ranks the United States 48th in quality of mathematics and science education.
- Sixty-nine percent of United States public school students in fifth through eighth grade are taught mathematics by a teacher without a degree or certificate in mathematics.
- The United States ranks 27th among developed nations in the proportion of college students receiving undergraduate degrees in science or engineering.
- Forty-nine percent of United States adults do not know how long it takes for the Earth to revolve around the Sun.
- The United States ranks 20th in high school completion rate among industrialized nations and 16th in college completion rate.

- Sixty-eight percent of U.S. state prison inmates are high school dropouts or otherwise did not qualify for a diploma.
- The United States has fallen from first to eleventh place in the proportion of 25-34 year olds that has graduated high school.
- According to the 2008 ACT College Readiness report, 78 percent of high school graduates did not meet the readiness benchmark levels for one or more entry-level college courses in mathematics, science, reading and English.

Gathering Storm concluded that, "Without a renewed effort to bolster the foundations of our competitiveness, we can expect to lose our privileged position. For the first time in generations, the nation's children could face poorer prospects than their parents and grandparents did."[8] As Aristotle observed long ago, "The fate of empires depends on how they educate their children." Along with other reviews of education and economic competitiveness, *Gathering Storm* helped build bipartisan support in 2007 for America COMPETES, legislation encouraging investing in innovation through research and development to improve American competitiveness.[9]

Tough Choices or Tough Times: The Report of the New Commission on the Skills of the American Workforce

In 2007, the New Commission on the Skills of the American Workforce, a group of American business, government and education leaders, proposed a new framework for American education to boost student performance and raise the overall efficiency of the educational system.[10] The commission recommended dramatic changes to America's education and training system so that the nation can maintain its standard of living as it advances through the 21st century. These recommendations included:

- Prepare everyone for college;
- Make more efficient use of resources by reprogramming funds for higher payoff;
- Recruit teachers from the top third of high school graduates going on to college;
- Develop standards, assessments, and curricula that reflect today's needs and tomorrow's requirements;
- Provide high-quality, universal early childhood education;
- Give strong support to the students who need it the most;
- Create personal competitiveness accounts and regional competitiveness authorities to make America competitive;

- Create lean, performance-oriented management systems, incentives for schools to perform and innovate, and high performance schools and districts;
- Have school districts write performance contracts with 3rd party organizations to run schools.

The commission didn't just recommend improvements, it recommended a complete overhaul and restructuring of education. As the commission wrote, "The core problem is that our education and training systems were built for another era, an era in which most workers needed only a rudimentary education. It is not possible to get where we have to go by patching that system. There is not enough money at any level of our intergovernmental system to fix this problem by spending more on the system we have. We can get where we must go only by changing the system itself."[11]

While it focused on economic performance, efficiency and student achievement, the commission, like the National Commission on Excellence in Education a quarter century earlier, also recognized the need to address societal goals beyond economic ones. It recommended creating a fair financing system so all kids have a good shot at success, investing in early childhood education for all 4-year-olds and low-income 3-year-olds, funding all public schools directly from the state, and uniform base funding for all students plus increments for lower income, non-English speaking, and disabled children.

This brief summary of several national efforts illustrates how the public value of prosperity drives our understanding of the core purposes of public schooling. As is true for liberty, equality and community, we will pursue this goal as long as we exist as a nation, for like the other core public values, the pursuit of greater prosperity has no end.

In the late 1980s the president and the nation's governors adopted Goals 2000 to restore America to its rightful place in the world by the end of the century. In the early 1990s, the federal government proposed voluntary national standards. In the mid-1990s voluntary standards began to morph into national testing. The early 2000s gave birth to *No Child Left Behind*, with its increased emphasis on standardized testing.

In 2009 the Obama administration launched *Race to the Top* to encourage educational innovation by asking states to compete for federal innovation grants. The administration also launched *Educate to Innovate*, a complement to Race to the Top, to encourage middle and high school students to pursue science, technology, engineering and math. The stated policy goal was to move the United States from the middle to the top in science and math over the next decade. If that sounds somewhat reminiscent of the *Sputnik* era, you've been paying attention.

A PROSPERITY-CENTERED VISION OF PUBLIC EDUCATION AND PUBLIC SCHOOLS

Many national and state-wide organizations advocate for greater economy, efficiency, performance standards and measurement, benchmarking, data-driven decision making, and applying market solutions to public policy problems. Examples of prosperity-based organizations that address public education and public schools include Americans for Prosperity and Citizens for a Sound Economy headquartered in Washington, DC, the Children's Alliance of New Hampshire, the Great Lakes West Comprehensive Assistance Center in Illinois, the Maryland Business Roundtable for Education, the North Carolina Business Committee for Education, Colorado's Public Education and Business Coalition, Oregon's Public Education Network, South Dakota's Alliance for Education, and the Wisconsin Information Network for School Success.

Based on the mission of these organizations and other organizations like them that promote education for the economy and on the dimensions of prosperity we described earlier, what might a prosperity-centered vision of public education and public schools look like that would emphasize education to prepare students for competing in a 21st century global economy and making America's schools number one in the world? Following is a composite prosperity-centered vision of public schools, drawn from a wide variety of prosperity-centered organizations across the country.

Emphasize a curriculum relevant to business that incorporates career preparation and is based on real-world learning. Encourage school-business partnerships, apprenticeship, summer work, and cooperative and vocational education. Support universal pre-K education to prepare children for academic success. Focus on competitiveness and meeting global standards to further economic progress. Emphasize a curriculum of science, mathematics, computers, and technology. Academic performance comes first, sports and arts second. Make America's public schools first in the world.

Use performance data to help parents evaluate educational outcomes. Employ grading, student testing, standards, assessment, rankings, teacher certification, and data-driven decision making to achieve continuous improvement in student achievement. Adopt pay for performance, teacher signing and performance bonuses, incentives, commercialization, advertising, contracting, employment incentives and sanctions to improve student achievement. Make each school accountable for the performance of each child.

Operate schools according to business principles. Use privatization, contracting, and public-private partnerships. Apply private-sector costing models to manage transportation, facilities, school construction and food services. Align planning and budgeting with efforts to increase student achievement. Maximize the use of school facilities and school calendars. Extend the school day and year.

This isn't a single vision, but a composite of the visions of many organizations and groups that believe prosperity is central to public schools and public education. As this description illustrates, a prosperity-centered vision of public education is built upon standards, assessment, measurement, competition, performance indicators and return on investment. The KnowledgeWorks Foundation, which helps school districts increase student performance and reduce costs, suggests that since schools are an important contributor to our economy, education should be viewed as an investment rather than a service that governments provide.

PROSPERITY AND PUBLIC SCHOOLS TODAY: EDUCATION FOR THE ECONOMY

Public schools serve as a principal gateway to individual and national economic success. When we look at public education through the economic lens of prosperity, we see ways in which schools can both enhance economic progress and operate in accordance with economic principles. The following examples address economic competitiveness and schools as marketplaces. They illustrate some of the ways in which prosperity matters in public schools.

Economic Competitiveness

There is a pervasive sense that America is losing ground. Our high school graduation rate, once the highest in the world, now ranks 20th. Between 2000 and 2005, the U.S. was the only industrialized country with no increase in its postsecondary graduation rate. For 25-34 year olds with college degrees, the U.S. ranked 1st in 1998, 7th in 2005, and 13th in 2008, behind Slovenia.

In 2006, the Connecticut Committee for Economic Development stated that "Businesses are the number one consumers of the education system. If we are to believe all the studies that consistently show that investment in early education is so critical, then we . . . need to invest in our children."

In 2010 the National Academies, the country's leading advisory group on science and technology, ranked the U.S. 27th out of 29 wealthy countries in the proportion of college students with degrees in science or engineering. The World Economic Forum ranked the U.S. 48th out of 133 developed and developing nations in quality of math and science instruction.[12]

The Education Trust reported that the United States is the only industrialized country in the world in which today's young people are less likely than their parents to have completed high school.[13] Barely a century ago, our principal educational challenge was getting children into public schools. Today, our challenge is to get them out, and with a diploma.

School as a Marketplace

A few school districts have tried operating schools and classrooms as a marketplace. One example is the MicroSociety School program, which seeks to replicate the world of work and business in the classroom. Participating schools pay students with micro dollars to attend class, require students to rent their desks and buy supplies, pay taxes to a school "town' government, run a student justice system, and operate according to rules that mirror the working lives of their parents.

As one school's principal explained, "Some people disagree with the idea that we should pay children to go to school, but we get paid to go to work. Kids always ask during class how they are going to use the lessons we teach them. At this school, they will use that information every day or they'll soon go broke."[14]

With universities competing in an educational marketplace, academic disciplines, teaching and research take on an economic value in terms of their exchange rate and the return on investment they generate.[15] Under increasing pressure to generate revenue, some public universities have proposed differential pricing as a replacement for university-wide tuition rates. Under differential pricing, courses and majors are priced in relation to the market value or those degrees and skills.

Public schools are not immune to market pressures. Demands for greater accountability drive up costs and demands for lower taxes constrain school funding. Some public schools have turned to selling naming rights, with prices reportedly ranging from $30,000 for an elementary school to $25 million for a high school. Some schools have also endorsed exclusive contracts with vendors, agreed to sell commercial products to students, and accepted commercial advertising.

HOW MUCH PROSPERITY SHOULD WE HAVE IN PUBLIC SCHOOLS?

Can we have too much prosperity, too much focus on economic-related outcomes? The following examples address schools as marketplaces, measuring and managing performance and differing views of children.

These examples illustrate some of the tensions that efforts to achieve greater prosperity can create with other public values.

Economy and Efficiency

Budget and cost-cutting pressures have led many school districts to forgo stand-alone auditoriums that traditionally have been part of middle and high schools. Some districts have adopted a new design that combines an auditorium and cafeteria into a cafetorium. A partition divides the larger space when small groups use the stage area. The partition is removed for large performances. To save money, the floor is flat. Proponents point out that using a cafetorium reduces the size of a single middle school by 2,000 square feet and reduces the cost by $300,000. Opponents argue that a cafetorium does not give legitimacy to theater arts in the same way an auditorium does.

Some school districts, faced with population growth that outstrips the capacity of taxes and bond issues to fund adequate school construction, have proposed or begun converting traditional calendar schools to year-round schools. Proponents argue that it maximizes the use of existing school buildings and educates more children at a lower cost since the need for new construction is reduced. Opponents cite the disruption of traditional summers and vacations, and the difficulty of coordinating different school schedules for siblings.

Standards, Testing and Certification

Despite the passage of No Child Left Behind in 2001 and the constant rhetoric about tougher academic standards in public schools, a study by the U.S. Department of Education shows that nearly a third of states lowered their academic proficiency standards between 2005 and 2007.[16] Lowering standards can help schools stay ahead of sanctions, but it can make it more difficult to accurately compare student achievement with other districts, states and countries.

Child care and preschool rating systems serve as a way to inform parents about the level of program quality they can expect and to encourage providers to strive for higher standards. Even though most parents and policymakers agree that pre-schoolers are too young to be graded on their academic work, some states are moving ahead with efforts to certify early-childhood programs according to how well children who go through those programs perform in kindergarten. Most states base their ratings primarily on literacy scores. But some advocates argue that skills such as following directions and sharing with classmates are as important, if not more important at that age than math and language skills.

In response to the clamor for academic improvement, most states have implemented end-of-year tests to determine student advancement to the next grade level. Despite their widespread adoption, parents, students, teachers, principals and school board members disagree on whether high stakes tests are a good idea and what test scores measure.

Supporters argue that testing increases accountability, demonstrates student mastery of fundamental academic subjects, and shows which schools are doing a good job and which ones are not. Testing helps equalize education at all schools, regardless of local neighborhoods or other factors. Standardized tests discourage social promotion, which essentially endorses inequalities among students. Academic standards ensure that high school graduates become productive members of the workforce and are better prepared for higher education. It is cheaper and more efficient to analyze the results of one standardized test than to try to analyze and compare the results of dozens of locally-developed tests.

Opponents argue that standardized tests don't take into account many of the important things students know or can do. Teachers spend too much time teaching to the test instead of teaching the curriculum. Teachers receive little support for hands-on activities or field trips which do not directly prepare students for tests. Testing widens achievement gaps by requiring that students who do not pass the tests be held back, increasing the likelihood that those students will drop out of school. Standardized tests widen the gap between more and less adept test-takers, a gap which is often divided along racial or ethnic lines.

Everyone has an interest in seeing students succeed. Setting standards and measuring performance require thoughtful consideration of the interplay among the values of community, prosperity and equality.

Instrumental and Developmental Views of Children

In the aftermath of Hurricane Katrina, many public schools engaged in campaigns to help the victims. Here are two different approaches from two different elementary schools, illustrating both instrumental and developmental views of children. One school distributed a flyer titled "Coins for Caring: Help for Hurricane Katrina Victims" to its students. The flyer read: "Hey kids!!! Collect some coins. Bring them to class. Watch our lobby container fill up. Feel good about helping others. Each classroom will have a container to collect the coins, and those can be emptied daily into the big container, which will be kept in the lobby."

At about the same time, another school included "A Message about Hurricane Katrina" in its monthly parent newsletter. It read: "Most mental health experts agree that with young children we should answer their questions about disasters but discourage their participation in any large relief drives because young children cannot separate themselves from the event. We will continue to answer their questions and encourage and support older children who work with their families to show their concern for the victims of the disaster. As a school policy, we do not support children being used in fundraising activities."

These are both elementary schools. The first school employs a traditional student achievement model emphasizing homework and pep rallies for state testing periods. The second school employs a whole child approach, emphasizing social, emotional and cognitive development. Both schools are public. Both schools administer state-mandated assessments. And both schools have a different view of what public education means, and what public leadership requires from those who assume the role of stewards of public schools.

A ROLE FOR PUBLIC SCHOOLS IN ACHIEVING PROSPERITY

Public schools play an important role in preparing the next generation of employers and employees. A greater standard of living is often cited as the reason why students should stay in school, and is used to justify a focus on student achievement more than on other goals. In 2007 the Organization for Economic Cooperation and Development released its Economic Survey of the United States, concluding that a country's ability to compete in a world economy depends on a highly educated workforce.

While a number of national commissions have described the economic context of education and the ways in which public schools contribute to economic progress, virtually every commission has also identified some set of broader purposes. The cross-cutting conclusion among these commissions is that the public good includes more than just economic prosperity, and the perpetuation of our democratic and economic republic involves multiple interests, including aspects of liberty, equality, and community. As Calvin Coolidge remarked, "Prosperity is only an instrument to be used, not a deity to be worshipped."

Too great a reliance solely upon student achievement, test scores and an instrumental view of education can have a crippling effect. When only results matter, then how we obtain those results sometimes takes a back seat to the results themselves. The alleged cheating scandal in the Atlanta school district is not the first to be reported during our renewed emphasis on measurable classroom performance, simply the most recent.[17] It certainly won't be the last.

Outside of the conglomerate of business organizations, public schools are one of the largest economic development institutions in the nation. But achieving national prosperity requires more than a focus on student achievement. For example, our current use of the concept of "achievement gap" takes many of the dimensions of inequality and checks them at the classroom door. It implies that issues of health, wealth, and safety don't matter inside the classroom other than to the extent they interfere with or can be shown to contribute to student achievement.

As our explorations of liberty, community, equality and prosperity have shown, the student achievement gap might also be viewed as a wealth gap, an income gap, an opportunity gap, an equality gap, a health gap, an environmental gap, a poverty gap, a nutrition gap, a housing gap, a safety gap, an incarceration gap, or an infrastructure gap. Without adequate levels of health, wealth and social networks for all children, student achievement serves as only a thin approximation of the prosperity that most business and economic leaders envision.

NOTES

1. National Commission on Excellence in Education. (1983). *A nation at risk: The imperative for educational reform.* Washington, DC: U.S. Department of Education, p. 13.
2. Ibid, p. 9.
3. Brown, P. R. (1990). "Accountability in public education." *Policy Brief No. 14.* San Francisco, CA: Far West Laboratory for Educational Research and Development.
4. National Commission on Excellence in Education, 1983, p. 9.
5. Ibid, p. 10.
6. Committee on Prospering in the Global Economy of the 21st Century: National Academy of Sciences, the National Academy of Engineering and the Institute of Medicine (2007). *Rising above the Gathering Storm: Energizing and Employing America for a Brighter Economic Future.* Washington, DC: The National Academies Press. Retrieved Mar. 8, 2011 from http://www.nap.edu/catalog/11463.html.
7. Ibid, p. 1.
8. Ibid, p. 13.
9. America Creating Opportunities to Meaningfully Promote Excellence in Technology, Education, and Science Act, Public Law 110–69, August 9, 2007.
10. National Center on Education and the Economy. (2007). *Tough choices or tough times: The report of the new commission on the skills of the American workforce.* San Francisco, CA: Jossey-Bass.
11. Ibid, p. 8.
12. Gerald and Haycock (2006).

13. *The New York Times* (2010). “48th is not a good place.” Editorial Page, October 26.

14. Simmons, T. (2003). “Charter school aims for big lessons in its microsociety.” *The News & Observer,* August 18.

15. Giroux (2008).

16. Urbina, I. (2010). “States lower test standards for a high school diploma.” *The New York Times,* January 12.

17. Severson, K. (2010). “Scandal and a schism rattle Atlanta’s schools. *The New York Times,* December 11.

Part III

Policy Goals and Values in Crestwich Public Schools

The Crestwich public school system was formed when Elkwich and Crestton public schools merged. Prior to merger, Elkwich was a small, sleepy city located in a mostly rural area. Elkwich relied heavily on government, universities, service industries and light manufacturing as its economic base. Crestton and several other smaller communities surrounding Elkwich relied heavily upon agriculture and agriculture-related businesses. But like many other areas of the country, Elkwich, Crestton and their surrounding communities would soon be transformed.

Agriculture, light manufacturing and textile mills were soon replaced by technology manufacturing, software development and support, and a host of other high-tech enterprises located largely in a regional research park. Elkwich and its suburbs became increasingly metropolitan due to migration from other parts of the country, which would continue for the next several decades. Over three consecutive decades, the population of Crestwich grew by 40 percent, 48 percent and 45 percent respectively, reaching a total population of just more than 900,000 residents.

The Crestwich school system grew similarly, making it the largest school district in the state and one of the 50 largest districts in the nation. At the beginning of the most recent school year, the district opened four new schools, bringing its total to 163 schools. It counted a total of 143,432 students, 49 percent of whom were non-white, and 31 percent of whom were eligible for free and reduced meals.

Population and growth, once centered within the city of Elkwich, shifted dramatically to the rural and suburban parts of the region. Before long, more than half of the region's population resided outside Elkwich, setting the stage for increased urban, suburban and inter-jurisdictional conflict. The subsequent political, economic and demographic changes that occurred transformed the region into a microcosm of contemporary America. These transformations gave rise and voice to divergent ideological factions, and helped usher in a political battle for control of Crestwich Public Schools.

In Part II we explored how the public values of liberty, community, equality and prosperity framed our visions of public education and public schools. In Part III, we explore how these values play out in the fictional Crestwich public school district. More specifically, we explore how these values frame policy goals, choices and conflicts involving educational opportunity, assigning student to schools and paying for public education.

We have two goals in this section. Our first goal is to show how policy problems as varied and complex as providing educational opportunity, populating schools, and funding public schools can be explained and understood in terms of the public values we described in Part II.

Our second goal is to show how and to what degree the choices made by Crestwich policymakers satisfied the values represented in these policy problems, and to identify some of the consequences of the value choices that were made. Crestwich could be any school district in America, and policy choices and trade-offs such as these occur in every school district at some time or another.

Chapter 5

Leveling the Playing Field

Who Gets Educational Opportunity?

The merger of Elkwich and Crestton public schools was big news across the state. The Associated Press proclaimed that the merger would receive final approval from the State Board of Education that day, ending more than a decade of passionate debate. Approval of merger appeared to be all but a formality, but the high drama that had characterized long-standing merger discussions in the two school districts would continue right up to the very moment of merger, and beyond.

The Elkwich Board of Education had unanimously approved merger of the two districts. But the Crestton Board of Education awaited a federal court ruling. Opponents of merger had requested an injunction to stop action by local elected officials that would lead to approval of merger. After a federal judge denied that request, the Crestton Board of Education voted 4-3 to approve the merger with Elkwich.

After several minor changes to the merger agreement proposed by the two boards of education, and after hours of consideration by elected officials and judges, the merger agreement was approved. A new district, the Crestwich school district, came into being. Despite eventual approval by the State Board of Education, the road leading to merger of the two school districts had been anything but smooth.

Several years earlier a non-binding referendum on merger was placed before the voters of Elkwich and Crestton. Proponents of merger passionately touted greater efficiency, cost savings and improved educational quality for all children. Opponents of merger passionately raised fears about increased integration, more busing, and argued that no child would benefit under such a plan. The referendum was soundly defeated in both communities.

Two years after the referendum, the local legislative delegation put forth enabling legislation to make merger possible. The legislation spelled out the terms under which the two school administrative units and two boards of education could be merged to form the Crestwich Public School System. But before consolidation could occur, the bill stipulated that each appropriate elected body must approve the merger by majority vote.

The legislature passed the enabling legislation, making it possible for the Crestton Board of Education, the Elkwich Board of Education and the State Board of Education to approve an action that had been rejected by Crestton and Elkwich voters just two years earlier. Why would state and local public officials pursue merger, particularly in the face of a clearly voiced direction by the people? In reflecting on the actions leading up to the establishment of the Crestwich Public School System, a local business leader said of the decision to approve merger, ". . . the voice of the people is the voice of finality. But not in this case."

Was voter rejection of merger a true reflection of what residents wanted? What people say they want and what they want are not always the same thing. As Abraham Lincoln observed, "What I want is to get done what the people desire to have done, and the question for me is how to find that out exactly." To answer these questions, we turn our attention to the goals and values that framed the place and time in which merger occurred.

POLICY GOALS AND VALUES OF EDUCATIONAL OPPORTUNITY

In the years prior to merger, the demographic differences between the Elkwich and Crestton school districts grew. So did the inequity between them. Three key factors contributed to separate and increasingly unequal school systems. One factor was white flight from Elkwich to Crestton, which led to declining enrollment in Elkwich public schools. Elkwich schools were becoming predominately black, and a number of schools were under-enrolled.

A second factor was the beginning of several decades of continuous growth. A regional research park began to see an influx of high technology firms and businesses. The siting of a major technology manufacturing facility became a tipping point in the growth of the area. Encouraged by strong economic development along with a favorable climate and location, business after business relocated to the area.

In the ensuing years, thousands of families moved to Crestton, Elkwich and the surrounding communities in pursuit of economic opportunities. For the most part, their children attended public schools. Crestton schools, especially the newer, more suburban schools, were rapidly becoming predominately white and over-crowded. One high school just beyond the Elkwich school district line had more students than its brick and mortar classrooms could hold. The front yard of the school became a parking lot for mobile classrooms.

Public funding was a third factor. Neither school district had local taxing authority, and municipalities did not levy taxes for schools. Both districts were dependent upon state funding for operations and county funding for facilities. Lower tax rates in the unincorporated areas of the region accelerated rural and suburban growth.

As the demographic differences between the two school districts continued to grow, the economic boundaries between Elkwich, Crestton and the surrounding communities began to blur. Jobs, transportation, and economic connections crossed political boundaries. Population growth created new neighborhoods and communities, some close to the city of Elkwich and some farther out in rural, unincorporated areas. Within a single decade five new municipalities were incorporated. Even though the number of jurisdictional boundaries increased, cultural, economic and environmental forces began to shape multiple jurisdictions into a single region.

As growth and demographic changes eroded the stability of past population patterns, issues of consolidation, economic growth and local control took center stage. The efficient use of existing schools to house students, the inequitable distribution of educational quality and opportunity, and the increasing racial segregation of schools became driving forces for many elected officials and business leaders. Leveling the educational playing field would require grappling with tensions among public values.

Most leaders in Elkwich supported merger, based in part on projections showing that the city's public school population would become predominately black in the near future. Many Elkwich residents feared that unequal school districts would translate into unequal opportunity. Their vision of public education might be described as ". . . a free and unsectarian public school in every ward and every village with its door wide open to children of all races and every creed."[1]

But some Elkwich leaders opposed merger, based on their fear of losing local control of schools, even segregated schools. And some leaders worried that merger might lead to less funding for Elkwich schools than for Crestton schools. For the residents of Elkwich, the possibility of merger raised concerns about equal educational opportunity, self-determination and local identity.

In contrast, many suburban leaders opposed merger, expressing concerns about the potential loss of educational quality if suburban schools were merged with city schools. Many families cited concerns about educational quality and academic achievement as reasons for moving out of Elkwich and into Crestton and its surrounding suburban areas.

For many business leaders, both in Elkwich and Crestton, the economic reality of a predominately black city school district and a predominately white suburban school district was something to avoid even though it meant taking some risks. Creating schools where all students can succeed, even if some students have to help others make the grade, might be good preparation for adult life in a commercial republic. But a preference for individual opportunity and achievement made many suburban residents skeptical of the benefits of merger and integration.

Urban and suburban residents shared one key concern. Both worried that merger and integration would result in increased busing of students, and that this would lead to the loss of neighborhood schools, local identity and a sense of community connection. Merger supporters understood these concerns. As a prominent business leader and supporter of school merger commented, "The hardest thing was being against neighborhood schools. That's like being against mom and apple pie." The desire for local autonomy and control of schools contrasted greatly with growing awareness of local interdependence and the need for greater regional collaboration, and would shape the platforms of many candidates for the board of education for years to come.

MERGING SCHOOL SYSTEMS

As growth transformed multiple jurisdictions into a region, the inequalities resulting from local school funding became more and more apparent. It became increasingly difficult, politically and financially, for public officials to approve tax increases to build new schools and add mobile classrooms in one district while at the same time funding under-utilized schools in another district. As the disparities between the two school districts became less acceptable, elected officials, business leaders and educators came together to establish a single school system that would equalize both school funding and educational opportunity.

Once merger was approved, the administrative aspects of implementation were carried out relatively easily and without much media attention. But political implementation, on the other hand, was fraught with potholes and land mines. Public officials soon became enmeshed in a web of competing values and goals: improving educational opportunity for all children, improving the quality of education for all children, increasing system-wide efficiency, ensuring more equitable funding, and maintaining families' sense of connection, belonging and identity.

Sufficiently broad local leadership support for these goals had made merger possible. The newly formed Crestwich Board of Education knew that a well-developed plan to integrate all of the schools in the newly consolidated district was critical. They also knew that such a plan must be implemented successfully, and must strike a reasonable balance among the multiple and sometimes conflicting goals of merger.

The two districts were moderately different in size, but other differences were more pronounced. Crestton schools were a mix of suburban and rural, with ample geographical separation between individual schools. As a result of the distances between schools, the smaller communities within the Crestton school district felt a strong sense of ownership of their schools. Each school was fairly autonomous, with established traditions and an individual identity.

Elkwich schools served a more urban population and a community that was much more densely populated. Compared to Crestton schools, the Elkwich schools were more bureaucratic and had more centralized decision making and control. The Elkwich Board of Education and central district staff made most key decisions and school building staff implemented them. The district, not individual schools, established city-wide traditions and identity.

In the Crestton schools, administrative authority and control were much more at the building level. More independent and autonomous schools resulted in two important differences between the two districts. Parents generally had greater involvement in Crestton schools, but educational quality was less consistent. Elkwich schools, whose administration was more centralized and standardized, had greater consistency among schools with respect to educational quality, but less parental involvement. In spite of these differences in organization and administration, both districts reflected the philosophies and values of their respective communities.

Because of the passion surrounding merger, efforts to achieve racial integration were delayed in order to allow time to focus on the logistics of merging the two districts. Both supporters and opponents of merger understood that the districts had distinct organizational cultures, business operations, and administrative procedures. It would take time to effect merger.

Not everyone was patient. Some supporters of merger were adamant that integration take place according to and as required by federal mandates. But the consensus of local leaders was that while administrative merger would not by itself achieve greater school integration, an unsuccessful administrative merger would most certainly derail integration. The new board of education, well aware of the political challenges and potential pitfalls, agreed that little change should be seen or felt at the classroom level that first year.

The decision was made to effect administrative merger first. School officials would be allowed time to work through the challenges of bringing together two very different school districts. Once the administrative tasks associated with merger were accomplished, the next and bigger step would be to develop an acceptable and workable district-wide plan to integrate Crestwich public schools.

INTEGRATING SCHOOLS

Integrating schools would require more than simply a physical and administrative merger of the two school systems. With the research park fueling an economic boom and families from all over the nation relocating to the area, the entire regional community experienced a shift in residential housing patterns as more and more affluent families moved to the suburbs.

Implementing public policy is subject to the law of unintended consequences. Things happen as a result of implementing change, but they are not always the things we want to happen. Early integration efforts had one such unintended effect.

Most suburban parents did not want their children to attend schools in urban neighborhoods. Schools in the former Elkwich district, although generally in good repair, were seen as less desirable by Crestton parents. Consequently, most of the students moved to begin integrating Crestwich schools were black. This had the unintended effect of spurring even greater white flight to the outer city limits of Elkwich and to the contiguous Crestton suburban areas.

In response, sixth grade centers were created in more urban areas of the merged district as part of an effort to bring white students closer to the center of the city. In spite of such efforts, city schools continued to have higher concentrations of black students while schools in more suburban areas had higher concentrations of white students. This early mixed experience with integrating schools would play a role in future integration efforts.

As the urban to suburban population shift continued, demands intensified for neighborhood schools, exacerbating the challenges of merger and jeopardizing fragile public support for integration. The district would need new approaches to organizing and delivering education in order to address these competing goals and sustain a unified and integrated school district. Since we are not born equal, equality comes about only as a result of human organization.[2] The newly merged district turned to magnet schools and multi-track calendars to help achieve its goals.

Magnet Schools

Prior to merger, efforts to balance the Elkwich schools racially were met with resistance and white flight. Some students in the school district were reassigned to other schools in an attempt to make individual school populations reflect the total population of students. Crestton schools, prior to merger, made little attempt to integrate schools.

The magnet school concept was introduced into the newly formed Crestwich public school district as part of the desegregation plan adopted after merger. Magnet schools have specialized themes such as environmental science or experiential learning that are intended to draw together children of different economic and racial groups.

Magnet schools were seen as an innovative way of not only populating schools efficiently but also as a means of enhancing educational opportunity for students. A substantial body of research has found that low-income and minority students learn more in magnet schools than in segregated, higher poverty schools because the quality of teaching and rigor of instruction are directly connected to segregation, particularly socioeconomic segregation.[3]

The board of education adopted a Schools of Choice program using magnet schools as the foundation. The purposes of the program were to integrate schools and improve educational quality. Twenty-eight schools featuring five different themes were designated as magnet schools to attract students. These schools offered programs and courses that were not available in non-magnet schools. One theme, for example, included a strong emphasis on the arts.

Seats in the magnet schools were not assigned based on interest, merit or desert[4] but rather through a lottery system. Parents lined up at post offices across the district to get a letter postmarked on the day the selection process opened, requesting a coveted seat in the magnet school of their choice. In principle, every student in the consolidated school district had an equal opportunity to attend a magnet program.

Some suburban families felt that magnet schools located within the city boundaries of Elkwich were too great a distance from their neighborhoods and therefore required excessive bus travel. In response to this concern, a handful of magnet schools were located in the outlying regions of the school system. These schools, referred to as equity magnets, offered some of the same special programs and were more accessible physically to suburban students.

The magnet schools program resulted in sufficient voluntary movement of white students to substantially integrate the consolidated school district. Targeted student assignment plans were still required to address new population growth and to use existing and new school capacity efficiently. The Schools of Choice magnet program became the foundation upon which the desegregation plan for the Crestwich Public School System was built.

Multi-Track Year-Round Calendar Schools

With a successful magnet program in place, the district commissioned a study of year-round schools in light of projected continuing population growth. Year-round calendars were designed initially as an innovative way to deliver education, but the district concluded that they also had the potential to provide a more efficient use of school buildings than a traditional calendar.

Multi-track year-round calendar schools have four tracks. Students are assigned to one of the four tracks and attend school for nine weeks, then have three weeks off. This continues throughout the entire year as a continuous cycle. At any given time, three of the four tracks are in session, and one is out. This allows for greater and more efficient use of facilities, especially if buildings are designed and constructed to accommodate such a calendar and configuration.

Faced with growing angst from a public tired of the increasing cost of a rapidly growing school system, Crestwich public schools opened the first year-round school in the state and the first year-round magnet school in the nation. A few years later, the National Education Commission on Time and Learning would recognize the important role that schedules and calendars play in public schools. "The school clock governs how families organize their lives, how administrators oversee their schools, and how teachers work their way through the curriculum. Above all, it governs how material is presented to students and the opportunity they have to comprehend and master it."[5]

Initially, the district assumed that year-round calendar schools would be created only as part of the magnet program, and that assigning students to these schools would take place using an application process. Parents who chose a year-round school as a magnet school would have a newly constructed, well-equipped building and a school calendar that better suited their needs. These families could have the benefits of greater choice, stability in school assignment, and convenience.

Within a decade there were nine schools operating on a multi-track calendar. Because this calendar's success depends so much on appropriate building design and capacity, multi-track year-round magnet schools tended to be new schools, located mainly in the suburban areas of the school system where growth was increasing fastest.

Unlike the Schools of Choice magnet program, year-round magnet schools had a very different impact on racial balance. Despite a strong recruiting effort and program incentives to ensure that year-round magnets mirrored the racial makeup of the school district, minority families did not apply in very large numbers to attend year-round magnet schools.

In retrospect, the benefits of the year-round multi-track magnet schools were greater for suburban families, because that was where new schools were most likely to be built. Most of the year-round schools were attended by students from whiter, more affluent and less diverse areas of the district. As was true for earlier integration efforts, increased bus travel and the loss of a sense of "neighborhood" schools mitigated some of the appeal of these magnet programs to black families. The addition of a nontraditional schedule compounded this problem.

THE UNFINISHED TASK OF EQUAL OPPORTUNITY

Elected leaders may at times find themselves supporting a public choice that they might not have supported if the choice was purely a personal one. This is testimony to Myrdal's observation that institutions tend to be more broad-minded on average than are the individuals who comprise the institution. In our Crestwich story, a plurality of state and local elected officials brought merger to fruition, even though a non-binding referendum indicated that a majority of individuals opposed merger. This is a powerful testament to the resiliency of democracy and the legitimacy of local decision making.

These state and local leaders, while anything but a homogenous group, affirmed several fundamental democratic principles. They understood what Jefferson meant when he argued that the best principles of our republic secure for all citizens a perfect equality of rights. They grasped Aristotle's argument that the only stable state is one in which all inhabitants are equal before the law. And they recognized Jefferson's proclamation that while our beliefs and our behaviors are sometimes at odds with each other, justice is and must always be the fundamental law of society.

A goal of integrated public schools involves multiple public values, and achieving such a goal requires multiple policy tools. Merger, magnet programs, and multi-track calendars helped further integration in Crestwich public schools. These tools were effective because they enhanced individual public values, such as opportunity and efficiency. They were successful because they reduced the degree of head-on conflict among values by shifting the way in which competing values intersected, and therefore better aligned, at least for a while, the aggregate interests of citizens, parents and students.

But tools alone cannot resolve the core public value conflicts involved in issues of racial segregation and equal opportunity. Multi-track magnet schools tended to be less integrated than earlier magnet schools, and therefore they did not accomplish as much on behalf of racial and socioeconomic balance. Efforts to recruit minority families and students showed some success, but not enough. It would take nearly another decade for greater integration to occur.

NOTES

1. Henry Cabot Lodge, statesman, historian, U.S. Senator from Massachusetts, conservative Republican politician and political foe of Woodrow Wilson.
2. Political theorist and philosopher Hannah Arendt, who fled Germany in 1933, immigrated to the United States in 1941, and held a number of academic positions at various American universities until her death in 1975.

3. Kahlenberg, R. (2010). "Charter vs. magnet schools. Taking note: a century foundation group blog," January 8. Retrieved July 30, 2010 from http://takingnote.tcf.org/2010/01/charter-vs-magnet-schools.html.

4. Factors that make a person deserving. For example, a person might be deemed deserving by virtue of need, qualifications or experience. This concept is explored more fully in Michael Walzer (1983). *Spheres of justice: A defense of pluralism and equality.* New York, NY: Basic Books, pp. 23–26.

5. National Education Commission on Time and Learning. (1994). *Prisoners of time.* Washington, DC: Author, p. 8.

Chapter 6

Assigning Students

Who Goes Where, with Whom and Why?

The question of who goes to school where is a fundamental issue in K–12 public education. This question arises in any school district which has more than one elementary, middle or high school. How students come to attend one school and not another school in the same district is the result of a process commonly referred to as student assignment.

In smaller districts, assigning students to school buildings is a relatively simple logistical matter. But as districts grow in size, student assignment becomes more than just an administrative challenge. It also becomes a public values problem. To uncover the policy goals and values involved in assigning students to schools, we might ask who attends school where, with whom and why?

Student assignment can have any number of variations based on district size, growth or decline in student population, funding for school buildings and geography. Schools can seat only so many students at any one time. They are expensive to construct and to operate. Because public schools are built with tax dollars, the public expects that buildings will be used efficiently. With the amount of capital funding available for constructing and renovating schools often limited by tax pressures, districts look for ways to increase the capacity and efficiency of existing facilities.

Both underutilization and overcrowding decrease operational efficiency, and can impact learning negatively. In communities with relatively stable or declining populations, some schools end up with fewer and fewer students as school-age children move from elementary to middle to high school and then leave home for post-secondary education or to begin work. In some cases, school district enrollment declines overall.

In districts with a growing population, the student population also grows. Creating new space for these students requires a process for filling the additional seats. Historically, districts have looked to add seats to relieve over-crowding by building new brick and mortar facilities, adding to existing facilities and using mobile or modular units on a school campus. These measures expand the number of seats arithmetically to meet growing numbers of students. They increase capacity, but do not necessarily improve efficiency. And inevitably, increases and decreases in student populations require some form of redistribution in order to use school buildings as efficiently and effectively as possible.

In this chapter we explore the policy challenges involved in assigning students that resulted from implementing merger and integration. We look at three very different policy solutions for achieving an equitable and efficient assignment of students. Each solution reflects a different balancing of the tensions and trade-offs among the four public values of liberty, equality, community and prosperity. And each policy solution results in a different answer to the question of who goes where, with whom, and why?

POLICY GOALS AND VALUES OF STUDENT ASSIGNMENT

The rapid pace and uneven distribution of growth would complicate the Crestwich Board of Education's efforts to integrate schools and use classrooms efficiently. Growth in the suburban and outermost urban neighborhoods resulted in too few seats for students. At the same time, a number of school buildings in the city core were under-utilized. And if the challenges of merger and integration weren't daunting enough, the board was faced with the prospect of purchasing mobile units and constructing new schools to address rural and suburban growth, while at the same time closing some city schools to reduce operating costs and avoid wasting resources.

Some students would have to be reassigned, not only to integrate schools but also to achieve the most efficient use of facilities possible. Simply put, white students could be reassigned to predominately black schools to fill and diversify them, or black students could be reassigned to predominately white schools to achieve greater racial integration. Given the dual dilemma of both overcrowding and underutilization, some combination of the two would be necessary.

Regardless of how student assignment would be carried out, a plan and process for doing so would have to satisfy multiple goals and values. First, it must facilitate the administrative merger of the school systems. Second, it must help integrate schools. Third, it must help use buildings as efficiently as possible. Fourth, it must show promise for improving educational opportunity, quality and achievement for all students. And fifth, it must meet federal requirements for desegregation.

To achieve these goals, the district would employ three student assignment strategies—the first would involve administrative assignment, the second would involve parental choice, and the third would be based on socioeconomic balance. But no matter how well the district crafted an assignment plan, reassigning students would result in some degree of family, social and neighborhood disruption.

To achieve integration, use facilities efficiently and hold down the costs of growth, a sizeable number of families within the district would have to bear the opportunity costs of reassignment. Some of these families were unlikely to see the benefits. The delicate political coalition that had made merger possible would have to withstand the inevitable pushback that reassignment would produce. This challenge would become herculean when the goal of moving as few students and creating as little disruption as possible was added.

DISTRICT-DIRECTED STUDENT ASSIGNMENT

Because of the need to address both growth and integration and because of the physical and geographic scale of the school system, the board of education adopted a student assignment policy based on administratively-directed assignment. With the help of an outside consultant, guidelines and a plan were developed with input from board members, district staff and community leaders.

For planning purposes, the district was divided into 550 small geographical areas called "nodes." District staff identified the demographic characteristics of the cluster of students within each node. The assignment plan called for populating schools at or near the district-wide percentages of black and white students, which in this case meant having a target of 71 percent white students and 29 percent black students in each school. Sixth grade centers and magnet schools were incorporated into the assignment plan to attract white students to schools that otherwise would be predominately black.

In addition to supporting district-wide merger and integration, the plan identified several other objectives. These included keeping students close to their homes, limiting busing, ensuring student safety, maximizing the capacity and utilization of buildings, and keeping students together throughout their public education years.

The board took the plan to the community. During a series of public hearings, choices were questioned, issues were raised, and decisions were explained. Adjustments were made to the plan as a result of public input, and a final plan was adopted by the board. Despite soliciting public input and adopting revisions, two polar views of student assignment emerged.

The first view coalesced around the importance of merger, integration and efficient utilization of buildings. Proponents of this view tended to see schools as district schools, and therefore all schools should be open to all students. The second view emphasized the importance of parents, families and a sense of community. Proponents of this view tended to see schools as neighborhood and community schools, and therefore schools should be open only to students who lived within that neighborhood or community.

Initially, the board adopted the first view. What began as a process for filling seats in some schools morphed into a larger process for achieving racial balance in all schools. Student assignment shifted from being an administrative process to a political process. The tension between these competing views of schools would continue for decades.

Faced with directed reassignment, some families refused to send their children to their newly assigned schools. In other cases, parents protested which students were assigned to a specific school. This was most likely to occur if the assignments involved changing the racial composition of the school. The question of who goes to school where, with whom, and why occupied much of the board of education's attention.

The district found itself in the challenging position of responding to individual family desires and concerns while trying to implement a district-wide plan. Implementation was made even more difficult by the fact that many school buses in service at the time were unreliable due to age and wear. There simply weren't enough buses to transport all of the students who would need transportation to achieve the board's policy goals for student assignment.

In the meantime, growth accelerated. More than 400,000 residents now resided within the district's boundaries. The number of students enrolled in Crestwich schools increased by more than 30,000, a population larger than many other school districts in the state.

To accommodate the dramatic growth, twenty-three new schools were constructed during the next decade. Since new school construction inevitably lags student population growth, temporary solutions such as the use of mobile classrooms became common. During their peak use, nearly 13,000 students attended school in mobile classrooms.

Mobile classrooms help alleviate overcrowding, but they create other problems. Parents invoked claims of equity and fairness when their children attended class in mobile units in over-crowed schools. They raised concerns about safety when severe weather threatened and about social and physical isolation from other students and from school buildings and activities.

Building and filling new schools also raises concerns. As many as 3,000 students were reassigned each year in trying to address overcrowding, integration and efficient use of classroom seats. While "reassignment" was the administrative term used by the school district, "shuffling" was the term the media used. Hyped by the media and dreaded by families, annual reassignment plans created anxiety and uncertainty. Who would be moved? Where will we be assigned next? How long before the next reassignment? Will my child have to go to a school where she has no friends or where most of the students don't look like him? What are our choices? These were just some of the questions that parents and the media asked the board and district staff each year.

While most residents seemed to appreciate the economic benefits of growth, the social costs of regular student reassignment began to wear on some parents and local communities. Tensions began to grow between those pursuing district-wide schools and those pursuing neighborhood schools.

Merger, integration, and student assignment were district-wide policy tools adopted to achieve the goals of greater educational opportunity and equality for all students and greater economic efficiency throughout the school system. These goals clashed with more individual and local preferences for choice, control, self-determination, connection and stability.

The first official pushback against district-directed student reassignment came in the form of election of a new board member who campaigned on a promise to represent parents who felt unheard by the board of education and return to neighborhood schools. This election marked the beginning of a growing campaign for seats on the board that invoked the spirit of John Stuart Mill when he wrote that "The only purpose for which power can be rightfully exercised over any member of a civilized community, against his will, is to prevent harm to others." This refrain, composed during the time of merger, would be sung louder during each subsequent campaign, achieving full voice in the election of four new board members described in the Prologue.

CHOICE-DRIVEN STUDENT ASSIGNMENT

Choice, although it focused on just a few schools, was an integral part of the very first assignment plan for the new Crestwich Public School System. The district incorporated a choice component in its first magnet schools, a gifted and talented program and an extended day program at two elementary schools.

A majority of the earliest magnet schools were located in former Elkwich City Schools that were under-enrolled. Parents in other parts of the district could choose to attend a magnet program and apply for a seat through a selection process. Demand quickly outstripped the seats available. It was clear that magnet schools were desirable to parents, and that the district could make use of more magnet programs.

The board of education's approval of the Schools of Choice program increased the number of magnet schools in the district. In addition to increasing parental participation and choice, the Schools of Choice program was designed to help address several other challenges, including:

- Overcrowding and under-enrollment of schools;
- Equalizing educational opportunity;
- Achieving racial balance; and
- Improving overall educational quality.

Nearly thirty schools were made magnet schools under the Schools of Choice program, most of them formerly Elkwich schools that had become predominately black schools. In many cases the schools were completely reconstituted. Principals and staff were reassigned along with students. New magnet themes included gifted and talented, classical studies, international studies, and an extended day program.

"It is vain to talk of the interest of the community," wrote Jeremy Bentham, "without understanding what is the interest of the individual." The board of education and staff shared information about the Schools of Choice program with parents in meetings held across the district. Parents saw that they would have new opportunities to apply for specialized programs, courses and innovative approaches for their children. Carefully selected principals and teachers would serve in the magnet schools. Parents responded enthusiastically—and in great numbers.

In offering families the most choice and control since before the school system merger, the board of education shifted some of the decision making about who goes where and why to parents, who could choose whether or not to participate in the magnet program. Parents could seek a magnet program seat by postmarking a request within a certain time period. Some parents were known to stand in line at post offices the night before the opening of the magnet request period to insure a timely postmark.

The Schools of Choice program restored a degree of control, self-determination and stability to parents and families. A seat in a magnet program generally insulated a student from reassignment due to growth. The program also accelerated the integration of Crestwich Public Schools. White parents now demanded that their children attend school in areas of Elkwich that just a few years earlier had experienced white flight.

The movement of white students from suburban and rural areas of the school system to more urban schools had two key impacts. It improved the utilization of existing schools within the city limits of Elkwich, and it greatly improved the racial balance of magnet schools. To open seats in urban magnet programs, some black students were reassigned to rural and suburban schools, improving the racial balance of formerly predominately white schools.

As the popularity of magnet programs grew, parents surfaced new concerns about travel time and distance and the safety of rural roads used for bus transportation. In response to these concerns, the board of education designated a handful of magnet schools across the district as equity magnet schools. These schools were made available to students for whom travel time and distance posed a serious obstacle to their participation in magnet programs. But even with the equity magnet option, school bus travel time could exceed an hour each way. Despite the time and distance involved, many parents still chose magnet schools.

As popular as magnet programs had become, they could not satisfy the competing goals of choice and racial balance alone. Continuing growth meant ongoing school construction and reassignment of students to fill new schools. Growth also demanded reconfiguration of the areas from which magnet schools could draw students from other schools in the district. The reconfiguration of draw areas had the same downsides as the process of student reassignment. Current magnet students were guaranteed the same (or a similar) magnet program, but not a particular magnet school. Parents reacted with some of the same frustration they had regarding student reassignments.

Growth also upset the delicate racial balance magnet programs had helped achieve. The board of education had established targets of no more than 45 percent and no less than 15 percent minority students in any individual school. These were district-wide targets representing a range 15 percentage points above and below the district's minority population of 30 percent.

District-wide goals for racial balance were undermined by different local government land use, zoning and economic development practices, which stimulated greater growth in some areas than others. Uneven growth increased demographic differences in the multiple communities served by Crestwich Public Schools. As growth continued, more and more schools became unable to meet the board's racial balance goal.

The board of education had little choice but to reassign students in order to mitigate further overcrowding and racial imbalance due to growth. This prompted more and more parents to seek magnet seats as a refuge from potential reassignments. In one particular school year, with a large reassignment scheduled for the following year, over 7,000 magnet school applications were submitted, nearly twice the number of available magnet seats. The district was forced to deny more than three thousand requests. The promise of choice had become greater than the reality.

New schools continued to open in the high-growth suburban areas of the district. Municipalities annexed new housing developments and created instant communities. As the suburban population grew, more and more families sought the benefits of magnet programs without the opportunity costs associated with travel. The longer bus rides for specialized courses and programs in magnet schools, acceptable to many parents at first, stretched out due to growth, construction and congestion. The luster of the initial trade-off of convenience for opportunity faded for some.

As suburban parents began to back away from the increasing travel and uncertainty associated with magnet programs, some parents opted to keep their children closer to home in their neighborhood schools rather than accept long bus rides to magnet schools. Other parents sought to replicate versions of magnet programs in newer, suburban schools. The result was that the exclusivity and prestige of the original magnet programs diminished somewhat. Even with several substantial federal grants to bolster magnet programs and strengthen their draw of white students, by the end of the decade the appeal of magnet schools was flagging.

SOCIOECONOMIC-BASED STUDENT ASSIGNMENT

The goals crafted at the time of merger provided a policy framework for student assignment that lasted nearly thirty years: use school buildings and student seats efficiently, integrate the schools, and move as few students as possible. But court decisions across the nation were making it clear that the use of race as a factor in assigning students to schools would result in legal challenges. To improve racial balance and diversity in district schools, the board of education would need a new approach to student assignment that avoided potential legal problems associated with race-based assignment.

Drawing upon research on educational opportunity,[1] the board dropped racial balance as a goal and adopted instead a goal of socioeconomic diversity based on student qualification for free or reduced price meals to use in assigning students to schools. Because U.S. Department of Agriculture regulations prohibited the use of individual student data related to qualification for free or reduced price meals, the district applied the data by geographic node to each school to determine its degree of socioeconomic diversity.

The board of education adopted two key measures of socioeconomic diversity to guide student assignment decisions. The first was a target ceiling of no more than 40 percent of students eligible for free and reduced price meals in any school. The second was a limit on the percentage of students below grade level in any school, as measured by end-of-grade tests. Although the district's student assignment process was equally focused on achieving optimal use of school buildings and other resources, socioeconomic balance and student achievement received the greatest attention in the media and from parents.

The board of education's new policy direction evoked mixed reactions from the community. Supporters championed the policy for continuing to ensure racial balance in schools and provide educational opportunity for every student. Opponents derided the policy as social engineering, calling for a return to neighborhood schools and an end to "forced busing" for diversity. Had Rip van Winkle awakened after a 25-year sleep, he would have easily recognized both the district's goals for diversity and the countering arguments for neighborhood schools and choice.

Crestwich became the largest school district in the nation to use socioeconomic diversity and student achievement in student assignment. In the face of court challenges, many other school districts had already abandoned efforts to ensure racial or socioeconomic diversity in schools. With a new policy direction to guide their efforts, district staff began work on the first ever socioeconomic-based multi-year assignment plan for Crestwich Public Schools, a plan they hoped would achieve the board's goal and give parents a respite from assignment overload.

District staff conducted community engagement sessions to share draft plans and solicit public input prior to presenting a formal plan to the board. After months of community meetings and planning with the staff of schools most likely to be affected by reassignment, a multi-year assignment plan was presented to the board of education.

After receiving the plan, the board scheduled a series of public hearings and work sessions. Board members discussed the impacts and consequences of growth and explained why growth would require continuing reassignments. Parents shared stories about reassignment, emphasizing why greater predictability and stability would be best for their children.

After numerous public hearings and work sessions, the board approved a student assignment plan that spanned three years. By linking the assignment plan to the capital plan, the district could better inform parents about which schools their children would attend, and for how long. The new three-year plan meant that for the first time in decades parents, students, school board members and staff would be able to take a break from the much-dreaded annual reassignment.

The new policy approach improved predictability, but stability was still a concern, as some amount of ongoing reassignment was necessary to accommodate continuing student growth within the district. However, proposed changes could be communicated earlier than in the past, and parents had greater assurance that once students were reassigned, they would remain at their schools for a longer period of time. But the effort to create some breathing room in the scheduled process of populating schools was unsuccessful as far as parents were concerned. Apparently, knowing your child would attend a different school in three years was little better than knowing such a change would occur next year.

POLICY CHOICES AND VALUE TRADE-OFFS IN STUDENT ASSIGNMENT

At the time of merger, the city of Elkwich was home to a majority of the population of the region. For many residents at the time of merger, a consolidated school system held out the hope of greater educational opportunity and equality. In the years following merger, Crestwich Public Schools would take steps to fulfill that vision, achieving a record of academic success and socioeconomic diversity that was the envy of districts throughout the state and nation.

As new communities and municipalities sprang to life in Crestton in the years following merger, Elkwich's proportion of the total population in the district fell to less than half. By the time of the most recent school board election, nearly two-thirds of the region's residents lived in one of a dozen independent municipalities. Although some school board members issued frequent public reminders that Crestwich schools were district schools and not neighborhood or municipal schools, most residents identified with their neighborhood first, their municipality second, and their school district third.

For thousands of new residents who flocked to the area in search of the good life, a consolidated school district came to symbolize social engineering and the arbitrary exercise of bureaucratic authority that emphasized equal opportunity and aggregate equity at the expense of choice and individual opportunity. "Freedom from" inconvenience and instability became a rallying point for a growing number of residents who found it burdensome to be part of a consolidated school system that emphasized collective responsibility for public education.[2] Part of that collective responsibility meant being willing to populate schools to help achieve district-wide goals.

Minus other goals, virtually all Crestwich families would prefer their elementary school children to attend a school within five miles of their home. Such a preference is reasonable on the surface. But it is a logistical and political challenge in a district encompassing 832 square miles, with a population approaching 1 million, and with the competing political goals we have described. As the most recent school board election demonstrated, the district was unable to reconcile the trade-offs between parental choice, convenience, stability and personal responsibility on one hand, and equal opportunity, racial balance, socioeconomic diversity and collective responsibility on the other. The new board will face the same challenge.

NOTES

1. Coleman, James S. (1966). *Equality of Educational Opportunity*. Washington, DC: U.S. Department of Health, Education and Welfare.
2. Godwin, R. K., and Kemerer, F. R. (2002). *School choice tradeoffs: Liberty, equity, and diversity*. Austin, TX: University of Texas Press.

Chapter 7

Funding Schools

Who Pays for What, How, Why and for Whom?

Public education combines children and money. For many citizens, what they think about their public schools is greatly influenced by what schools do or propose to do with the children and money of parents and taxpayers. Parents are passionate about the care and development of their children, especially when that care and development is placed in the hands of those in charge of public schools. Taxpayers are passionate about how tax dollars are spent.

In public education, every policy decision has a fiscal impact, the consequences of how and why public dollars are spent. While it might seem that taxation, funding and spending decisions are driven by the public value of prosperity, any or all of the other public values of liberty, equality and community are likely to be in play. In some cases these values align, in others they collide. In either case, when children and money are involved, the expression of public values is infused with passion and emotion.

Much time and energy is spent in Crestwich addressing questions of school funding. Who should pay for public school facilities and programs? How should revenue be generated? Which schools and students will or won't benefit? What return should residents receive on the investment of tax revenue in public education? The questions of who, how and why with regard to school funding are fairly well established in state law. They are generally accepted, although sometimes reluctantly, by local policymakers. Over the years, the district and the players have changed, but the questions have remained the same.

As population and economic growth transformed the Crestwich area in the twenty-first century, funding public infrastructure, especially public school construction and maintenance, became a growing political and financial challenge. The system of taxation for funding public schools would become a driving factor in the changing relationship between residents and their public schools. In Crestwich it turned out to be the question of "for whom" that would transform fiscal decisions about taxation, funding and investment into political ones.

TAXATION TO PROVIDE FOR PUBLIC SCHOOLS

The fiscal system for generating revenue to support public schools in the state was developed in the 1930s during the Great Depression. Many local school systems could not afford to provide or operate facilities to support a free public education for all children as required by the state constitution. The governor at the time commissioned a study to recommend a world-class system for generating revenue to operate the state, including public schools.

The resulting legislation provided for the bulk of funds to support the instructional operation of schools to come from revenue generated by the state. The creators of this legislation must have understood what Thomas Jefferson meant when he wrote that "The tax which will be paid for the purpose of education is not more than the thousandth part of what will be paid to kings, priests and nobles who will rise up among us if we leave the people in ignorance."[1]

Local boards of education would have general administrative responsibility for educational funds provided by the state and federal governments. Funds to provide and maintain school facilities would come from revenue generated by county governments, which operate in many ways as extensions of the state. This funding model places local boards of education in a position of fiscal dependency with respect to counties and the state. Forward-thinking in the 1930s, the tax structure has remained virtually the same, while the economic base that supports state and local government and public schools has changed dramatically.

With the exception of funding to maintain schools within the operating budget of school districts, there is no statutory requirement for county governments to provide additional funding to public schools. There is wide disparity across the state in the amount of funding individual school districts receive each year, reflecting in large part differences in wealth, tax base and attitudes towards government and public schools in different areas of the state.

The questions of who funds public schools, by what means, and why are answered in legislation in every state. State funding provides a foundation level of support to ensure a sound basic education. As is the case in most states, the foundation level of funding is based on student membership in each district. In addition, the state provides categorical funds to address the needs of smaller and low-wealth districts, as well as funds for all districts to address the needs of students identified as economically disadvantaged, gifted or special needs. While there are idiosyncratic differences among states, the answers always reflect a combination of the core public values of liberty, equality, community and of course, prosperity.

VALUE TRADE-OFFS IN FUNDING CRESTWICH PUBLIC SCHOOLS

Prior to merger, Crestton struggled to fund new classrooms in its rapidly growing schools, while Elkwich struggled to pay for under-utilized schools. Unless existing school buildings and facilities could be used more efficiently to offset rising costs, county officials would be forced to consider increasing property taxes. A funding dilemma was brewing.

In addition to rising capital costs, other factors contributed to the funding dilemma. Business leaders recognized the negative economic consequences that would result if Elkwich continued to lose white families. Elected leaders recognized the negative electoral consequences they would likely suffer if they raised taxes to pay for new classrooms while existing classrooms went unused. Business and elected leaders joined together to promote merger as a solution to escalating capital costs and a growing tax burden.

In promoting merger, proponents argued that consolidating school administrative offices would reduce the size of central administration and thereby reduce the cost of schools operations. They also argued that demand for new facilities would be reduced by increasing utilization of existing facilities, thereby reducing or at least slowing the rise in capital funding. Overall, greater economies of scale would be realized by increasing the size of the system serving all students in the Crestton and Elkwich school districts.

Several efficiencies were realized once merger was approved. Two superintendents were replaced by one. Two sets of senior leaders in areas such as instruction, facilities and maintenance, finance, human resources, transportation and food service were replaced by one. Entire departments were streamlined and operated with fewer employees in a single, larger school system. A new uniform system for reporting school budgets and expenditures was implemented along with computerized recordkeeping, something that had not been done prior to merger as neither district felt the cost could be justified.

Not all efficiencies were easily achieved. As part of right-sizing building capacity for students, the district closed a handful of schools that were underutilized and in need of significant repair or renovation. Such schools were neither safe nor inviting, and they were relatively costly to operate. It made little sense financially to keep such schools open. However, the schools involved served mostly black students in Elkwich. Reasonable efficiency and cost-savings arguments conflicted with equally compelling arguments for preserving a sense of belonging, identity, heritage and tradition.

In the years following merger, the need for new seats for students moved from a steady beat to a drum roll, keeping capital needs at the forefront of school funding discussions and decisions. At the same time, the growing district required new and expanded programs to support equity, educational innovation and to improve educational outcomes for all students. Issues of cost, equity, value and return on investment framed funding requests and decisions.

VALUE TRADEOFFS IN FUNDING CRESTWICH PUBLIC SCHOOL FACILITIES

Capital improvement programs purchase land, construct new schools and additions to existing schools, and purchase and locate mobile or modular classroom units to increase capacity for students. Such plans involve tens or even hundreds of millions of dollars. Capital plans can also include renovating and reconfiguring buildings, deferred maintenance, school technology and support, purchasing equipment, and replacing heating, cooling and power systems. In Crestwich, capital improvement plans are typically funded through either a bond referendum requiring voter approval or by certificates of participation or pay-as-you-go financing not requiring voter approval.

During the decade following merger, voters approved two bond referenda which, combined with previously dedicated capital funds, totaled nearly $300 million and funded the construction of 16 new schools and additions and renovations to 54 existing schools. These bonds were approved by 86 percent and 85 percent of voters, respectively. Voters also approved a tax increase to repay the debt incurred to build schools.

Growth and capital investment go hand in hand. Growth requires additional capacity either through new schools or additions to existing schools. New schools and additions encourage increased population growth and economic development which in turn require more new schools and additions. As the economic impact of schools contributed to growth, and as the construction of new schools increased the attractiveness of the area, growth and capital investment began to snowball. In Crestwich, capital investment in public schools was certainly a cost of growth, but local leaders also touted it as an investment in quality of life and future economic growth.

Renovations, on the other hand, are not a direct cost of growth but an investment in equity. They are needed to improve the safety, functionality, attractiveness and desirability of existing schools. Since merger, the combination of underfunded capital needs and rapid growth had resulted in a growing number of schools that were now at or beyond the life cycle for such facilities. As the number of schools grew, so too did facility costs.

In addition to protecting the economic investment already made in existing schools, renovations help maintain a sense of fairness and equality for families whose children are assigned to older school buildings. Renovation makes new and older schools more comparable, a critical consideration in light of the importance of creating a single, unified and equitable district after the two school systems were merged.

Replacing and updating equipment and technology in existing schools is another example of capital investment as equity. New schools usually open with all the bells and whistles that come with updated technology. Funding new technology for older schools keeps them on a par with newer schools. Parity, equity and comparability became important political considerations in Crestwich in deciding whether, when and how to fund renovation and replacement.

Crestwich voters seemed to prefer a bond referendum to a tax increase. Bonds that included money for renovations, additions or equipment upgrades had tangible purposes voters could understand, making them more difficult to oppose. And specific purposes kept public focus more on the purpose of the bond than on the cost. Property tax increases, on the other hand, were usually proposed for unspecified operating costs. They generated far more political opposition.

Strong support for these bond referenda suggested that Crestwich voters agreed with Franklin Delano Roosevelt when he remarked that, "The school is the last expenditure upon which America should be willing to economize." But like the seasons, this too would change.

FROM INVESTING TO COST-CUTTING

With enrollment in Crestwich public schools growing at around 3,000 students annually, new schools were needed and the list of additions and renovations needed at existing schools lengthened. A new capital plan with an estimated $938 million cost was developed to purchase land for new schools, construct 15 new schools, fund renovations to 58 existing schools, and fund significant new investments in technology. To support the plan a $650 million bond referendum was placed before voters.

As the economic prosperity of the area grew, so did the cost of living and the cost of government. Citizens railed more loudly against tax increases. Many local elected officials ran on "no tax pledge" campaigns. The more than one-half billion dollar bond referendum came to symbolize the seemingly insatiable appetite of the school system for taxpayer money.

An anti-tax group organized and funded a campaign to defeat the bond, tapping into the growing anti-tax and anti-government sentiment of voters with the slogan of "There's a Better Way!" The better way, never articulated, seemed to sway voters. For the first time since merger, the public did not support a school bond referendum. As Jefferson noted, "Excessive taxation will carry reason and reflection to every man's door, and particularly in the hour of election."[2]

Although the anti-tax group successfully defeated the bond, they were unsuccessful in preventing future tax increases in the face of continuing overcrowding in schools. With the bond referendum defeated, Crestwich officials had little choice but to raise property taxes to support the growing cost of the consolidated school system. The bulk of the tax increase was designated to fund a scaled-down capital improvement program to address school crowding. The remainder was designated to support the general operations of the school system.

As the number of seats needed for the projected growth of students continued to climb, it became clear that the next capital improvement program would dwarf those that had come before. Adding to this cost was a legislatively-mandated reduction in class size in elementary grades, increasing the number of classrooms and seats needed. The growing inventory of renovations, additions, major maintenance projects and equipment upgrades added still more. As the school district developed capital scenarios, the initial cost projections exceeded $1 billion.

With public attitudes shifting away from investment and toward cost reduction, local leaders began calling for cost-cutting and cost control. Responding to growing public sentiment for no new tax increase, elected and business leaders had but one message for the board of education—too much, scale it back. It now seemed that voters were more likely to agree with Samuel Butler when he wrote that, "A drunkard would not give money to sober people . . . they would only eat it, and buy clothes and send their children to school with it."

POLICY TOOLS AND APPROACHES FOR ADDRESSING ECONOMY AND EFFICIENCY

As Crestwich residents became more aware of the costs of growth, cries for tax relief, cost-cutting and cost savings grew more audible. The public, the media and policymakers became increasingly skeptical about the district's projections of population growth and the increasing size and cost of the school system. Thomas Paine's admonition that "The continual whine of lamenting the burden of taxes, however successfully it may be practiced in mixed governments, is inconsistent with the sense and spirit of a republic"[3] fell on deaf ears. Rebuilding voter confidence and support would be an essential next step.

To respond to this changing political climate, Crestwich public schools used a variety of policy tools and approaches to achieve greater efficiencies and reduce and control costs. Each of these tools and approaches satisfied some aspect of the value of prosperity. And each tool or approach supported or conflicted with one or more of the other public values. The overarching lesson for citizens, policymakers, and administrators is that just as policy choices involve public values, so do policy tools. And just as there are no one-value policy choices, there are also no one-value policy tools.

Citizens Facilities Advisory Committee

The board of commissioners and the board of education formed a joint 31-member Citizens Advisory Committee to review school facility needs and make recommendations to both elected bodies. Meeting over several months, the committee reviewed all aspects of school design, construction, maintenance and operations. The committee developed 28 recommendations to be considered in developing the next capital improvement plan. Key recommendations included:

- Meet classroom needs first;
- Plan for approximately 11,000 additional classroom seats;
- Reduce space standards;
- Use more efficient construction methods and reuse existing building plans;
- Open more year-round schools to make the most of available space and reduce new construction costs; and
- Do not raise taxes to build or improve schools.

The committee provided independent confirmation of the school district's facilities needs. It also provided political legitimacy for local elected officials to sponsor and support two new bond referenda to meet capital needs, both of which were approved by voters.

Magnet Schools and Magnet Programs

As we described previously, magnet schools in the Crestwich district were designed primarily to support efficient use of buildings and desegregation efforts. Desegregation and utilization went hand in hand. The most efficient way to both desegregate and fully utilize schools would be to assign students directly to a school. But the Crestwich magnet program was a choice program, meaning integration could only occur if parents, in large enough numbers, decided voluntarily to move their children from their assigned schools to a magnet school.

There is a cost to desegregating schools and increasing utilization through choice. To create sufficient incentives and demand, magnet programs required resources beyond those provided to non-magnet schools. The Crestwich magnet program would not have become nationally recognized without the investment of considerable additional resources, including additional teachers, equipment, funding, transportation and administrative support.

Magnet programs also created some opportunity costs. To maintain the draw and special appeal of magnet programs, the district prohibited non-magnet schools from duplicating special programs and offerings found in magnet schools. This created perceptions of unequal treatment. Parents and students in non-magnet schools wanted the opportunities available in magnet schools, but without the cost of having to leave their assigned school. These value conflicts were an unintended consequence of having created a unified district in which all taxpayers supported a single school system, and in which the board worked to make the health and quality of schools comparable through the use of system-wide policy tools.

Joint Funding Agreement

The county commission and board of education differed sharply over the level of local funding needed by the school system. The early years of growth had produced excess tax revenue and allowed the county commission to decrease the property tax rate. This short-term benefit to taxpayers would be wiped out by escalating operating and capital costs as the county and school system grew.

Unable to resolve this funding dispute through the normal appropriation process, the board of education requested mediation, as permitted under state law and as required prior to taking legal action. The mediation process requires consideration of the entire school system budget by both boards in an attempt to resolve their differences.

After lengthy discussions, the two boards signed a joint funding agreement, the first of its kind in the state. The county guaranteed the school system a minimum appropriation tied to the growth of the tax base. Part of the total county property tax rate was designated for operational costs and part for capital expenditures. If the tax base increased, so would the amount of funding. The board of education could request an increase in the tax rate, and the board of commissioners could approve or deny the request if five of the seven commissioners voted to do so.

Community-Wide Goal Setting

Recognizing that funding differences were likely to persist for quite some time, the Crestwich Education Partnership, a local education foundation supported by the business community, proposed a community summit to help refocus public attitudes after the funding dispute between the elected county and school boards. Their goal was to create a common focus for public schools and unify the community around a common educational goal.

As had occurred in many districts, high stakes testing and accountability initiatives intensified in Crestwich. Student test scores in grades 3 through 8 determined grade-level performance or proficiency. Testing data was disaggregated and shared across the state to compare schools and districts and to highlight the performance of sub-groups of students.

The result of the summit was a community-wide goal, adopted by the board of education, that "Within five years, 95 percent of students tested will be at or above grade level as measured by state end-of-grade testing for grades 3 and 8." At the time of the summit, the average reading and math scores in the district were more than 20 percentage points lower than the goal. The district had no funding available to dedicate specifically to this goal.

But as allowed for by the recent joint funding agreement, the county commission approved a two-cent tax increase requested by the board of education to support this goal. The district re-purposed and re-prioritized funding to provide targeted financial resources to schools. The district created a specialized learning program to provide not just remediation but acceleration for students who did not score proficient on end-of-grade tests. Afterschool and Saturday school programs were created to assist struggling students.

The community goal was not met, but it did have some positive outcomes. The district's test scores rose enough to make Crestwich Public Schools one of the highest performing districts in the state, as measured by statewide student testing. It led to creating programs to help students with greater needs, thereby addressing some of the equity challenges in a large and diverse district. And it created a more shared sense of ownership of public schools throughout the community, and reinforced the district's accountability to the community.

Curriculum Management Audit

As might be expected after such an intensive effort to raise academic performance, student achievement began to plateau after a period of years.

To revitalize and refocus its efforts on behalf of every student, the district commissioned a national organization to conduct a curriculum management audit, based on a proven model utilizing business principles. The entire instructional delivery program, from the boardroom to the classroom, was audited to identify discrepancies between standards and practices throughout the school district. This effort was designed to fine-tune and better align administrative and instructional systems to improve district-wide performance.

The audit team reviewed 50,000 pages of documents, interviewed nearly 500 people, and visited and observed nearly 4,000 classrooms in preparing a 400-page report for the board of education and the superintendent. The curriculum management audit report contained eight major recommendations addressing opportunity, consistency, governance, management, evaluation, budgeting, instruction, and organization. The recommendations included 47 actions addressing district governance and 70 actions addressing district administration.

The eight major recommendations were presented in order of importance as defined by the audit team. The first and most critical recommendation was to "Implement district plans and goals to provide equal access to comparable programs, services, and opportunities to impact student success. Eliminate the achievement gap between ethnic and socioeconomic student groups. Take further steps to allocate resources on the basis of need."[4]

Most audits focus on improving financial management, strengthening internal controls, or achieving greater administrative efficiencies. In this instance the district received an audit report calling for improving equal access, eliminating unequal outcomes, and allocating resources more equitably, all as ways of increasing student success.

Mandatory Year-Round Schools

Faced with declining public support for a new bond referendum, the board of education and district staff struggled to identify ways to reduce capital costs and still provide the space needed. The district listened to ideas and suggestions from both supporters and opponents of previous bonds. Only one option emerged with broad support from both groups—scale back the number of new schools planned for construction and increase overall capacity by opening all new elementary and middle schools on a year-round calendar.[5]

Technical analyses suggested that a year-round calendar school could yield up to 30 percent greater student capacity than the same building operated on a traditional calendar. The district had already begun opening some new elementary and middle schools on multi-track year-round calendars. Now, all new elementary and middle schools would operate as year-round schools.

But staff analyses of updated growth projections also showed that even if all new elementary and middle schools opened on a year-round basis, there would still be insufficient capacity. The board of education was hooked on the horns of a trilemma. The board did not have sufficient political support to finance the new seats needed to continue traditional calendar schools. By law, the district could not go directly to voters with a bond referendum for building additional capacity to meet growth. And opening only new elementary and middle schools as year-round schools would reduce but not eliminate the shortage of seats.

To resolve this trilemma, an even more radical proposal surfaced—convert existing traditional calendar schools in high growth areas to year-round schools. The math was simple, even if the politics were not. The more schools that were converted to year-round, the greater the increase in capacity and the lower the cost of the next capital improvement plan.

Seeing no other alternative, the board of education directed district staff to develop a plan to convert a sufficient number of existing traditional calendar schools to year-round schedules. After discussing a variety of options, the board committed to opening all new elementary and middle schools on a year-round basis and agreed to convert 22 existing elementary and middle schools to year-round calendars.

A decade or so earlier, magnet programs were located primarily in schools within the city limits of Elkwich to draw more suburban and more white families to less-utilized urban schools. But in converting traditional calendar schools to year-round schools, few urban schools were even considered. Existing urban schools tended to be older and smaller than suburban schools. Consequently, converting these schools to year-round would yield relatively little extra capacity.

The board's decision to convert existing schools increased projected capacity just enough to reduce the amount of the next supporting bond referendum to $970 million, just under the $1 billion figure that produced sticker shock throughout the district. The board of county commissioners endorsed the district's capital improvement plan and placed it on the ballot for voters to decide. This school bond referendum, the largest in the nation at the time, passed. The political fallout from mandatory conversion did not.

It did not take long for families in higher growth suburban areas to understand the consequences of year-round conversion. When magnet programs were placed in more urban schools, suburban families clamored for the same opportunities without having to leave their neighborhoods. Now targeted for conversion to year-round because that was where the greatest number of students lived and were projected to live in the future, they demanded that year-round conversions take place somewhere else. Families and neighborhoods felt pitted against each other. Convert them, not us, they told the board and staff.

Resistance to year-round calendar schools began to escalate. Fault lines appeared as some suburban municipalities began to push back against the very idea of a unified county-wide school district. What had started out as a cost-effective fiscal decision seeking to satisfy dimensions of efficiency and cost control within the value of prosperity became an issue of freedom, rights and choice. As it always does, liberty spoke loudly.

Parental complaints and protests led to a legal challenge. A lower court ruled that students could not be required to attend a "mandatory year-round" school, as they had a right under the State Constitution to attend a traditional calendar school. The court required the district to obtain consent from parents before reassigning students to year-round schools.

The district appealed the ruling. It was overturned by a higher court that ruled the board was not legally required to obtain prior consent. The district sought to accommodate unhappy parents by allowing transfers to traditional calendar schools, but families that took advantage of this option were often assigned to a different school than the one they had attended previously. To many families, these efforts were seen as too little, too late.

Multi-track year-round schools, originally opened in small numbers as part of the district's magnet program to enhance equality through greater integration and later relied upon to produce desperately needed efficiency through greater utilization, had become a source of great contention among many Crestwich families. They would become a focal point for supporters of neighborhood schools and parental choice.

In retrospect, the financial costs that were avoided by expanding year-round schools were not worth the political and social costs of mandating them. Freedom isn't free, or cheap. As the district's experience with these tools and approaches for improving efficiency illustrates, greater return on investment seldom comes without greater investment.

EFFICIENCY IS A MEANS, PROSPERITY IS THE GOAL

While some of these approaches are unique to Crestwich Public Schools, one thing that is not unique is the lesson of how fiscal decisions driven by the public value of prosperity complement or conflict with other public values and goals. Tax dollars are a resource, but taxation is a policy tool.

And no policy tool used to satisfy one particular value is without unintended consequences for other public values.

The Crestwich school district's most recent operating budget, including state, local and federal funds, exceeded $1.2 billion. Serving 144,000 students, the greatest portion of the operating budget, more than 80 percent, pays salary and benefits for employees. The public and their elected representatives want public institutions held accountable for the efficient use of public dollars. Despite being a means rather than an end, efficiency is frequently cited as a goal or rationale for pursuing a course of action designed to reduce costs.

Although Crestwich compares well to other districts on any number of cost and efficiency measures, there are continued calls to reduce the size and cost of the system. Numerous audits, usually led by outside professionals and business experts, have found a generally efficient and well-run organization, albeit always with recommendations for improvement and calls to run the school system more like a business. The district has responded to these recommendations in a variety of ways, including adopting a form of zero-based budgeting to justify every category of expenditure and by implementing a multi-year budget planning process.

Another lesson is that citizens seem to pay greater attention to taxation than to spending. In other words, citizens tend to pay more attention to how they will be asked to pay for public education than to what education they are being asked to pay for. Each year, the board of education holds a public hearing before forwarding its budget request to the board of commissioners for consideration. Relatively few members of the public attend.

When the board of commissioners holds its annual public hearing on the county budget, which includes the appropriation for the school system and any recommended tax increases, the number of speakers often grows quite large. Decisions to increase or decrease taxes that rest with county commissioners draw much more public attention than the budget request and spending plan of the board of education.

Every policy decision has a fiscal implication, and vice versa. Decisions about how to raise revenue, how much revenue to raise and how to allocate the costs and benefits of that revenue have impacts beyond issues of just cost, productivity and efficiency. Issues of liberty, equality and community will also arise. Public school leaders cannot escape debates about how much to spend and how much is too much or too little. We suggest they keep in mind this advice from writer and journalist Walter Lippmann who observed: "We are quite rich enough to defend ourselves, whatever the cost. We must now learn that we are quite rich enough to educate ourselves as we need to be educated."

Adequate school funding can be determined using a variety of calculators, formulas and algorithms. But ultimately adequacy is a political construct, not a numerical one. Any numbers that school districts use to justify increased funding or to demonstrate cost savings are ultimately judged by the public in terms of being too much, too little, or about right. Goldilocks may no longer be allowed in the classroom, but she sits front and center in the boardroom.

NOTES

1. Thomas Jefferson to George Wythe (1786).
2. Thomas Jefferson to John Taylor (1798).
3. Thomas Paine, *Rights of Man.*
4. Phi Delta Kappa International (August 2007). *A curriculum management audit of the Wake County Public School System.* Bloomington, IN: Author, p. 349.
5. A proposal to open new high schools on a year-round calendar was considered, but short-lived. Few high schools in the nation operated year-round. The principal disincentives included reduced course offerings, large student populations, the administrative burden and logistical limitations on student participation in athletics and extra-curricular activities.

Part IV

Leading and Governing Public Schools

Policy arguments surrounding educational opportunity, parental choice and taxation and school funding can be found in any school district. As we have shown, these policy arguments are framed by the core public values of liberty, equality, community and prosperity. When we argue for or against a particular policy solution, we are expressing a preference for a particular value or combination of values over other values or other combinations. We can use the example of assigning students to schools by directed assignment and through parental choice to illustrate this principle.

Supporters of district-directed student assignment base their arguments on dimensions of liberty, equality and prosperity. They argue for liberty in terms of increasing educational opportunity. They argue for equality in terms of addressing equity and fairness in assigning students, populating schools at or near district-wide demographic profiles, increasing racial integration, achieving socioeconomic diversity, and distributing the benefits and costs of economic growth more equitably. And they argue for prosperity in terms of making the most efficient and cost-effective use of existing schools possible to reduce the cost per student and redistributing student populations to minimize overutilization or underutilization of classrooms.

Supporters of parental choice in student assignment base their arguments on dimensions of liberty, community and prosperity. They argue for liberty in terms of giving families their choice of schools and letting families decide. They argue for community in terms of neighborhood schools, keeping students close to their home, keeping students together throughout their public education years to maintain friendships, greater safety, creating a greater sense of connection and belonging, and increasing families' sense of stability. They argue for prosperity in terms of providing incentives for families to choose schools for their children that they otherwise would not have chosen, and letting market forces determine school enrollments.

Supporters of both directed and choice student assignment draw upon liberty and prosperity. In this example they are expressing a preference for different dimensions of the same values rather than different values. The key difference between proponents of each form of student assignment is that supporters of directed assignment draw upon equality, while supporters of choice assignment draw upon community.

Directed assignment equalizes differences between all families and communities, but in doing so it reduces the commonality and connection among and within some families and communities. Parental choice does just the opposite. It allows for connection among and within some families and communities, but it is not likely to contribute toward equality between all families and communities. This tension between the good of individuals and the good of the community runs across and through many policy choices in public education, including educational opportunity, assigning students and funding public schools.

So far in this book we have been descriptive, laying out how Americans think about public schools, exploring the competing visions and values underlying public education, and illustrating how policy conflicts in public schools are framed by choices from among these visions and values. In the following chapters, we shift gears to follow Henry Wadsworth Longfellow's advice that in this world one must be either anvil or hammer. We now shift from the anvil of description to the hammer of prescription.

The questions we address in Part IV are the "so what" questions. In Chapter 8 we explore the essential features and characteristics of public policy problems. What do they look like and how can we recognize them? What choices do policy problems present to us? How do public values frame policy problems and choices in public schools?

In Chapter 9 we explore the challenges of policy leadership in public schools. What is the essential leadership task of public school leaders? How can they help their districts discuss and understand policy problems and choices? What process can public school leaders use to identify the values represented in a given policy problem and forge policy solutions that respond logically to core values and democratic principles?

In Chapter 10 we address the challenges of governing public schools. In most states, we govern public schools with locally elected boards of education. Why do we elect citizens to govern public schools? Why do we elect citizens individually and then require them to serve on a board with other elected citizens? What does it mean to govern? What decisions should boards make? How can boards distinguish policy decisions from administrative decisions? What obligations do those who govern public schools have to those they govern?

As we have shown, supporters and opponents sometimes invoke different values and sometimes the same values when they argue about policy problems and solutions. How can this be? What does this paradox mean for leading and governing public schools? These questions matter, as does how we choose to answer them. "America's future will be determined by the home and the school," said Jane Addams. "The child becomes largely what he is taught; hence we must watch what we teach, and how we live." It is to these questions that we now turn our attention.

Chapter 8

Policy Problems in Public Schools

Like all public institutions, public schools are confronted with two basic types of problems—positive and normative. Positive problems are problems of fact. We solve positive problems by using legal, scientific and technical knowledge. Given a list of households with children who need to be picked up by a school bus, what is the most efficient (quickest, shortest), cost-effective (cheapest) and least risky (safest, legal) route for the bus driver to take?

To solve this problem, we need to know about housing and traffic patterns, zoning practices, transportation corridors, and the fuel efficiency and student capacity of our school bus. We also need experts who possess legal, scientific and technical knowledge and who understand how to apply that knowledge to problems like this one.

We may choose from among the available routes based on technical criteria, such as time or distance. If time is more important than distance, we may choose a longer route if it gets us to our destination more quickly. If driving less or saving fuel is more important than saving time, we may drive a shorter route even if it takes longer to arrive at our destination. Technical choices involve positive or factual statements. Route A is shorter in distance. Route B takes less time. Solving positive problems does not require leadership.

Normative problems are problems of values. We solve normative problems by using moral, ethical and political knowledge. Given a list of all children within a school district, which children should be eligible to ride a school bus? We could decide that all children are eligible, thereby treating every child equally. However, the cost of transporting every child might be so great that we can't afford it without taking money from other areas of schooling. Should we offer more transportation at greater cost, or limit transportation to reduce the cost?

Some children live close to their school. Picking up and transporting children who live close by may take longer than if they walked or their parents drove them. Should we adopt a minimum physical distance to be eligible to ride a school bus? What about children who live farther away? How long should a child ride a bus? Should we adopt a maximum amount of time a child should spend on a school bus?

Exercise is good for children. This is a positive statement based on fact. Should we require or encourage children who live close by to walk if they are physically able? This is a normative question based on values. How safe are the streets for walking? Are there sidewalks and adequate crosswalks and traffic signals? What should we do about children who live close by but for some reason are unable or unwilling to walk to school?

Not all parents may want their child to ride a school bus. Should parents or the district be responsible for transportation to school? Is transportation to school a public responsibility, a private responsibility, or both? If it is both, how should that responsibility be divided or shared?

As this example shows, the essence of the *public* in public schools is normative, meaning it is value-based and political. Leadership is essential to preserving the public in public schools. Some reformers call for removing political issues from the classroom to better focus on teaching and student achievement. Others call for removing political issues from the boardroom to better focus on the business of learning.

Such arguments presume that we can remove politics and policy conflicts from either the classroom or the boardroom without harming the public in public schools. We cannot. To do so would remove the *public* from public schools. It might reduce policy conflicts, but it would also remove the very values that all of the purposes of public education and all of the rationales for public schools rest upon. Policy problems, conflicts and choices in public schools are about the *public* in public schools. They involve technical issues, but they are not technical problems. They are normative or value-based problems. In this chapter we examine the key features of policy problems and how public values frame policy problems and choices in public schools.

KEY FEATURES OF POLICY PROBLEMS

Policy problems involve both facts and values. We may know many different facts about a policy problem. But when we argue about how best to resolve a policy problem, we are likely to select those facts that support the values we already prefer. The U.S. Supreme Court has ruled that school districts may conduct random drug testing of students involved in extracurricular activities.

In light of this ruling, districts must decide how to balance concerns about safety, classroom productivity and social and moral order against concerns about privacy, fairness, and the cost of drug testing.

Proponents of student drug testing are likely to argue that illegal drug use among students leads to accidents, injuries and criminal behavior. Opponents are likely to argue that there is relatively little illegal drug use among students and that the expected benefits from drug testing don't outweigh the legal, social and economic costs of testing. Both sides cite studies and facts to support their arguments.

When we argue for or against a particular policy solution, we are likely to make both positive and normative statements. "Vegetables contain vitamins" is an example of a positive or factual statement. Normative statements are value-based statements about how things should or ought to be. "Schools should serve children more vegetables" is an example of a normative statement. The more strongly we believe normative statements, the more likely we are to state them as if they were facts. Just because a statement is value-based doesn't preclude some people from holding it to be true.

In deciding which policy choices we prefer, we weigh the relative importance of the values involved, and decide which value is most important. Technology may solve some problems but it can also create new ones. Cell phones, for example, give students greater individual freedom and provide parents with a greater sense of safety, security and connection. But cell phones, particularly ones with cameras, video capability and text messaging, can raise privacy concerns and interfere with an orderly and productive learning environment. Should school districts permit, restrict or ban student cell phones in schools? We resolve problems like these based not on a single right answer, but rather on the answer we think is most important.

Policy problems arise when individuals or groups pursue different public values. They occur in public settings where we engage each other as fellow citizens rather than as private individuals. And they require us to use normative statements. Below are some examples of policy problems in public schools. See if you can argue for a particular choice using only positive or factual statements:

- Should schools teach evolution, teach creationism, creation science and intelligent design, or teach all of these?
- Should schools adopt an anti-bullying policy that includes and protects everyone?
- Should we fund schools with property taxes based on the wealth of each district, should we subsidize lower-wealth districts, or should we fund all school districts equally regardless of their wealth?

- Should schools teach sex education to all age-appropriate students with parental consent, teach abstinence only, or leave sex education up to parents?
- Should school districts offer employment benefits to domestic partners of district employees?
- Should school districts link teacher pay and retention to student performance on standardized tests?

It's impossible to discuss these choices, let alone argue for or against any of them, without using normative or value-based statements. Each policy choice involves at least two of the core public values of liberty, equality, community and prosperity. If there was only one core value involved, there would be little to discuss, no choice to make, and nothing to argue about.

When citizens and public school leaders debate normative issues such as these, inevitably they discover that they have value differences. They are likely to assume that their value differences arise because they hold different values. They do not. They hold the same values, the core public values of liberty, equality, community and prosperity. Their differences arise not from different values, but from different priorities among these core values.

We are so passionate about these core values that we sometimes make multiple but conflicting claims of each value. In the preceding chapters about educational opportunity, student assignment and school funding, we illustrated how individuals or groups attached priority to different core public values and sometimes to different dimensions of the same core value. In doing this we create a marvelous policy paradox.[1] Here are three examples.

It's difficult for people to feel independent without some degree of security, but increasing people's security can also increase their dependence. This paradox arises in debates about teacher tenure, in which some people argue that productivity and innovation decline when teachers have more security.

We value the independence and freedom to make our own choices, but sometimes we ask government to restrain people from acting voluntarily in ways that can harm them. This paradox arises in debates about whether schools should ban or allow the sale of soda, snacks and fast food in order to earn revenue or protect the health of students.

Efficient and innovative organizations require a certain degree of freedom of choice, but free choice results in a certain degree of inequality. This paradox arises when public school districts seek to achieve and maintain equality, because to do so often requires a large bureaucracy which some people argue is wasteful and inefficient.

We wouldn't feel so strongly and so passionately about our own policy preferences that are often different from those of other people if we didn't also hold these values in common with them. If we held different values, our value differences would just be different. The passion behind policy arguments suggests conflict over different values, but the paradox of difference is that it is the values we have in common that give rise to our policy conflicts.

Public values of liberty, equality, community and prosperity unite us as Americans in ways that nothing else can. Most of the ways we describe ourselves as a people divide us. Language, religion, music, cuisine, geography, occupation, education, race, ethnicity, gender, and income are just some of the ways in which we express and describe our differences.

It is through public values that we express our commonality as a people and as a nation. Seemingly simple concepts like liberty and equality suggest a common goal, a common purpose. But the more we struggle to define precisely what we mean by these concepts, the more tensions we uncover between the values and the more we sacrifice their commonality.[2]

Consider Thomas Jefferson's assertion that "There is nothing more unequal than the equal treatment of unequal people." This simple statement offers us opportunities for hours of discussion and debate about the meaning of equal and unequal, and their relative importance and priority in different situations. Such is the dilemma we face when trying to understand policy problems.

PUBLIC VALUES FRAME POLICY PROBLEMS AND CHOICES IN PUBLIC SCHOOLS

Like a photographer who uses a camera lens to frame and focus a landscape, we frame policy problems and focus policy solutions through the lens of our values. Because different values give us different views of the problem, we tend to also see different solutions. Before we can decide how to solve a policy problem, we must first be able to see the problem in terms of its core values.

Once we know which values are involved, we can better understand the choices available to us to solve the problem. Sometimes we are reluctant to look at different points of view, either because we are convinced that our view is right or because we prefer not to make room for different views. To paraphrase Aristotle, an educated mind should be able to entertain an idea without having to accept it.

The following examples of policy problems involve determining appropriate student dress and making acceptable classroom reading assignments. These examples illustrate how public values frame policy problems, how both supporters and opponents use fact-based and value-based arguments, and how the policy choices available to us involve trade-offs among the public values represented in each problem.

Student Dress Codes

Virtually all public school districts have adopted student dress codes. Some prohibit T-shirts and clothing with non-school logos and lettering. Some limit clothing to mostly solid colors, such as khaki or navy blue. Students are often subject to disciplinary action if they violate their district's dress code. Some parents and students support dress codes. Some do not. And for others, it depends on the specific dress code in question.

In general, supporters of dress codes believe that students are too concerned with name-brand clothing. They believe dress codes decrease violence and theft that occurs over designer clothing, and prevent gang members from wearing gang colors and insignia at school. They argue that too much attention on fashion leads some students to judge other students solely on how they look rather than who they are.

Students who cannot afford "cool" clothing can feel inferior to students who are able to buy the latest fashions. Different dress can sometimes lead to feeling excluded, less equal and even to fighting. Supporters believe dress codes help parents and students resist peer pressure, emphasize commonality rather than difference, and help students concentrate more on school work.

Parents who support a dress code might say: "Kids make fun of other kids if they don't wear cool, name-brand clothes, and it can be very hurtful and damaging to their self-esteem. If this puts an end to that, then I'm all for it." Students who support a dress code might say: "Wearing the same clothes doesn't start fights, and no one picks on you, because you're all wearing the same thing. The clothes aren't really cool, but they're OK."

In general, opponents of dress codes argue that kids are people too, and they deserve to be treated as individuals. They believe clothing is an important way for students to express themselves as individuals, and that dress codes stifle students' development as individuals. They believe that requiring students to wear the same type of clothing is coercive and unfair because it restricts their freedom to be children. In some instances dress codes may also conflict with religious and cultural beliefs.

Opponents also argue that schools are seeking a quick fix for deeper behavioral problems among some students, and that students are being discriminated against if there is no similar dress code for teachers and other school employees. Parents who oppose a dress code might say: "This dress code policy takes away children's individuality and attempts to make them clones." Students who oppose a dress code might say: "This dress code policy is against the rights of students and prevents them from being kids."

The choices we face in deciding upon a student dress code are not simply choices between colors and logos. Most of the time, deciding what to wear is a private matter and an individual decision. But deciding what to wear to school becomes a policy problem when it affects others in public settings and involves public values.

How much freedom to choose what students wear to school should parents and students have? Are students better off having more freedom to choose or being more equal? We value both freedom and equality, but when it comes to student dress, some parents and students value freedom more than equality, while others value equality more than freedom.

When parents and students decide what clothes to wear to school, their decisions can affect other students. One purpose of public schools is to provide educational opportunities for all students. Clothes that offend some students or distract students from learning may make it more difficult to achieve equal educational opportunity. To resolve policy problems resulting from student dress, we must decide how to balance the rights of students as individuals with their responsibilities as classmates to other students.

If we adopt a dress code, students will have less freedom to choose how to dress, but they will be more equal in their dress. If we don't adopt a dress code, students will have more freedom to choose how to dress, but they will be less equal in their dress. If we favor having more equality, then we must be willing to give up some freedom. But if we favor having more freedom, then we must be willing to accept less equality. All things being equal, we want as much freedom and as much equality as we can have. But we disagree on how to balance freedom and equality when policy problems require us to choose between them.

Classroom Reading Assignments

A 15-year-old high school sophomore objected to some of the language in an assigned book. She shared her reservations about reading the book with her father. "The book had a bunch of very bad language in it," she said. "It shouldn't be in there because it's offending people. . . . If they can't find a book that uses clean words, they shouldn't have a book at all."

The student's parent filed an objection with the district regarding *Fahrenheit 451,* written by Ray Bradbury and published in 1953. He requested that the district remove the book from the curriculum. "It's just all kinds of filth," he said, adding that he had not read the book. "The words don't need to be brought out in class. I want to get the book taken out of the class." He looked through the book and found the following things wrong with the book: discussion of being drunk, smoking cigarettes, violence, "dirty talk," and references to the Bible and using God's name in vain. He said the book's material goes against his family's religious beliefs.

The district's assistant superintendent said that *Fahrenheit 451* poses a warning to society about the importance of preserving and passing on knowledge. It asks whether government should do the thinking for people, and raises important questions about individuality, conformity, freedom of speech and the consequences of losing it, the importance of remembering and understanding history, and technology as both help and hindrance to humans.

The district uses a selection process for materials other than textbooks. Materials must meet specific standards, be appropriate for the course subject, age and social and emotional development of students, and motivate students to examine their own attitudes and behavior. *Fahrenheit 451* has been used in the curriculum for nearly twenty years. The district said it was unaware of any other challenges to *Fahrenheit 451,* and has not received challenges to any other books in the past four years.

Some students circulated a petition in support of the book, and wore t-shirts expressing their views. "This was probably one of the greatest eye openers that we've had in our school curriculum," said one student. "A lot of the students who signed our petition said that of all the books they had to read in class, this was the one they enjoyed most. It really makes you think about society and our current situation," said another student.

Each year, school districts across the nation must decide how they will respond to objections they receive from students and parents regarding the content of reading assignments. This example raises two key policy questions. First, who should determine reading assignments for students? Should it be the district, or should parents and students have a say in determining reading assignments? Second, what criteria should be used to select the books to be read?

The first question involves determining who should make reading assignments. If we believe that the district should make reading assignments, we are likely to argue that the district has greater knowledge and expertise, and can ensure that students gain the greatest educational benefit possible. This argument invokes the public value of prosperity. If we believe that parents and students should have a greater voice, we are likely to argue that the authority and responsibility to determine reading assignments should be shared, and that parents and students should have voice and choice in determining assignments. This argument invokes the public value of liberty.

The second question involves determining the criteria that should be used to select the books to be read. If the district selects reading assignments, it might develop standards for selecting content that is age and developmentally appropriate, has social and literary relevance and supports the educational goals of the district's curriculum. Again, this approach would support the value of prosperity over other values.

Alternatively, the district could recommend reading assignments, which would then be screened through a community review process. Such a process would need to address three key issues: first, how to respond to any community objections that are raised; second, whether parents and students should be allowed to opt out of a reading assignment they deem objectionable; and third, how parents and students who are allowed to opt out should address the educational goals identified by the district. This approach still supports the public value of prosperity, but also seeks to satisfy dimensions of freedom and choice included in the public value of liberty, and dimensions of social and moral order included in the public value of community.

IT'S NOT THE SIZE OF THE PROBLEM THAT MATTERS, BUT THE SIZE OF THE VALUES

First Amendment freedoms and concerns about censorship and social and moral order are big issues. While any school district may encounter this problem at some time, most districts don't deal with it regularly or frequently. But it doesn't require a big policy issue to raise questions that involve public values. Sometimes what seems like a relatively small issue can have big policy consequences. Here are two examples.

In one small school district the separation of childhood friendships and community ties became a public issue when parents raised concerns about the district's proposal to change school boundaries. The district has two elementary schools, one over-utilized and one under-utilized. Growing by about 100 students a year, the district proposed reassigning students so as to have each school at 90 percent of actual capacity to leave a little room for additional growth from year to year.

A district spokesperson stated that setting boundaries is "difficult work" and "we can't accommodate everybody to a true neighborhood school."[3] This example demonstrates that it's not the number of students that get reassigned that raises public values, but the reassignment itself, because it involves issues of choice, control, neighborhood schools, and residents' sense of community and connection.

Massachusetts became the first state to require preschools to teach children how to brush their teeth and educate them about oral health.[4] A study commissioned by the state concluded that dental disease at an early age can have negative long-term impacts on a child's health and quality of life, and found that one in four kindergartners in the state had dental disease. The study also found that kindergartners with dental disease were more likely to be poor and minority.

Dental hygiene may be a private matter at home, but in programs and facilities licensed by the state it becomes a public matter because it raises issues of parental responsibility and government intervention. Some parents and caregivers praise the regulations while others oppose them. "We don't need the state mandating every little thing in our lives. Let parents be parents," said one caregiver. "When you teach children oral health at a young age, they'll be able to maintain good dental hygiene for life," said a parent of a preschooler. Parents who feel strongly opposed to the regulation can opt out.

Safety and health concerns have also been raised. Pre-school programs are working to apply very little toothpaste so that it is safe for children to swallow. Some parents and teachers are concerned about the spread of germs through toothbrushes and spitting. "I don't want someone's hand in my child's mouth," said a pre-school teacher and mother.

Already busy pre-school schedules just got a little busier. "We need to start early," said a pre-school director. "We're supposed to have rest time, and now we have to eat a little earlier so there's enough time for the children to brush their teeth."

This example involves parental responsibility, freedom of choice and mandates (liberty), disadvantaged and minority children (equality), safety, health, disease and hygiene (community) and the use of time and resources (prosperity). Few people would ever think that teaching pre-schoolers about four-way brushing could become a four-value policy problem. Now you know it is, and now you know why.

WHY POLICY PROBLEMS MATTER

In this policy framework, policy problems represent opportunities to affirm public values, determine the relative priority of each value, and decide how best to satisfy each of the values represented. While policy problems may appear very different on the surface, underneath lie configurations of the same core public values. For all practical purposes, there are nearly an infinite variety of ways to combine the various dimensions of these core public values.

This recombinant property of public values makes it appear that there are nearly an infinite number of policy problems. Instead, our model suggests a rather finite number of policy problems that can take on a nearly infinite number of variations.

Because policy problems are value-based and not technical, they are seldom solved in any permanent sense. At best they are resolved for some period of time. Most important policy problems emerge again and again. How long a specific policy solution lasts is influenced by many factors, not least of which is how well all of the values represented in the most recent configuration of the problem were satisfied. In the next chapter we present a problem solving and decision making process for achieving good policy solutions.

NOTES

1. Stone (2002).
2. Ibid.
3. Compton, T. (2010). "Renton School Board considering changes to elementary school boundaries." *Renton Reporter,* Dec. 2.
4. Zezima, K. (2010). "Preschools add brush-and-spit to day." *The New York Times,* January 29.

Chapter 9

Public Leadership

Policy Problem Solving and Decision Making

Public schools are more than simply schools paid for with public dollars. Similarly, public leadership is more than simply leadership in public organizations. For our purposes, public leadership is the art and science of solving policy problems, making policy choices and crafting policy solutions on behalf of the public good.

In Part III we described how fundamental policy problems such as how to allocate educational opportunity, assign students, and fund public schools are framed by the core public values of liberty, equality, community and prosperity. As we saw, there was little consensus about how to resolve those policy problems. As British historian James Bryce noted, "There is in the American Government . . . a want of unity. . . . The Sailors, the helmsman, the engineer, do not seem to have one purpose or obey one will so that instead of making steady way the vessel may pursue a devious or zigzag course, and sometimes merely turn round and round in the water."[1]

This lack of consensus makes addressing the competing visions and values of public education the essential leadership challenge in public schools. Because policy problems involve the values of the public good and affect us as citizens, we do not make these choices alone. We engage each other in collective public decision making, and we must do so consistent with democratic principles. Meeting this leadership challenge involves three significant tasks for public school leaders.

The first task of public leadership is to create a shared understanding of policy problems and choices. Without a shared understanding, we are more likely to harm the public good than to do good. The second leadership task is to craft policy solutions that achieve the greatest possible public good. We do this by striking the best possible balance among all of the competing public values. The third leadership task is to use democratic means to accomplish the first two tasks. This requires arts and skills of democracy such as inclusion, participation, representation, deliberation and facilitation.

PUBLIC LEADERSHIP IN PUBLIC SCHOOLS

Policy problems always involve a tension between at least two public values. There are no single-value problems. More than one value means there is more than one solution. Policy choices represent possible solutions to a policy problem. Policy decisions are the solutions we choose. We use the term *public problem solving* to mean peeling the policy layers to find the values represented, defining a collective goal and crafting an integrative solution.

Agree on the problem before solutions. Ask people what they like and don't like about a particular problem, issue or solution. Hear all of the arguments, identify all of the values. Recognize value differences. Make room for others. Distinguish between means and ends, and between the how and the what. Public problems have multiple solutions but no single right answer. Good choices are both technically feasible and politically acceptable.

Watch out for false choices such as solutions disguised as problems. Beware one-value problems and solutions. Since every public problem involves at least two values, we cannot solve a public problem by using just one value. A solution that satisfies fewer values than are represented in the problem is a less good solution.

Seek best rather than right solutions. No one value is always better than the other values. Every policy solution favors one value over the others, but we don't, and shouldn't, favor the same value every time. Seek to optimize all values involved rather than maximize one value. Think long-term. Benefit the community as a whole. The best solution to a public problem is one that expands the realms of liberty, equality, community, and prosperity simultaneously.

No one person, organization or unit of government owns a policy problem alone. Competing public values means that people have differing visions of the public good and differing ideas about how to solve the problem. Because policy problems are problems of the public good, they are less about deciding how to do a good thing rather than a bad thing than they are about how to do a good thing without jeopardizing another good thing.

PUTTING PRINCIPLES INTO PRACTICE: SUMMER VACATION OR SUMMER LEARNING?

Summer vacation is part of American folklore. Children associate the school year with "oppression and the summer months with liberty and nothing is more American than liberty. Summer is red, white and blue. It's flags and fireworks, hot dogs and mustard, cold watermelon and sweet corn. School is work and regimen, while summer is creativity and play."[2]

In recent years a policy debate has emerged over the benefits of summer vacation compared to what educational experts refer to as summer learning, a way to prevent the loss of learning or "summer slide" some researchers claim summer vacation precipitates. Or as an unknown pundit said, "The bigger the summer vacation the harder the fall."

With proponents on both sides of this issue, what is the public good involved, and how might we craft a policy solution that achieves and preserves that good? In the following section we describe an approach for creating sufficient public space in which we can engage our fellow citizens in addressing challenging and meaningful public policy problems.

STEP 1: PREPARE FOR PUBLIC TALK

Let us assume that concerns about summer slide have been raised in our district. We have assembled a group of interested citizens—parents, teachers, students, business and community leaders—to participate in a policy problem solving process to address these concerns. The broader practice of public engagement warrants more attention and space than we can give it here, but here are a few keys to success.

Be clear about why you want to engage your community. Identify who the public is for this particular issue, what you expect to gain by engaging them, what they need in order to participate effectively, what you want them to learn, and what you want to learn from them. Choose an initial engagement tool such as surveys, interviews, or focus groups that is appropriate for the issue you have chosen and for the time and resources available.

Critical mass matters, as does diversity. Encourage broad-based participation. Reach out to organizations in your community that are most likely to represent the faces not usually seen and the voices not often heard. Do more than simply invite people. Look for ways to reduce barriers that might prevent invitees from participating, e.g., transportation, child care, or translators.

Use small groups instead of large public hearings to help people share their experiences. Provide a structure and format for small-group discussions to analyze policy options and discuss how families and community organizations can play a role in improving education for young people. This helps participants make progress on their task or topic, ensures plenty of air time for everyone, and results in participants feeling that their time was well-spent.

Structure your process to avoid debating solutions until everyone has a sufficient understanding of the problem. Move from exploration and understanding to planning and action. Be clear about what has been done in the past, what has been useful, what was or was not implemented, how this effort will improve on previous ones and what result you want to achieve.

Regardless of how or why we start this conversation, policy problems are about what we value and what we believe. We cannot discuss policy choices without talking about policy values. There may be many relevant facts, but it's what we think and feel and the value we place on facts that matter most to us.

Solving policy problems requires that we engage each other in public talk. Discourse and discussion are our tools in trade. We seldom learn anything from people who agree with us, and we are often reluctant to engage people who disagree with us. The best way to learn about a policy problem is to engage each other in conversation. When citizens are invited to discuss and learn rather than argue and debate, they display a thoughtfulness and depth of understanding that contributes to good decisions and solutions.

STEP 2: PEEL THE POLICY ONION

Policy problems are like onions. They have layers. Because policy problems are value-based, peeling the layers to identify the public values involved is the key to crafting solutions that make collective decisions possible.

We tend to jump to solutions rather than take time to talk about the layers of policy problems. This can quickly narrow our choices to yes-no and either-or. If we convene a group of citizens to discuss summer slide, someone would be quick to say, "Here's what we should do. We should adopt summer learning!" Of course, someone else will say, "Wait a minute, what we should do is preserve summer vacation!" The problem isn't that we can't see the solution, it's that we can't see the problem.[3]

Since a policy problem always has more than one solution, reducing our choices to yes-no, either-or makes sense only if we've identified all the possible alternatives. If we haven't fully explored the problem, and the solution we are ready to debate is the sixth best choice, then we're less likely to achieve the good we seek, regardless of the decision we make. We can avoid this dilemma by peeling our policy onion. To do this we must ask questions. To truly understand a policy problem, it's better to know some of the questions than all of the answers.[4]

In this example, we'll designate summer vacation as our existing policy. The questions we will ask address what we value about summer and summer vacation and the disadvantages of summer vacation. We'll designate summer learning as our proposed policy. The questions we will ask address what we hope to gain by adopting summer learning and what good we currently have that we might harm or diminish by adopting summer learning. Drawing upon citizen conversations and the views of a range of public educators, following is a synopsis of typical responses.[5]

What We Value about Summer and Summer Vacation

We value fun, freedom, play, recreation and leisure time, quality of life, family time, trips and travel to new places, vacations, and romantic visions and nostalgic memories associated with our experience of summer vacation. We value lower school operating costs, the importance of developing the whole child, and knowing that children start the school year refreshed and ready to learn. Brief reviews each fall of where students left off in the spring can be beneficial for all children. Summer is a gift of time in which children can explore new hobbies, work a summer job, or gain independence.

Running, playing, swimming, camping, and learning important interpersonal skills through activities with friends and sometimes with peers who are not so friendly are important developmental activities for children. Being able to come and go to the library and read as they please, looking at the sky or a bug or a leaf or just day dreaming, and the sheer joy of having time to wonder and wander are good for developing minds. "What is childhood for? Do we value it for its own sake, or for its instrumental worth in service to some other end?"[6]

Disadvantages of Summer Vacation

The long summer vacation creates "summer slide." It disrupts the rhythm of instruction, leads to forgetting, and requires time to be spent reviewing old material when students return to school in the fall. It can widen achievement gaps, require remedial education, and increase the number of students at risk of not graduating. Academic losses can become cumulative and greater for poorer children and other children at risk, particularly when children are playing while their international peers are studying.

There's not enough time in the traditional school year to teach students everything we want them to learn. For many children growing up in poorer families and diminished neighborhoods, the Tom Sawyerish ideal of summer gives way to a different reality, one characterized by boredom, inactivity, danger and isolation.[7] Achievement test scores tend to decline between spring and fall as out-of-school activities offer fewer opportunities to learn and practice academic skills.

Potential Benefits of Summer Learning

Children learn best when instruction is continuous. They are less likely to fall behind, to experience "summer slide," and to need remedial education. An increased investment in children means that children are more likely to graduate, have smaller achievement gaps, and experience less boredom, inactivity, and isolation. Continuous learning helps level the playing field, increases knowledge and skills, helps prepare children for the real world, and improves the ability of children to compete with other children around the world.

Potential Harms or Losses Related to Summer Learning

Children and their families would lose some freedom and recreation and leisure time. There would be less family and social time, fewer trips and family vacations, and competition with businesses tied to the cycle of summer. We may overburden children with homework, and they may become burned out and resentful. There may be higher tax and cost implications. We may have fewer opportunities to develop children as neighbors, citizens and friends, and not just as learners. Studies show little or no correlation between homework and standardized test scores or long-term achievement in elementary school and only a moderate correlation in middle school.

Summer learning steals time away from other important learning such as play, which helps children master social skills and teamwork. Children will spend fewer hours being physically active, which is essential for good health, weight control, and proper brain development.

Students don't necessarily enjoy doing homework during the school year but they understand it is part of their daily routine. In summer, students expect and often need a break from this routine and the daily pressures that usually accompany it. Structured activities can stifle creativity and stunt natural thought processes. Children don't have to have all of their time structured and regimented in order to become well educated.

Notice that we have asked some questions that are reverse images of each other. This serves an important purpose by providing sufficient opportunity to explore and discuss this issue. It also facilitates decision making, which we'll discuss shortly. Those who become most impatient with this process are usually those who think they already know the answer. By structuring our discussion this way, we give people a chance to peel enough layers of the policy onion to create a shared understanding separate from argument and debate. "Freedom from the desire for an answer is essential to the understanding of a problem."[8]

STEP 3: IDENTIFY THE PUBLIC VALUES REPRESENTED

The arguments for and against summer vacation and summer learning are based on public values. This means that we should be able to organize these arguments according to the values they represent. Once again, we peel this layer of our policy onion by asking questions. Which values do the arguments for summer vacation represent? Which values do the arguments for summer learning represent?

Public Values Represented by Arguments for Summer Vacation

Supporters of summer vacation are concerned primarily with the values of liberty and community. Supporters express the value of liberty in the following ways—having time, freedom and opportunity to play and recreate, explore, have fun, travel, have new experiences, develop as a person, work a summer job, gain independence, have fewer burdens and responsibilities, read for pleasure, daydream, wonder, socialize, be physically active, and be creative.

Supporters of summer vacation express the value of community in the following ways—recreation and leisure time, quality of life, family time, trips, vacations, romantic visions and nostalgic memories, learning important interpersonal skills by creating activities of their own with their friends and sometimes peers who are not so friendly; and opportunities to develop children as neighbors, citizens and friends, and not just as learners.

Public Values Represented by Arguments for Summer Learning

Supporters of summer learning are concerned primarily with the values of prosperity and equality. Supporters express the value of prosperity in the following ways—increase knowledge and skills by offsetting the shortage of time in the traditional school year to teach everything students need to learn; increase instructional efficiency and productivity by ending the negative cycle of long summer vacation that disrupts the rhythm of instruction, leads to forgetting, and requires time be spent reviewing old material when students return to school in fall; reduce the need for remedial education, increase high school graduation rates, make an increased positive investment in children, prepare children for the real world, and improve children's ability to compete with other children around the world.

Supporters of summer learning express the value of equality in the following ways—reduce "summer slide," reduce the likelihood that some children will fall behind, close achievement gaps, level the playing field between children from poorer and wealthier families, and counter the academic losses that can be cumulative and greater for poor children.

STEP 4: DEFINE A COLLECTIVE POLICY GOAL

Having peeled our policy onion, how might we move towards a mutually acceptable policy solution? Our next step is to define a policy goal that addresses all of the values represented. In other words, define a policy goal that supporters of summer vacation and supporters of summer learning can both get behind. And yes, we do this too by asking a question. What is the public good we seek by adopting summer learning and preserving summer vacation?

We begin by asking participants to draft a goal that captures the essence of what they want to achieve and what they want to preserve. Since we have identified a four-value policy problem, we seek a four-value policy goal. If people limit their choices only to what seems possible or reasonable, they risk disconnecting themselves from what they truly want, and all that is left is compromise or domination. We also ask participants to frame their goal as an affirmative statement. This gives people time to consider what's important to them, and to recognize why they need the people on the other side of the issue to frame a viable policy goal.

While groups will vary in what they emphasize and the language they use, a sample collective goal might look like this: provide summer learning to reduce learning loss and improve achievement for all children while preserving the fun, play and opportunities that summer vacation provides for family and social time and exploring new things.

STEP 5: CRAFT AND IMPLEMENT AN INTEGRATIVE SOLUTION

We could choose to adopt summer learning and ignore the consequences for summer vacation. Conversely, we could choose to preserve summer vacation and ignore the consequences for summer learning. However, we would have to make either choice by force.

In either case, our community would be different, but not necessarily better. Sometimes different is better. Sometimes different is just different. We may like one of these choices better than the other. But that doesn't make it a better choice. The goal of our policy decision should be to strike a balance among the competing public values that makes our community and schools better. The ability to balance our actions is one of the things that makes us human.[9]

The previous steps in our policy problem solving process helped us define the *why* and the *what* surrounding summer learning and summer vacation. We drew upon what people value about summer learning and summer vacation to identify the good that people want to achieve and preserve. We also drew upon what concerned participants about summer vacation and summer learning to identify the harm people want to prevent.

Once we have crafted an integrative policy goal, we must address how to implement our policy solution, which involves the *how* and the *who*. In public decision making, "once the *what* is decided, the *how* always follows. We must not make the *how* an excuse for not facing and accepting the *what*."[10]

Based on our discussions, we know what we want (provide summer learning and preserve the fun, play and opportunities of summer vacation) and we know why we want it (reduce learning loss and improve achievement for all children). We need to ask just one more question: How might we achieve the good we seek (summer learning) without harming the good we already have (summer vacation)? This question helps us identify principles and criteria we can use to define *how* we want to carry out summer learning and *who* needs to be involved.

If we look back at our discussions in peeling this policy onion, we can identify the following *how* and *who* principles to guide implementation. Achievement test scores decline between spring and fall because out-of-school activities offer fewer opportunities for children to learn and practice academic skills. Children learn best when instruction is continuous. Summer learning should reinforce key academic concepts and skills, especially for lower achievers who are more likely to be students of color and from poorer families.

Studies show little or no correlation between homework and standardized test scores or long-term achievement in elementary school and only a moderate correlation in middle school. Our summer learning program should provide choice with guidance, be embedded in projects and activities that have a real purpose, and integrate thinking with doing. Assignments and activities should support children in exploration, discovery, curiosity and wonder. Children don't have to have all of their time structured and regimented in order to become well educated.

Make participation desirable to children and families. Offer choices and voluntary activities. Avoid a sense of being forced to participate. Make summer learning appealing so that kids and families choose to participate. Ensure that children from all backgrounds and socioeconomic levels have equal opportunity to participate. Flexible scheduling can ensure a robust learning experience while also preserving opportunities for personal and family adventures. Motivation plays a central role in student achievement and if students are given choice and voice in the learning process they are more likely to want to learn and retain what they have learned.

Summer learning should be a time for personal and social growth. Connect students to social and learning networks. Provide opportunities for self-growth, socialization, relationship building, collective problem solving and decision making, and time for reflection. Rather than duplicating traditional classroom learning and homework, immerse students in small but intensive learning communities that last four to six weeks. Combine the experience of summer camps, vacation and learning, and allow teachers to also be mentors, advisors, counselors, and guides.

View summer learning as an investment, not just a cost. Look for ways of funding it within current tax, budget and cost levels. Structure programs and schedule activities to take advantage of holidays, traditions, celebrations, recreation and businesses tied to the cycle of summer. Engage business and community organizations in creating opportunities for older children to integrate learning and working and to generate a return-on-investment to offset additional costs.

Peeling our policy onion to discover the *what* and the *why* helps us understand the problem we're trying to solve. Peeling our policy onion to discover the *how* and the *who* helps us understand what a good solution looks like. "Too many problem-solving sessions become battlegrounds where decisions are made based on power rather than intelligence."[11] In policy problem solving, a solution is a problem everyone understands!

POLICY PROBLEM SOLVING REQUIRES EDUCATED CITIZENS

The purpose of policy problem solving is to make a good decision. A good policy decision does three things. First, it identifies a policy direction by choosing which value has priority and explaining why this value matters to everyone affected by the problem. We chose to pursue summer learning because of the greater good it could provide for everyone.

Second, a good policy decision defines how the other values represented in the policy problem will be satisfied relative to our priority value. This means protecting and preserving other values to the extent possible, not ignoring or discarding them. We identified elements of summer vacation that we wished to preserve, so as not to create harm in trying to achieve the good of summer learning.

Third, a good policy decision describes how we are better off with this solution than we were previously or would be if we chose a different solution. In this case we are better off with the benefits of both summer vacation and summer learning than we were with just summer vacation or would be with just summer learning.

Technical problem solving skills are useful and necessary for many endeavors, but they are inadequate for addressing policy choices involving the public good. The process we have described requires educated citizens, but not just in the sense that citizens are educated in reading, writing, math and science. An educated citizen also possesses the arts of liberty.[12]

The first art of liberty involves connecting rights and responsibility, e.g., the right to a trial by a jury of our peers depends upon our willingness to serve as a juror. In a democracy, rights are not freedoms from things, but freedoms of things. The right to a public education imposes certain responsibilities on parents and students.

The second art of liberty involves understanding that differences matter and should be incorporated into all institutions and aspects of American life, especially public schools. This art has allowed us to assimilate generations of immigrants and sustain a diverse society. "The highest result of education is tolerance," observed Helen Keller. Seeing difference as a strength and tapping into the power of difference are two of the keys to effective policy problem solving.

The third art of liberty involves engaging our fellow citizens in exploring the meaning of community. This can be difficult to do, especially when people afraid of diversity are trying to build walls between suburbs and cities, rich and poor, and white and nonwhite. In our Crestwich narrative, it turns out that the drive for a return to neighborhood schools had several layers, including a push by some suburban parents to move minority children assigned to suburban schools back to schools in their urban neighborhoods.[13] "The surface of American society is covered with a layer of democratic paint," observed Tocqueville, "but from time to time one can see the old aristocratic colours breaking through."

The fourth and most difficult art of liberty is the seemingly simple act of listening. How else will we hear each other and find common ground? Working together to find common ground helps us create a shared understanding of policy problems and craft collective solutions. Responsible democratic discourse involves more than allowing others to speak. It requires that we listen to each other and make room for differences. Conflict and difference are the essence of the democratic process. Leaders cannot decide whether or not to have conflict and difference, but they can decide what to do with them.

If we allow public schools to become simply schools paid for with public dollars, then public education will become simply education that occurs in public schools. Developing the educated leaders and citizens we need to preserve and sustain our republic requires an education that goes beyond technical knowledge and skills. It requires learning the arts of liberty, the skills of democracy, and the process of public problem solving and decision making.

Assuming that public education as it is currently constituted leads to an educated public is not just wrong, it's potentially dangerous to the health of our republic. As some critics argue, channeling the education of the young in accord with a prevailing world view that perceives economic advancement as the nation's only educational imperative endangers the future of the work in progress referred to as democracy.[14]

Public schools must expand their understanding of public education to encompass the idea of educating the public, including citizens and public leaders. Public schools cannot teach the arts and skills of democracy if public school leaders cannot practice them.

WRAPPING UP: LESSONS FOR PUBLIC LEADERS

To make a good decision about a problem that affects us individually, we must first understand the problem. To make a good decision about a problem that affects us collectively, we must not only understand the problem, we must also agree on the problem. Agreeing on the problem does not mean agreeing on the solution. Agreeing on the problem means we understand which values are involved and that a good solution requires addressing each of these values.

Agreeing on the problem does not guarantee that we will agree on the solution, but not agreeing on the problem does guarantee that that we won't agree on the solution. To borrow from Voltaire, in solving policy problems, right is the enemy of the good. Focusing on finding the right solution can limit our ability to discover a good solution.

When we favor a particular solution we tout its benefits and try to convince other people that they will be better off if they adopt our solution. As a corollary, we may assume that people who don't support our solution disagree with us. They may disagree, or they may just prefer a different value more than the value we prefer. They may also be more concerned about what they will give up than the benefits they will get from our solution.

Because public problems are value-based, they cannot be solved in any final and permanent sense, other than by force. This means they will re-appear over time. We may not realize that the problem we're trying to solve today is likely to result from a solution chosen by people preceding us to address a similar policy problem.

If done well, public problem solving yields a solution that has legs, meaning it can stand on its own and doesn't depend upon a particular advocate or agenda. And it has shelf life, meaning that it has sufficient support to give it a certain degree of staying power. A poor problem solving process usually means that the solution we choose will have neither legs nor shelf life, and we're likely to find ourselves trying to solve the same problem again.

Anyone who has ever played a game of pinball learned that the true measure of success isn't the score itself but winning the chance to play another game. In public problem solving, the true measure of a good policy solution is that it helps get us to the next iteration of the problem. As our discussion of student assignment illustrated, there will always be another iteration.

Moral and ethical choices are implicit in the practice of democracy. One such choice is how we choose to treat those values, colleagues and fellow citizens with whom we disagree. If we accept that all four values contribute to the public good, and that no one value is always better, it follows that extreme positions involving any one value are simply unjust.[15] We propose policy solutions in order to do good things. In seeking to do a good thing, we may promote one value to the neglect, exclusion, or harm of another. True public leaders look for ways to do a good thing without harming other good things.

The process we have described is important because the public is losing confidence in itself to address public challenges. A dwindling majority (57%) say they have a good deal of confidence in the wisdom of the American people when it comes to making political decisions and the proportion who agrees that Americans "can always find a way to solve our problems" has dropped 16 points in the past five years.[16]

In a democratic society, how we decide matters as much as the decisions we make. This is why solving public problems is both art and science. We have laid out a framework that explains the science and describes the art. This process takes practice. There is no shortcut to knowledge or democracy.

NOTES

1. James Bryce (1888), British historian and ambassador to the United States, *The American Commonwealth.*
2. Von Drehle, D. (2009). "The case against summer vacation." *Time,* August 2, p. 36.
3. G. K. Chesterton.
4. James Thurber.

5. *The New York Times* (2009). "The crush of summer homework." August 30.

6. Goodlad, J. I. (2000). "Education and democracy: Advancing the agenda." *Phi Delta Kappan,* September, p. 87.

7. Von Drehle.

8. Jiddu Krishnamurti.

9. St. Augustine and St. Thomas Aquinas.

10. Pearl Buck.

11. Margaret J. Wheatley.

12. Benjamin R. Barber (1993). "America skips school." *Harper's Magazine,* 287, 1, 39–46; and Leslie Blair (2000). "The Arts of Liberty: Absent from School Today." *Southeast Educational Development Laboratory Letter,* Putting the Public Back into Public Schools, May.

13. Hui, T. K. (2010). "SE Raleigh students to stay put next year." *The News & Observer,* Dec. 15.

14. Goodlad, 2000.

15. O'Toole, J. (1993). *The executive's compass: Business and the good society.* New York, NY: Oxford University Press.

16. "Trends in Political Values and Core Attitudes: 1987–2007." Washington, DC: Pew Research Center for the People and the Press, March 22, 2007. Retrieved Mar. 12, 2011 from http://people-press.org/report/?reportid=312.

Chapter 10

Governing Public Schools

Who Shall Rule?

On the anniversary of the September 11 attacks, a high school principal told a student to remove her American flag stars and stripes t-shirt. Under a school rule, students are not allowed to wear clothing displaying flags from any country, including the United States. According to the district's superintendent, school officials imposed the ban because of problems with students wearing flags on their clothing. Some students were using flags to show their gang colors, leading to fights and other disruptions.

The student's parent objected to the school's policy. "We're in America, and we've got to stand up for what's right. We are the land of the free. What are they going to take way from us next?" In support of the student, the American Civil Liberties Union sent a letter to the school district requesting that the high school reverse its policy of banning students from wearing clothing that depicts the American flag or any other flag. "The school has no right to prevent this student—or any other student—from wearing a flag on her clothing. The high school is violating students' First Amendment rights to free expression."

Responding to local pressure and national attention, the district lifted the high school's ban. The superintendent announced that "from this point on, all dress code changes will be made at the school board level." Why did the district lift the high school's ban? Why did the superintendent shift future decisions about dress code changes from school administrators to the school board? And why should student dress warrant the attention of the board of education? As this example and these questions suggest, governing is a political enterprise.

THE POLITICAL CONTEXT OF SCHOOL GOVERNANCE

Public schools began as a function of local government with an explicit political purpose. Rooted in rural, religious communities, "common" schools were intended to prepare responsible citizens through nonsectarian and nonpartisan moral and civic instruction. Free schools open to all children and subject to local control would provide a common experience for the children of a people who reflected multiple religions, languages and nationalities, who were mostly from somewhere else, and who had relatively little experience in living and working together.[1]

The free part of public schools was carried out rather easily through local property taxes. State funding emerged to support a growing investment in public education and to offset local differences in wealth. The "open to all children" part took more effort. Immigration strained the existing social and economic order. Compulsory schooling became a way to relieve some of the economic strain while preparing a new generation to take its place in a free society and market economy.

Public schools became a means by which to "Americanize" immigrants. The U.S. Supreme Court's *Brown vs. Board of Education of Topeka* decision helped transform public schools into policy vehicles for remedying discrimination, segregation and the vestiges of slavery. Public education, initially focused on individuals, was expanded to create equal opportunity for groups.

Political, military and economic competition helped transform the purposes of public schools from social and civic development to economic development. As the Education Commission of the States concluded, "The idea of education as 'moral development' has departed from most public discourse about education. The concept of education for civic virtue, the overriding concern of the common school movement in the 19th century, seems to many a quaint echo from an irrelevant past. The dominant rhetoric of schooling today is about economic growth, productivity and efficiency."[2]

Most school board members are local elected officials. Board members are often elected more for their willingness to serve than for their ability to govern. There are a small number of appointed school boards, but being appointed rather than elected makes little difference in the kinds of policy problems boards face and the value choices they must make. Local control by lay school boards, which can trace its origins to colonial Massachusetts, is perhaps the most unique aspect of American public education.[3]

As a legacy of this heritage, school boards face two critical governing challenges. The first is learning how to transition from campaigning to governing. Learning to govern within the context of representative democracy is essential to developing the capacity of citizen boards to govern public schools. The second governing challenge is to establish a balance between our contemporary emphasis on economic and instrumental goals and the traditional moral, civic and democratic purposes for which schools were originally created.[4]

The development of public schools in America parallels the development of the republic itself. Public schools operate in a political environment that is fueled by our efforts to satisfy the public values of liberty, equality, community and prosperity in pursuit of the good life, the good society and the American Dream. If the context of public school governance is political and value-based, what form of governance is best suited to address policy problems framed by the values of the public good? The question of governance is not simply one of who controls schools, but also what is the ideological basis for that control.[5] To answer these questions, we must address one of the oldest and most fundamental questions in politics—who shall rule?

WHAT IS GOVERNANCE AND WHY DOES IT MATTER?

"Governance matters," declared the National Commission on Governing America's Schools. "Without good governance, good schools are the exception, not the rule."[6] What is governance? What does it mean to govern? Is governing a structural arrangement, a technical exercise, a political process, or all of the above? What constitutes good governance?

Governance is the process of governing. Government, including school districts, is the institution in which governing occurs. For public schools, governance involves choices and decisions about how to allocate and use resources to achieve value-based educational goals. Five key features distinguish governance from management and administration. Governance is political, collective, horizontal, democratic, and uncertain.

First, governing is political. It involves making decisions about the fundamental purpose, goals and means of public schools. As we have demonstrated, these are value-based choices, not technical ones. The school principal made what he thought was an administrative decision in applying the standards of the school's dress code to an individual student's dress. But this decision also involved freedoms and rights, which are political issues. The broader governance decision facing the district involved how best to balance the freedom of students as individuals with the collective social order of the school as a community.

Second, governing is collective. The public interest is diverse. It is composed of many interests. In Federalist No. 10, James Madison argued that the regulation of these various interests forms the principal task of legislative bodies. Administrative authority can reside in an individual, but governing authority cannot. Once dress code concerns were identified as governance rather than administrative issues, they properly became the province of the school board rather than the school principal.

Third, governing is horizontal. It is broader than management and leadership because it reaches beyond organizational boundaries to encompass political issues of policy, rights and powers. Its legitimacy typically depends upon representative election rather than selective appointment. It requires consideration of multiple interests, points of view and solutions. Representing the public interest requires a horizontal governance structure and process that can equalize power differences among diverse and competing interests. Dress codes involve multiple interests which is why the superintendent announced that future dress code changes would be made at the school board level.

Fourth, governing is democratic. "Governments derive their just powers from the consent of the governed," proclaimed Jefferson. Governing requires boards to use democratic processes such as facilitation, participation, and deliberation to identify and understand the needs and interests of the public. It requires processes of negotiation, mediation, adjudication and legislation to transform public needs and interests into policy and practice. In our t-shirt example, the board engaged parents, school administrators, the media and a public interest group, the ACLU, to address the public interest represented in this policy problem.

Fifth, governing is uncertain. Management and administration are about authority, control and predictability. To govern means to rule without absolute power. Those who govern cannot predict or guarantee a specific outcome. There's no telling who will participate, how or why. Uncertainty is not a very comfortable idea, but then a democratic republic, which is built upon citizen participation, is the epitome of discomfort.[7]

WHAT SUPPORTERS AND DETRACTORS OF SCHOOL BOARD GOVERNANCE SAY

Elected boards derive their authority from public law, but they derive their legitimacy from the democratic political process. Public images of their legitimacy have historically been anything but flattering. Mark Twain is famously quoted for having said, "In the first place, God made idiots. That was for practice. Then he made school boards." Author Kurt Vonnegut remarked that "True terror is to wake up one morning and discover that your high school class is running the country."

Twain wasn't the only observer to impugn the legitimacy of school boards, merely one of the first. A 1939 city management text characterized the urban school board as "one of those instruments of tortuous propensities which, beaming with unbecoming and reflected wisdom, wanders in a twilight zone between civil squander and political connivance. Undoubtedly, some future public appraisal, beyond the board's discernment, will snuff it out."[8]

Other observers are even less kind. Calling for the end of school boards, two critics described them as resembling "a dysfunctional family, composed of three unlovable types: 1) aspiring politicians for whom this is a rung on the ladder to higher office; 2) former employees of the school system with a score to settle; and 3) single-minded advocates of one dubious cause or another who yearn to use the public schools to impose their particular hang-up on all the kids in town."[9] In all fairness, school boards do sometimes resemble these remarks, fueling challenges to their legitimacy and capacity to govern.

Critics question the very need for local boards of education and the capacity of ordinary citizens to govern public schools. They point to growing global economic competition and the demand for a technologically literate work force as evidence that school boards are a hindrance to quality schooling and student achievement and are obsolete in a 21st century global society.[10]

Critics also cite the increasing complexity of school curricula and state and municipal takeovers of local school systems as proof that local school governance is outmoded and antiquated. Some suggest that local school governance should be redesigned, restructured, reinvented or re-engineered.[11] Others suggest that school boards be abolished and replaced entirely with a different model of governance.[12] While most critics acknowledge that school boards are not likely to be replaced, some, like the Center for Leadership in School Reform, nonetheless urge school boards to "eliminate politics in favor of continuity of purpose."[13]

For some critics, trying to get politics out of public schools isn't enough. They also advocate getting educators out of education. They see boards and superintendents as creatures of an educational philosophy unprepared for the critical task of preparing a work force for a technological society and a global economy. "What if we were to declare local boards and superintendents to be archaic, living fossils of an earlier age? What is the local education agency except another instance of middle management of the sort that most modern organizations are stripping away in the name of efficiency and productivity."[14]

There are many arguments for abolishing local school boards. The rise of a global marketplace, increasing economic competition, technological literacy, and a desire to create a seamless school-to-work connection argue for reexamining our current system of school governance, and perhaps replacing it with one more suited to a global society. Critics ask if we dare risk leaving school governance in the hands of amateurs when surely challenges such as these can be met best by professionals. Some observers, pointing to the growing influence of governors, state boards, vouchers, and business-sponsored reforms, suggest that, at least in practice, local boards may have already been abolished.

The arguments of school board supporters seem to pale in comparison to the arguments of detractors. Supporters argue that elected local boards of education remain relevant as a form of governance.[15] They acknowledge challenges and weaknesses, but recommend that school boards, rather than being abolished or replaced, should strengthen their leadership role.[16] School boards can improve their governance skills through board development and training.[17]

The arguments of both supporters and detractors show clearly that the legitimacy and capacity of school boards to govern are under attack. Whether this attack will prevail depends upon two things. First, school boards must reinvigorate their representative democratic role and reconnect to citizens to prevent being perceived as self-serving rather than serving the public.[18] Second, school governance associations must invest in the democratic knowledge and skills, not just technical knowledge, that board members need to lead and govern.[19] If boards and their associations fail to do this, critics won't need to kill off school boards. They will die of decay.

IF NOT SCHOOL BOARDS, THEN WHAT?

Whenever Americans grow dissatisfied with public institutions, they tend to blame the way those institutions are governed.[20] The same holds true for public schools, "for governance is intimately involved with the how and why as well as the what of public schooling."[21] Critics of locally elected school boards have proposed a variety of alternatives for governing public schools. The following examples briefly describe five governance alternatives involving privatization, centralization, decentralization, separation and mayoral control.

Privatize Public Education and Public Schools

Privatization redefines the roles, responsibilities and relationships of states, school districts, and private organizations.[22] Approaches can vary, but in general districts would fund, authorize and oversee the performance of schools, but not operate them. Instead, districts would contract with independent entities, both profit and nonprofit, to run schools in much the same way they currently do with charter schools.

States and districts would establish clearly defined goals for schools and provide them with the resources, tools and support they need to succeed. School staffs would have greater autonomy and flexibility, but would be held more strictly accountable for producing results. This system would employ incentives and rewards for success and penalties and sanctions for failure. Teachers, principals, and parents would have considerable freedom to design, create and operate schools, limited only by state and federal laws and the terms of their contract with the district.

Parents would be allowed to enroll their child in any school receiving public funds, not just traditional public schools. Districts would be allowed to reward or penalize individual schools by granting or withholding funding. School boards would be transformed into chartering boards empowered to authorize, fund, oversee and hold schools accountable for performance.

Centralization: Replace Local Governance with State Governance

In one state legislators appointed a task force to take a comprehensive look at how the entire public education system—from kindergarten through college—was governed. The change was prompted by a constitutional amendment that altered K-12 governance structures at the state level.[23] The task force was guided by a set of principles which mandated that the new governance structure must be a coordinated, seamless system for kindergarten through graduate school education; be student-centered in every facet; maximize education access and academic success for all residents; safeguard equity; refuse to compromise academic excellence; and emphasize local control of institutions. Based on these principles, the level of governance may change, but the goals remain much the same.

In another state public schools are governed by a single statewide board of education. A recent ballot proposal asked voters to replace the elected state board with a board appointed by the governor. Proponents argued that an appointed board would be more likely to work together and would give principals more authority and control over their schools. Opponents disagreed. "There are no valid arguments except emotional ones to having an appointed board. There's no evidence that an appointed board would be any different, so why take people's vote away?"[24]

Decentralize School Governance: Put Parents in Charge

As school districts become larger and more complex, frustration with bureaucracy and the governance process can fuel discontent with public schools and school boards. School reformers in one state proposed a ballot initiative that would abolish local school boards, sending state money directly to "parental advisory councils" at each school.[25] Most money was to be earmarked by the state for personnel costs, but parents could spend the rest on programs and activities of their choice.

Proponents touted the benefits of local control and responsiveness to parents. Opponents argued that wealthier, well-connected schools would gain an advantage over schools in poorer areas where parents usually have less time and resources to get involved. "It could lead to class warfare all over again" said one voter. "We have enough problems today with trying to keep things equitable."

Separate Policy from Administration

Separating politics and administration, a cornerstone concept in administrative theory more than a century ago, has been dismissed by practitioners and most theorists.[26] Nonetheless, it has become a mantra preached by both boards and superintendents and their respective associations to protect their turf from each other.[27] Despite any practical way to clearly separate and delineate executive and elected responsibilities, many reformers believe that clearer lines of authority and responsibility will improve school governance.

Proponents argue that school boards will be more effective if board and superintendent responsibilities are more clearly delineated in state law, if boards focus on student achievement, and if superintendents act and are treated as chief executives and educational leaders of their districts.[28] This argument is appealing, particularly to those who yearn for a less messy form of governance. The challenges lie in implementation. In a survey of board-superintendent relations, three out of five board members and three out of four superintendents said they did not know where to draw the line between policy and administration.[29]

Replace Elected School Boards with Mayoral Control and Appointed Boards

In this model, the mayor assumes responsibility for public education, and appoints a local board of education to oversee schools. Proponents argue that establishing mayoral control over school systems, particularly "in the case of dysfunctional urban districts, seems to offer clear advantages for coherence, political leadership, and accountability."[30]

Supporters make several other arguments: Low voter turnout for school board elections is not particularly democratic and results in boards that do not reflect the makeup of the community. Marginal voter attention and participation make it difficult for citizens to hold board members accountable and allows mobilized interest groups to exert disproportionate influence.

Elected boards are prone to focus on short-term issues and achievements at the expense of longer-term goals. Boards tend to exhibit a lack of discipline, a tendency to micromanage, an inability to handle the essential tasks of governance and to operate in relative isolation from mayors and other political and civic leaders.

Opponents of mayoral control and appointed boards counter with arguments of their own. Mayoral control takes away the public's right to elect school leaders. The voices of business leaders and commercial interests will override concerns of parents, teachers and grassroots community leaders. Appointed boards are less likely to reflect the makeup of the community. They propose that political leaders should look for ways to strengthen local boards of education rather than disenfranchising the community by eliminating school boards.

There is no empirical evidence that one system is more effective than the other. Researchers have found no relationship between electing or appointing board members and student achievement.[31] Superintendents and elected school board members generally describe their relationships with each other as more cooperative than contentious, and say that relatively few board members represent only very specific and narrow interests.[32] Proponents acknowledge the lack of evidence, saying "We would be wise to reject the notion that there is a single best model of school governance."[33]

Supporters and detractors of school boards agree on the basic elements of good governance: clearly defined responsibilities and decision making authority, a shared vision and purpose, specific goals and objectives, mechanisms for oversight and assessing progress, transparency, accountability and processes for engaging various publics, such as parents, citizens, and business and civic leaders. These elements, no matter how technically sophisticated they may be, are determined and carried out politically.

Political leaders can change the form and structure of governance, but the fundamental questions of who decides, how decisions are made, and what criteria decisions are based upon remain. Most of the criticisms of elected school boards can also be made about representative democracy in general. No one has yet proposed replacing governors and legislators with mayors and appointed lawmakers.

WHY A DEMOCRATIC REPUBLIC NEEDS SCHOOL BOARDS

In 1930 there were some 200,000 school boards in the United States. Nearly one of every 500 citizens sat on a school board, and most citizens knew a school board member personally.[34] Today, there are nearly 15,000 local school boards and nearly 100,000 local school board members, 96 percent of whom are elected by their communities.[35] Only about one out of every 20,000 citizens sits on a school board today, and it is rare for a citizen to know a school board member personally.[36] School boards, once an opportunity for citizens to fulfill civic obligations, have instead become targets of our democratic discontent.

How, critics ask, can we possibly entrust governance of public schools, with all that we have riding on the success of schools, to citizens who in some cases could not pass the end-of-course and end-of-year tests we require of prospective high school graduates? Academic achievement does not guarantee better governance. As political journalist David Brooks points out, "There is a craft to governance, which depends less on academic intelligence than on a contextual awareness of how to bring people together."[37] So why do we have locally elected school boards, and why do we elect ordinary citizens as board members?

As a form of government, school boards must address two fundamental political questions. First, what is the purpose of any legitimate form of government? Second, who shall rule? In the beginning of this book we drew upon a number of political theorists and philosophers to suggest that the purpose of any legitimate government is to help its citizens create and achieve the good life, the good society. We now address the second question.

Throughout human history, across all kinds of civilizations and cultures, we have invented but four basic ways in which to rule a society: (1) a god, deity or religious leader; (2) a king, queen, or dictator; (3) a group or an elite; and (4) the people.[38] From socialism to communism, from patriarchy to matriarchy, from meritocracy to democracy and from totalitarianism to oligarchy, all forms of rule are variations on these four types. From time to time in our debates over how best to govern public schools, we can see and hear the arguments of those who would prefer rule by a god, by a king, or by a group or elite to rule by the people. Of course, these arguments beg the question of whose god, whose king, and which elite?

All societies, and their various levels of government, must choose one of these forms. For Americans, this choice brings with it a particular dilemma. Our dilemma lies not in choosing between a god, a king, an elite or the people. We have already made that choice. Our dilemma lies in that having rejected the other alternatives, we have no choice but to make rule by the people work. If we fail to make rule by the people work, one of the other forms must take its place. Politics, like nature, abhors a vacuum. Which alternative should we choose?

We could, for example, establish a national education czar. Classroom education, however, is a decentralized enterprise. If we want to operate public schools centrally, we have to nationalize them. With few exceptions, nationalization has seldom been acceptable, and with even fewer exceptions, popular. Fifty state governments and 15,000 school districts are unlikely to agree to cede their power and control. Keep in mind the passion raised by reading assignments and student assignments. Imagine that passion focused on a single unit of government.

Rule by a god or deity is more appealing, and therefore more challenging. But resolving the issue of whose god is likely to prove difficult. While a sizeable number of Americans see no practical reason for maintaining separation of church and state, no doubt the exclusion of someone's religion would serve as a tangible reminder. And because freedom of religion requires equality of religion, only a form of rule without its own religion can be trusted to safeguard such a freedom for everyone else.

This leads us to the question of whether some group or elite might not govern public schools better than school boards. As we have seen, the policy problems and choices that arise in public schools are primarily value-based, not technical. If only one value mattered, then any group supporting that value could govern public schools. But if public schools are repositories and stewards of the values of the public good, then we need a form of governance that can address all four public values. Elected representatives give us the best chance of doing this. From the U.S. Congress to state legislatures to county commissions to city and town councils to school boards, governance is a collective and representative enterprise, because only as a group can we represent all of the values of the public good.

School governance has taken the form of elected school boards because we prefer rule by the people to other types of rule. As Tocqueville noted, "The people reign in the American political world as the Deity does in the universe." A board composed of people with the same characteristics or background may see things more similarly, but it will be less representative. Whose views and whose values should we leave out?

We have state legislatures, city councils and school boards not because rule by the people is efficient, harmonious, predictable or always attractive to watch, but because all of the alternatives are worse. "Democracy is the worst form of government," remarked Winston Churchill, "except all those other forms that have been tried from time to time." We have adopted rule by the people in the form of elected governing boards not because it is the best form of governance, but because all the other forms of governance are worse.

To make rule by the people work requires knowledge of and knowledge in the arts and skills of democracy. As Thomas Jefferson pointed out, "I know of no safe depository of the ultimate powers of the society but the people themselves; and if we think them not enlightened enough to exercise their control with a wholesome discretion, the remedy is not to take it from them, but inform their discretion by education." This is why we elect citizens to govern public schools, and this is why school boards matter.

GOVERNANCE LEADERSHIP MATTERS MORE THAN GOVERNANCE STRUCTURE

Citizens experience real problems and frustrations in dealing with public schools and school governance. But most of the problems and frustrations citizens experience occur because each school board, like each city council, county commission and state legislature, is part of a much larger fragmented and open political system.

This is precisely the condition reformers want to change when they advocate for an alternative governance structure for public schools. Some reformers think changing the governance structure will change governance. It won't. "Democracy is a political method, that is to say, a certain type of institutional arrangement for arriving at political, legislative and administrative decisions and hence incapable of being an end in itself."[39]

Bureaucracy is not an obstacle to democracy but an inevitable complement to it.[40] The greatest mistake citizens can make when they complain about bureaucracy is "to suppose that their frustrations arise simply out of management problems; they do not—they arise out of governance problems."[41] And governance problems cannot be solved solely by technical means, including structural solutions.

Because public schools play an important role in achieving our vision of the good society, rule by the people is the only way we can ensure that all the values of the public good are represented in decisions about the purposes and goals of public schools. Rule by the people is seldom pretty, efficient, smooth, orderly, quiet or easy. It is, however, extraordinarily effective in preventing any single group from imposing its values on everyone else. "Which is the best government? That which teaches us to govern ourselves."[42] In which case, what really matters to us is leadership, not structure.

A national study of education governance confirmed that structural reform is not a panacea. It concluded that leadership quality matters more than leadership structure, that political representation and public engagement must be part of any governance system, and that successful governing boards can be found within a range of governance models nationwide.[43]

The study's authors concluded that individual state demographics and educational needs are far too varied to identify any single preferred structure of educational governance. Experience shows that there are no "magic bullets" and that simplistic, abrupt governance reforms can have unintended consequences that create new difficulties. The study also found that effective education governance derives from both legal authority and intangible factors, such as the credibility and quality of board members and other key education leaders.

This study illustrates two immutable laws of public school governance. First, we cannot remove political choices from a public enterprise such as public schools because by virtue of being public, schools give rise to value choices which are inherently political. Second, regardless of whether districts operate schools or contract for schools, public demands for oversight and accountability will require some form of representative mechanism to address policy goals, means and outcomes, which in turn will require allocating and satisfying public values.[44]

There is only one governance alternative that can remove public values and political considerations from school governance entirely. That alternative is complete and total privatization, in which case, this book would end here.

NOTES

1. Kaestle, C. F. (1983). *Pillars of the republic: Common schools and American society, 1780-1860.* New York, NY: Hill & Wang.
2. Education Commission of the States. (1999c). *The invisible hand of ideology: Perspectives from the history of school governance.* Denver, CO: Author, p. vii.
3. Russo, C. J. (1992). "The legal status of school boards in the intergovernmental system." In First, P. F., and Walberg, H. J. (Eds.). *School Boards: Changing Local Control.* Berkeley, CA: McCutchan, pp. 3–18.
4. Cremin, L. A. (1980). *American education: The national experience, 1783–1876.* New York, NY: Harper & Row.
5. Education Commission of the States, 1999c.
6. National Commission on Governing America's Schools. (1999). *Governing America's Schools: Changing the Rules.* Denver, CO: Education Commission of the States, November, p. 9.
7. Saul, J. R. (1995). *The unconscious civilization.* Concord, Ontario: Anansi Press.
8. Hodges, Henry G. (1939). *City management.* New York, NY: F. S. Crofts and Company, pp. 680-81.
9. Finn, C. E., Jr., and Keegan, L. G. (2004). "Lost at sea." *Education Next,* Summer, 15–17, available at www.education-next.org, p. 15.
10. Harrington-Lueker, D. (1996). "School boards at bay." *American School Board Journal, 183,* 18–22; Toch, T., and Glastris, K. (1994). "Who's minding the schools? The once stalwart board of education is today often a hindrance to quality public schooling." *U.S. News & World Report,* April 10, 78–80; Wagner, R. F., Jr. (1992). "The case for local educational policy boards." *Phi Delta Kappan, 74,* 228–229.

11. Cronin, J. M. (1992). "Reallocating the power of urban school boards." In First, P. F., and Walberg, H. J. (Eds.). *School boards: Changing local control.* Berkeley, CA: McCutchan, pp. 37–70; Danzberger, J. P. (1994). "Governing the nation's schools: The case for restructuring local school boards." *Phi Delta Kappan, 75,* 367–374; Finn, C. E., Jr. (1992). "Reinventing local control." In First, P. F., and Walberg, H. J. (Eds.). *School Boards: Changing Local Control.* Berkeley, CA: McCutchan, 21–25; Lewis, A. C. (1994). "Reinventing local school governance." *Phi Delta Kappan, 75,* 356–358; Wong, K. K. (1995). "Toward redesigning school board governance." *Teachers College Record, 96,* 569–577.

12. Finn, C. E., Jr. (2004). "Who needs school boards?" *PRISM, 4,* 1, pp. 12–13; Marcus, L. R. (1997). "Whither school boards?" *On the Horizon, 5,* 13–14; Mathews, J. (2001). "Are school boards really necessary?" *Washington Post,* April 10, p. A19; Miller, M. (2008). "First, kill all the school boards." *The Atlantic Monthly,* January/February. Retrieved December 31, 2009 from http://www.theatlantic.com/doc/print/200801/miller-education; Whitson, A. (1998). "Are local school boards obsolete?" *Childhood Education, 74,* 172–174.

13. American Association of School Administrators (1999). *Preparing schools and school systems for the 21st century.* Arlington, VA: Author, p. 74.

14. Finn, Jr., 1992, p. 22.

15. Danzberger, J. P., Usdan, M. D., Cunningham, L., Carol, L. N., Kirst, M. W., and McCloud, B. (1986). *School boards: Strengthening grass roots leadership.* Washington, DC: Institute for Educational Leadership; Miron, L. F., and Wimpelberg, R. K. (1992). "The role of school boards in the governance of education." In First, P. F., and Walberg, H. J. (Eds.). *School boards: Changing local control,* pp. 151–175. Berkeley, CA: McCutchan; Reecer, M. (1989). "Yes, boards are under fire, but reports of your death are greatly exaggerated." *American School Board Journal, 176,* 31–34; Twentieth Century Fund Task Force on School Governance. (1992). *Facing the challenge: Report of the twentieth century fund task force on school governance.* New York, NY: Twentieth Century Fund Press.

16. Bolman, L. G., and Deal, T. E. (1992). "Images of leadership." *American School Board Journal, 179,* 36–39; Campbell, D. W., and Greene, D. (1994). "Defining the leadership role of school boards in the 21st century." *Phi Delta Kappan, 75,* 391–395; Danzberger, J. P., and Usdan, M. D. (1992). "Strengthening a grass-roots American institution: The school board." In First, P. F., and Walberg, H. J. (Eds.). *School boards: Changing local control.* Berkeley, CA: McCutchan, pp. 91–124; Gemberling, K. W., Smith, C. W., and Villani, J. S. (2009). *The key work of school boards guidebook,* 2nd ed. Alexandria, VA: National School Boards Association; Smoley, E. R., Jr. (1996). *School board development: Needs and opportunities.* Washington, DC: National Center for Nonprofit Boards; Tallerico, M. (1993). "The professional development of school board members." *Journal of Staff Development, 14,* 32–36.

17. Banach, W. J. (1989). "These eleven traits are the hallmarks of winning school board teams." *American School Board Journal, 176,* 23–24; Bolman, L. G., Deal, T. E., and Rallis, S. F. (1995). *Becoming a school board member.* Thousand Oaks,

CA: Corwin; Campbell, M., Carr, J., and Harris, D. (1989). "Board members needn't be experts to play a vital role in curriculum." *American School Board Journal, 176,* 30–32; Chait, R. P., Holland, T. P., and Taylor, B. E. (1996). *Improving the performance of governing boards.* Phoenix, AZ: American Council on Education and Oryx Press; National School Boards Association. (1996). *Becoming a better board member: A guide to effective school board service.* Alexandria, VA: Author; Poston, W. K., Jr. (Ed.) (1994). *Effective school board governance.* Bloomington, IN: *Phi Delta Kappan*; Smoley, E. R., Jr. (1999). *Effective school boards: Strategies for improving board performance.* San Francisco, CA: Jossey-Bass.

18. Urschel, J. (2004). "Fed up! Can school boards reconnect with communities in order to govern education and learning?" PRISM, 4, 1, 14–15.

19. Education Commission of the States. (1999a). *Effective school governance: A look at today's practice and tomorrow's promise.* Denver, CO: Author.

20. Education Commission of the States, 1999c.

21. Ibid., p. v.

22. National Commission on Governing America's Schools.

23. Bracey, G. (2009). *The Bracey Report on the Condition of Public Education.* Boulder and Tempe: Education and the Public Interest Center & Education Policy Research Unit. Retrieved Oct. 31, 2010 from http://epicpolicy.org/publication/Bracey-Report.

24. Education Week (2010). "Hawaii may stop electing school board members." November 1.

25. National Association of State Boards of Education (2001). "Florida's new system of education governance." *State Improvement Initiatives, 6, 4,* June; and Flannery, M. E. (2003). "Plan would scrap school boards." *Palm Beach Post,* May 27.

26. Goodnow, F. J. (1900). *Politics and administration.* New York, NY: MacMillan.

27. Ziebarth, T. (2002). *The roles and responsibilities of school boards and superintendents: A state policy framework.* Education Commission of the States, September. Retrieved Mar. 21, 2008 from http://www.ecs.org/clearinghouse/13/59/1359.html.

28. The Education Policy and Leadership Center (March 2004). *Strengthening the work of school boards in Pennsylvania: Report on K-12 governance.* Harrisburg, PA: Author.

29. Wagner (1992).

30. Hess, F. M. (2008). *Assessing the case for mayoral control of urban schools.* Washington, DC: American Enterprise Institute for Public Policy Research, No. 4, August, p. 7.

31. Land, D. (2002). "Local school boards under review: Their role and effectiveness in relation to students' academic achievement." *Review of Educational Research*, 72, 2, 29–278;

32. Farkas, S., Foley, P., and Duffett, A. (2001). *Just waiting to be asked: A fresh look at attitudes on public engagement.* New York, NY: Public Agenda.

33. Hess (2008), p. 6.

34. Meier, D. (2003). "The road to trust." *American School Board Journal, 190,* 9, 18–21.

35. Education Commission of the States (1999a).

36. Meier.

37. Brooks, D. (2009). "The great gradualist." *The New York Times*, August 28.

38. Saul.

39. Schumpeter, J. A. (1950). *Capitalism, socialism and democracy.* New York, NY: Harper & Row.

40. Ibid.

41. Wilson, J. Q. (1989). *Bureaucracy: What government agencies do, and why they do it.* New York, NY: Basic Books, p. 376.

42. Johann Wolfgang von Goethe.

43. National Association of State Boards of Education. (1996). *A motion to reconsider: Education governance at a crossroads.* Report of the NASBE Study Group on Education Governance, October. Alexandria, VA: Author.

44. Boyle, P. (2004). "School boards and public values." *American School Board Journal, 191,* 6, 22–27.

Part V

Preserving the Public

"Perhaps this is our strange and haunting paradox here in America," wrote Thomas Wolfe, "that we are fixed and certain only when we are in movement." While Wolfe was not speaking about public schools, his insight applies just the same. Public schools are subject to the same political and ideological winds that sweep across the American landscape. We designed our republic to allow many different people with many different beliefs to live together. Public schools reflect, and in some cases amplify, the same forces and tensions that characterize us as a nation.

In Chapter 10 we described some of the arguments behind efforts to change public school governance. Such efforts are not restricted to public schools. Dissatisfied with the process and outcomes resulting from many of our institutions, we are drawn like moths to a light to yes-no, either-or and black and white solutions that promise quick and easy relief for difficult public problems. Consider early voting.

Extending the voting period by allowing citizens to vote in advance of election day should help alleviate scheduling conflicts, reduce long lines at polling places and increase voter turnout. Except that it doesn't. Recent studies have found that contrary to common expectations, early voting does not increase voter turnout, and in some cases, actually depresses turnout.[1]

Early voting did not increase the percentage of Georgians casting ballots in the first non-presidential general primary since the state initiated a seven-week voting period. Despite having 45 days prior to the election in which to vote, only 21 percent of registered voters participated, the same percentage as voted in the 2006 general primary. It turns out that politics, including the simple act of joining with other citizens to vote, is a "creative and valuable form of social existence."[2]

Georgia's results are consistent with research done on the impact of early voting periods in Texas. The rationale for extending the voting period seems obvious and logical to most people. If you extend the voting period time you increase voting. It turns out not to work that way. More convenience and more time do not lead to more voting. Freedom from the inconvenience of voting is not the same as freedom to vote.

In their vision of the good society as they hoped it would evolve in the new republic, the founders and framers were committed to creating freedoms of, such as speech, religion, assembly and suffrage. Knowing their work was incomplete, they left to future generations the obligation to expand these freedoms.

Today we find ourselves at odds with this vision, with government and public leaders often leading the way in chipping away at freedoms of and offering in their place a plethora of freedoms from. From sales tax holidays to public education lotteries to "no tax" pledges to early voting, the freedom we offer citizens most is freedom from the inconvenience of responsibility.

This is hardly new, particularly among republics. It is a prime element in their demise. We would do well to consider the words of the historian Edward Gibbon regarding the fall of Athens: "In the end, more than they wanted freedom, they wanted security—they wanted a comfortable life and they lost it all—security, comfort, and freedom—when the Athenians finally wanted not to give to society but for society to give to them, when the freedom they wished for most was freedom from responsibility, then Athens ceased to be free."

As a number of foreign observers have noted, Americans are passionate about the moral and ethical beliefs that constitute the American Creed. Our identification with these beliefs is so strong that whenever our behavior is at odds with what we profess we eventually take steps to remedy the situation. Perhaps this is what Winston Churchill meant when he remarked that "Americans always try to do the right thing after they've tried everything else." In this final section, we attempt to describe the "right thing" needed to preserve the public in public schools in Crestwich and throughout the nation.

As we approach the end of our exploration of the *public* in public schools, we hope that every reader will come to better understand and appreciate their role in our political drama that is now well into its third century. No policy choice we face today could exist without the efforts and deliberations of those who preceded us. In the story of the American experiment, tomorrow's chapters are blank pages today.

Democracy, wrote John Dewey, has to be born anew every generation, and education is its midwife.[3] The true contribution public school leaders can make to the public good in public schools lies not in achieving a final resolution to the thorny policy problems we have described, but rather in making possible future public conversations about these same timeless questions and choices.

NOTES

1. Burden, B. C., and Mayer, K. R. (2010). "Voting early, but not so often." *The New York Times,* October 24.
2. Stone, 2002, p. 8.
3. Dewey, J. (1900). *The school and society and the child and the curriculum.* Chicago, IL: Centennial Publications of the University of Chicago Press, republished 1991.

Conclusion

Public Schools for the Public Good

More than any other institution, public schools serve as a political lightning rod in American society. For public schools today, a partial list would include the following: school choice, dress codes, school prayer, high-stakes testing, zero tolerance, suspension policies, home schooling, achievement gaps, social promotion, bullying, bilingual education, vouchers, charter schools, school violence, overcrowding, class size, physical exercise, school lunch, nutrition, integration, evolution, intelligent design, sex education, the Pledge of Allegiance, school transfer policies, student assignment, redistricting, background checks, cameras in the classroom, seat belts on buses, student driving and parking, drug testing, dropout rates, and property tax relief.

We cannot help but be struck by the sheer volatility of these issues and the high degree of passion they evoke. Many public school leaders strive to limit or remove controversy from public schools. But political and religious controversy is educative in its own right.[1] It should serve to remind us that something very fundamental about the American essence is at stake. Controversial issues offer us opportunities to rediscover and reclaim the public in public schools.

Education should embrace controversy, but within a context that promotes dialogue as a means to achieve progress through how we educate our children.[2] The goal of education for democracy is not to offer solutions to all of the problems plaguing our educational institutions, but to consider ways of resolving those problems that are compatible with a commitment to democratic values.[3]

In doing so, public education should serve to "cultivate the skills and virtues of deliberation" so that we teach children what they need to know to participate intelligently as adults in the political processes that shape their society.[4] Shouldn't education not only prepare children for this world but also develop their potential to help make a better one?

THE PUBLIC GOOD WE EXPECT FROM PUBLIC SCHOOLS

Based on our discussion of public values and the kinds of policy issues and choices these values give rise to, how might we craft a vision of public schools that encompasses a more complete and inclusive view of the public good? What might a four-value vision of public education and public schools look like?

In terms of liberty, public schools would help create and perpetuate a nation of free individuals dedicated to self-government and capable of exercising rights, freedoms, and choice responsibly. They would preserve and pass on knowledge about what it means to be an American. Public schools would seek to provide a voice and become the schools of first choice for everyone. Through public participation and engagement, public schools would provide opportunities for citizens to learn and practice the arts and skills of democracy.

In terms of community, public schools would extend the boundaries of home and help socialize children and teens to assume roles and responsibilities as adults, citizens, neighbors, spouses, parents and members. They would transmit the values and mores of American society to ensure adequate social and moral order to preserve the republic. Public schools would help weave and maintain the social fabric of the nation by providing for a common democratic experience for all children.

In terms of equality, public schools would serve as the great equalizer in American society. They would include everyone, equalize educational opportunity, teach children tolerance and fair play, model fairness and treating people justly, and cultivate an acceptance of differences in preparing students for life in an increasingly diverse society. Public schools would serve as the primary public means by which we mitigate the effects of socioeconomic inequality.

In terms of prosperity, public schools would prepare each individual to be economically self-sufficient in a competitive national and global market economy in whatever form that self-sufficiency might take. Schools would teach future producers, employers and consumers to balance individual self-interest with concern for and contribution to the general welfare.

Preserving the public in public schools is also about preserving democracy, for the two go hand in hand. Democracy requires an educated citizenry to protect against tyranny; a common, equalizing, and democratizing social experience to create citizens who can transcend their many differences; and the capacity of citizens to act together on Tocqueville's notion of self-interest "properly understood" to ensure the common good.

We believe this vision to be in jeopardy. As David Mathews and the Kettering Foundation have concluded, we have lost our sense of the *public* in public schools, and in some instances we have lost the public themselves.[5] Public school leaders need to rebuild a public for public schools, and the public needs to reclaim their public schools in order for democracy to survive. For this to happen, we need a more complete view of the *public* in public schools.

TOWARD A MORE COMPLETE VIEW OF THE *PUBLIC* IN PUBLIC SCHOOLS

In our discussion of the visions and values of public education, we showed how different values rose to prominence during different social, political and economic times. The normative focus of education has shifted from liberty during our founding years to community during the rise of modern American society to equality after World War II to prosperity during the emergence of a global economy. Each of these values is always present, but not each value is equally valued all time.

In the minds of most people, our predominant view of public education today is a utilitarian view in which student achievement is seen as the quintessential purpose of public schools. We have argued in this book that student achievement, like efficiency, is a means to an end, and not an end in itself. It is a means to the good life. If it doesn't help lead to the good life, then what purpose does it serve? Some prominent proponents of testing, choice and student achievement have begun to ask the same question.[6]

We ask this question because a prosperity-centered vision of public education cannot be achieved without addressing the other competing visions and values that comprise the *public* in public schools. The danger that can accompany separating these values is illustrated by our loss of production and manufacturing capacity in recent years. Everyone knows this has happened, and the most frequently mentioned culprits include global economic competition, offshore tax advantages and cheaper foreign labor.

Less frequently mentioned is the notion that Americans might have come to value the physical and material things we produced more than the art of producing them. It may surprise some readers to learn that Tocqueville warned us about how excessive love of prosperity can do harm to it nearly two centuries ago.[7] Business leaders certainly should advocate for sufficient emphasis on math, science and engineering. But they should also be among the strongest advocates of the arts and creative learning in public schools.

While these visions and values compete with each other for supremacy, the bottom line is that we cannot achieve the elements of the good life without a vision of public schools that encompasses all four values of the public good. Educating students to protect America's ranking in patents, for example, is certainly a worthwhile goal. But so is protecting our heritage of political and religious freedom. A good case can be made that these are complementary and interdependent goals, and not conflicting or mutually exclusive ones.

What then, we might ask, does a more complete view of public education look like, and how might we achieve it in public schools? We might start by recognizing some of the weaknesses of an instrumental view of public education, and by identifying some ways in which we can strengthen the public good in public schools. What follows is not an exhaustive prescription by any means. Instead we highlight several key observations that help fill out a more complete view of public education and public schools.

A utilitarian view of public schools has led us to create a culture of measurement in which sometimes what we measure is what we value and sometimes what we measure is a proxy for what should be valued. Grades, for example, are best at predicting future grades. They do not help predict social responsibility, being a good neighbor, or leadership potential.

We have created an array of choices for parents and students, not as citizens but as consumers of education. In providing comparative data and greater freedom of choice we have diminished the responsibility of parents to be accountable for and to public schools. We should certainly expect policymakers to take individual desires into account, but we can't expect policymakers to satisfy only individual desires and still call that the public good.

A predominant focus on measurable outcomes absolves citizens, parents and public school leaders from discussing the broader and often less tangible purposes of public schools much beyond student achievement. It provides a single principle around which to organize policy and funding choices, a kind of grand unifying theory that greatly simplifies decision making and reduces the discomfort associated with trying to satisfy the competing normative goals of public education. For example, some schools might choose to steer clear of uncomfortable discussions about child hunger but choose to provide breakfast for students because research suggests it can improve school attendance and academic performance.[8]

Instrumental goals are well and good, but there are moral and ethical consequences of relying too heavily on an instrumental model of public education. We may be tempted to allow the means we use to obtain student achievement to take a back seat to education itself. There are several ways this can happen.

The first is to use any means necessary. The greater the pressure for higher test scores, the greater the temptation to use any means possible to obtain them. From classrooms to districts to states, if only the results matter, then how we get them is of less concern.[9] Helping students get the right answer becomes more important than helping students learn the right answer.

A second way is to lower the bar or defer action. For example, some states have been implicated in screening test-takers in order to increase the proportion of higher scores. Faced with data from practice tests indicating that large numbers of students would fail, many states softened standards[10] or delayed the requirement or added alternative paths to a diploma.[11]

A third way is to apply a one-value solution to a multi-value public problem. After making widely-publicized announcements proclaiming the end of social promotion, some states have conceded defeat, recognizing that there is more than one form of competency and more than one reason why schools might choose to graduate students.[12]

Student achievement is a means to an end, a means to the good life, and not an end in itself. "What we want is to see the child in pursuit of knowledge," remarked George Bernard Shaw, "and not knowledge in pursuit of the child." Some business leaders understand this better than public school leaders.

Writing about the knowledge society, business guru Peter Drucker describes how education both fuels the economy and shapes society. But it does so through its 'product,' the educated person, who is "prepared to both earn a living and lead a life."[13] For Drucker, it is not the measures of education that matter so much as how that person uses his or her education to solve problems and expand human capacity. Or as social philosopher John Dewey wrote, schools should focus on judgment rather than knowledge so that school children become adults who can "pass judgments pertinently and discriminatingly on the problems of human living."[14]

Democratic and economic goals may conflict at times, but they are not contradictory. Writing nearly a century ago about the relationship between education and democracy, Dewey suggested that "It is, of course, arbitrary to separate industrial competency from capacity in good citizenship."[15] When asked to identify what they expect from public education, most parents and public school leaders identify instrumental outcomes, but they also identify a model of schooling that aims to develop unique human beings.[16] Schools should help students learn to live and to work cooperatively with others, a common purpose which only education can achieve.[17]

All parents want some form of economic self-sufficiency and success for their children, but they understand that success in life takes many forms, and that economic success is not the measure of the value of one's life. As the authors of *The Good Society* conclude, "The idea of an education that simply gives individuals the methods and skills they need to get ahead in the world is almost certainly inadequate even as job preparation in an advanced technical economy, which requires morally and socially sensitive people capable of responsible interaction. It is even more inadequate in preparing citizens for active participation in a complex world."[18]

A more complete view of the public in public schools requires expanding the other values of the public good to ensure that public schools are aligned not only with economic goals, but also with democratic goals. Merely expanding one value does not by itself necessarily increase the overall public good. Sometimes expanding one value contracts another value. And sometimes merely expanding one value increases the conflict with another value, undermining the public good. The policy leadership challenge is to expand the other values without creating additional political conflict, without causing another value to contract and harming the overall public good.

For example, public schools might expand the value of community. In a letter to the President and Members of Congress about the importance of public education, the National Council of Churches of Christ wrote that "Our biblical heritage and our theology teach us that we live in community, not solely the marketplace."[19] The Council supported alternative forms of schooling, such as home schooling and private schools, as being part of a pluralistic society.

But the Council strongly encouraged the nation's leaders to preserve the fundamental purposes of public education in building a society that allows for political, cultural and religious diversity. This view of community involves more than simply safety and security, which schools already address. It encompasses civic competency, our obligations to each other as fellow citizens and as fellow human beings and fulfilling the potential for human development.

Public schools might also expand the value of equality. This involves more than providing equal opportunity to children once they walk through the school doors. It involves joining with other public leaders to address equal opportunity and redress socioeconomic imbalances outside the classroom. In Montgomery County, MD, for example, local zoning laws require affordable housing amid the suburban homes of Washington commuters.

A Century Foundation study showed that kids sharing air with their wealthier peers cut their achievement gap by almost a third in reading and half in math, even though lower-income schools had greater per-student funding.[20] The difference was attributed to environment—fewer disciplinary interruptions, more engaged students, and a more stable set of teachers. Money matters, but people, it seems, matter more.[21]

Fairness is a key dimension of equality. States that impose across the board budget cuts, for example, create challenges to fairness. Budget cuts scarcely affect wealthier districts that rely primarily on local taxes to support well-appointed schools. But they are likely to be devastating for impoverished districts that rely heavily on state aid. Sometimes treating everyone or every district the same is fair. But sometimes treating everyone or every district differently is fair. The art is knowing when and why to do one and not the other. It's an art of policy leadership.

Strengthening economic competitiveness is important. So is strengthening democracy. Public education has a moral and political obligation to introduce students to democracy not only as a concept and political arrangement but as a way of life.[22] As Eleanor Roosevelt remarked, "Our children should learn the general framework of their government and then they should know where they come in contact with the government, where it touches their daily lives and where their influence is exerted on the government. It must not be a distant thing, someone else's business, but they must see how every cog in the wheel of a democracy is important and bears its share of responsibility for the smooth running of the entire machine."

Civic preparation for democracy is not restricted to a civics class, but rather should be part of every activity of our life.[23] Some of the best leadership development occurs through integrating leadership into every learning experience, no matter how technical the subject matter. The same is true for democracy. The arts, skills and principles of democracy should be woven into every subject taught in public schools, regardless of whether it's a math, science, language arts or physical education class.

Learning to stand in line and wait one's turn, for example, is essential in a society which espouses belief in the fundamental equality of all citizens. Preparing citizens for their public roles and responsibilities is as important as preparing them for their private roles and responsibilities. A more complete view of public schools requires both.

PRINCIPLES FOR PRESERVING THE *PUBLIC* IN PUBLIC SCHOOLS

We believe the future of the *public* in public schools is in the hands of all Americans. If citizens and public school leaders fail to preserve public education for the public good they will fuel further calls for privatization, municipal and state takeovers, perhaps nationalization of public schools, appointed boards, legislated qualifications for school boards, and business and military leadership of schools. How might we preserve a vision of public education for the public good? We offer the following principles to all public school leaders.

Treat Each Other as Fellow Citizens

Treating each other as citizens means that we respect the individuality and competence of each other.[24] We show respect for others by adopting ground rules to ensure that we do not speak in ways that are hurtful and close down communication. Irresponsible discourse can have a variety of negative consequences, including distrust, disrespect, intolerance, frustration, anger, fear, lashing out, diminished enthusiasm and enjoyment, decisions with poor shelf life and a loss of community respect.

We agree to share all relevant information openly in a way that enhances trust. We respect each other by listening when others speak, not talking when others talk, and giving each other sufficient time to speak. We support each other by not taking cheap shots, calling each other names, labeling someone or their behavior, attacking each other or using hurtful language. We share our feelings, positions and convictions with each other, explain the reasons behind them, and accept others' perceptions and feelings as valid.

We discuss and debate issues as much as we need to, but we accept the collective decision once it is made. We don't use false appeals to cohesiveness or congeniality as a means for manipulating other members. When we disagree with each other we do so openly. An honest adversarial relationship, John Dewey suggested, is better than a false unity. Clearly this is hard work. As Thomas Paine noted many years ago, "Those who would enjoy the benefits of liberty must endure the fatigues of supporting it." Sometimes this includes our fellow citizens.

Understand that Relationships Matter

When we participate in governing we enjoy a special kind of relationship, a way of relating to one another that is consistent with and conducive to the democratic process. Aristotle likened governing relationships to a political extension of friendship.

When board members discuss what they want and expect from each other in their governing relationships, they often mention things such as: (1) being able to disagree and recognizing that disagreement isn't bad; (2) relationships are critical; (3) differences are a strength; (4) being able to communicate honestly with each other without being hurtful; and (5) being able to have fun in carrying out the difficult work of governing.

Satisfying governing relationships require inclusive membership, equally distributed decision making power, democratic deliberation, speaking rights and listening responsibilities. As Adlai Stevenson remarked, "The sound of tireless voices is the price we pay for the right to hear the music of our own opinions."

Make Room for Difference

We are elected or appointed individually, but we govern together. This gives rise to the most fundamental leadership challenge in governing—how to deal with difference. There's no question as to whether we will encounter difference. That's a given. The leadership challenge is what we will do with the difference we encounter. If we all agreed about everything, we wouldn't need democracy, and we wouldn't need to learn how to work out differences.[25]

Be careful not to ignore members' positions and interests just because they are in the minority. "If you find yourself in the majority," advised Mark Twain, "stop and think about it." And when we find ourselves in the minority, we need to be able to openly support the majority after the vote. We should not act as a "Lone Ranger," challenging publicly the wisdom and legitimacy of our colleagues. We can't impugn the legitimacy of our fellow board members without also impugning the legitimacy of representative democracy, the very process by which we each acquired our seats at the board table.

Be wary of refusing to change positions, of relying too heavily on compromise, of doing too much talking and not enough listening, or of substituting voting for building consensus. Governing is not a one-night stand. It requires repeated encounters with the same people. "The condition of our survival in any but the meagerest existence is our willingness to accommodate ourselves to the conflicting interests of others, to learn to live in a social world."[26]

Don't shut out difference because it is different, but welcome what is different, advised Mary Parker Follett, because through its difference it will make our lives and experiences richer. A school board that rejects creating a seat for a non-voting student representative is like a person who vows never to get into the water until he learns to swim.

Transition from Campaigning to Governing

Whether you are elected, appointed, or a volunteer, you are likely to have become involved in school governance because of a specific interest or issue. Advocating is different from governing. Advocating for a specific cause brings like individuals together around a particular issue. They do not have to have other things in common in order to associate with each other. Nor are they likely to have to deal with each other's differences.

But serving as a member of a governing board or a school committee is quite different. Members must agree on the very issues they will tackle and on how they will make decisions. They must ensure that all members have adequate opportunity to participate and to be heard. They must share power and authority. And they must deal with each other's differences.

In campaigns, some people win and some people lose. But in governing, when we play "win-lose" everybody loses. Campaigning emphasizes differences. Governing emphasizes commonality. Individual board members may come and go, but the relationship between the board and the community continues.

Candidates will likely articulate different visions of public schools and public education. But once the members of a board have been elected, the first and most important task of the board is to develop a collective vision that reflects the interests of the entire community. Great boards work hard to avoid splitting themselves and dividing the community. If you campaign well, it's your seat; if you govern well, your seat belongs to posterity.

Govern as Citizen Representatives

We contribute best to the process of governing when we avoid assuming the mantle of the expert, refrain from disregarding expert advice because it is expert advice, and stop trying to manage the public organizations and functions we have been asked to govern or advise. We may bring the knowledge, experience and credentials of a physician, an engineer, an architect, an accountant, or an artist to our task, but credentials are not why we were elected or appointed.

When we serve as a citizen representative, we serve as an expert in the values of our community. This is the basis of our legitimacy in representing and governing our fellow citizens. Newly-elected board members must overcome several early impediments, including a lack of understanding of what government does and why, expectations raised by single-issue advocates, and the consequences of campaigning against the board rather than for public schools. The longer elected officials serve, the less they tend to believe they know all of the answers.

Participating in a governing body teaches several important lessons. Policy choices evoke short-term passions but have long-term consequences. Change comes slowly in a political system intentionally designed with nobody in charge. We must be willing to think deeply about issues and sometimes accept a reality contrary to our own beliefs.

We represent all of the residents in our community, not just organized special interest groups or campaign supporters. We have a responsibility to respond constructively to the concerns of citizens, constituents, businesses, staff, community groups, spouses, children, neighbors and friends without creating a bigger problem for the folks whose job it is to try to solve the problem.

Voting Is Not the Same as Decision Making

We know the choices we have as voters. But in governing, we don't know what our choices are until we define the policy problem we're trying to solve. Impatient boards and win-lose boards are prone to voting on solutions to problems they don't understand, let alone agree on. This can lead to unintended consequences, which are often worse than the initial problem.

Voting is not so much a way of making decisions as it is a way of avoiding war. As Judge Learned Hand remarked, "While counting heads is not an ideal way to govern, I'm sure you'll agree that it's preferable to breaking them." Voting is like a thermometer—it measures the degree of difference in the room, but tells you little about why people agree or disagree. Make representative government, urged Benjamin Franklin, mean something more than two wolves and a sheep voting on what to have for lunch.

Develop the Leadership Skills Needed to Govern

It takes time to develop the leadership skills needed to govern democratically on behalf of our fellow citizens. Governing requires understanding the political context in which governing occurs, and the ability to bring different people together around different issues. Advocating for or against a particular position is not leadership. "Leadership is based on inspiration, not domination; on cooperation, not intimidation."[27] Creating common purpose and collective action is the true work of public leaders.

Citizens involved in school governance, from school boards to school committees to parent-teacher councils, want to make a contribution and make a difference. Public school leaders should be able to conduct effective meetings, engage colleagues in discussing school issues and challenges and facilitate collaborative problem solving and decision making.

Govern from Good to Great

When citizens come together, whether as committee volunteers to address a specific school issue such as off-campus lunch or as an elected board to govern an entire school system, they typically want to achieve tangible results and enjoy their time in the company of their colleagues. Boards and governing groups that are able to do both of these things are high-performing and high-satisfying, and have several characteristics in common.

Members feel responsible for results. Members share responsibility for process and outcomes. The board removes barriers to full and effective participation by members, who participate equally to the best of their abilities in planning and making decisions.

Members are aligned as to why the board exists and to its purpose. Conflicts and differences are used creatively to develop alternative solutions and inform collective decisions. Members practice authentic communication and create a climate of trust, openness and mutual respect.

The board is future forward, meaning that members are optimistic and opportunistic. They do not allow obstacles to prevent them from identifying and acting on opportunities. Members see change as an opportunity for learning and growth.

Build and Educate the Public

Public education must include educating the public. The very value differences that divide us create opportunities for practicing democracy and educating the public. We spend a great deal of money, time and effort in building the academic capacity of public schools, but considerably less time in building their public capacity.

James Madison tasked governing bodies in a democratic republic with responsibility for refining and enlarging public views by passing them through the medium of a chosen body of citizens whose collective wisdom would best discern the true public interest. Public leaders *choose* whether to enlarge or narrow the public view.

Leaders learn how to make room for difference without feeling like they must sacrifice their core values or compromise deeply-held beliefs. They learn that it is possible to hear and understand a fellow citizen's position without having to agree with them. And they learn that it is okay to explore a specific issue in public without having to take a position or push for an immediate solution or decision. Most importantly, leaders learn how to help citizens appreciate that "the spirit of liberty is the spirit which is not too sure that it is right."[28]

Practice Democracy

As citizens, we are all public educators in the broadest sense of the term. We serve as role models for the practice of democracy. Our words and actions convey to our fellow citizens a sense of whether self-government is worthwhile, whether democracy is worth the trouble and whether the American Dream is for all Americans or just some.

Public schools not only serve the public, they create the public.[29] What purpose does it serve to promote anti-bullying programs in public schools if students observe public school leaders bullying each other? Public school leaders cannot teach democracy if they cannot practice it. Here's a ten-point performance check-up any board or committee can conduct in just minutes.

- Are we clear about our purpose?
- Do we agree on our goals and priorities?
- Are we satisfied with our communication?
- What's our level of trust?
- Do disagreements become personal?
- Is there less tolerance for those who disagree?
- Have we stopped listening to some members?
- Do we ignore minority viewpoints?
- Do we play "win-lose" and "us and them?"
- Do we share responsibility for leading and hold each other accountable for doing so?

Demand Political Accountability, Not Just Technical Accountability

Public leaders are fond of calling for more accountability from public schools. How might we hold public leaders accountable? What should we expect from elected representatives? What should be the standard for the governing performance of a board of education? The National Commission on Excellence in Education distinguished between governance leadership involving persuasion, setting goals, and developing community consensus and organizational leadership involving managerial and supervisory skills.[30]

The Commission recognized that some managerial and supervisory skills are necessary, but recommended that school boards must consciously develop governance leadership skills at the school and district levels. Toward that end, we offer the following governance competencies and standards for public school leaders.

1. Articulate the meaning of democracy, identify the core values that underlie public policy choices, distinguish means from ends and understand the roles and responsibilities of an elected board within the framework of representative government.
2. Forge effective political relationships with citizens, business, community organizations and other governmental bodies.
3. Create public spaces within which and public processes by which citizens can come together to explore shared values, strengthen their sense of connection and belonging, and create a common vision of their future.

4. Demonstrate effective skills in communication, conflict resolution, collaborative problem solving, decision making, sharing power and coalition building. Teach citizens to appreciate that what we see as conflict is really the way the democratic process is designed to work. Help constituents and stakeholders see conflict in a new light, as a positive and natural tension that occurs when we attach priority to different core values in a given situation and struggle to come to terms with the values represented in the conflict and which value has priority.
5. Conduct a sincere search for consensus and for the public good, seek alternatives to "either-or," and seek integrative solutions before resorting to compromise or domination. Craft policy solutions that make your community better, not just different.

These standards are both political and moral. They are intended to help public school leaders practice democracy and preserve the public in public schools for everyone. Public school leaders need political and moral standards, because public schools are a political and moral enterprise. Public schools are political because we have decided as a people to publically fund public education. They are a moral enterprise because we expect them to contribute to helping create and sustain our vision of the good society.[31]

PUBLIC SCHOOLS AND DEMOCRACY: A LOOK AHEAD

Public schools matter to all of us because they are the principal means by which we perpetuate the revolutionary idea of a self-governing republic. They promote and preserve national knowledge and values. Through processes of democratic and educational socialization, they help each successive generation find answers to important questions about what it means to be an American and what it means to be a citizen. Local school boards and other school governance bodies serve as a means of preserving liberty and providing citizens with opportunities to learn and practice democracy.

Democracy is not an end in itself, but a means to the good life, a means of resolving political disagreements. Democratic elections don't always guarantee democratic representation, and democratic processes do not guarantee democratic outcomes. "Democracy is not a final achievement," declared John F. Kennedy, "but rather a call to an untiring effort."

There is one thing democracy can guarantee. As long as enough citizens understand the principles of democratic governance, volunteer to serve on public school boards and work to keep the spirit and practice of representative government alive, democracy will endure, and so will public schools. The destiny of our schools and the destiny of our democracy are intertwined. "Certainly there will be no liberty, no equality, no social justice without democracy, and there will be no democracy without citizens and the schools that forge civic identity and democratic responsibility."[32]

If democracy and public schools endure, your sons and daughters, grandsons and granddaughters will have new opportunities to rediscover and reinvent what it means to be an American, to recapitulate the founding arguments of the framers, and to learn firsthand what it means to believe in and practice democracy. Such knowledge and experience will be vital when they encounter their own versions of events like the following.

Two parents filed a free-speech lawsuit against their school district when their daughters were suspended for wearing the popular "I (heart) boobies!" bracelets. The American Civil Liberties Union believes the lawsuit is the first in the country over a school's ban on the bracelets, which are designed to raise breast-cancer awareness among young people. School officials argued that the slogan is distracting and demeaning and that it trivialized a serious illness.

A federal appeals court ruled that a state law requiring schools to schedule voluntary recitation of the Pledge of Allegiance does not unconstitutionally force religion upon students. The ruling came in a lawsuit brought by a couple who claimed the rights of their three young children were violated when elementary and middle school teachers led their classes in daily recitation of the pledge because it describes the United States as a nation "under God."

We can't predict which issue will be your next test of democracy in public schools. "You can't learn in school what the world is going to do next year," observed Henry Ford. We do know that as long as public schools survive, so will democracy, and therefore there will be a next test. There will always be a next test.

Public schools represent the single most powerful expression of the promise of American democracy. No one understood this promise better than Tocqueville, who concluded that America is great because she is good, and that if America ever ceases to be good she will cease to be great. "If the lights that guide us ever go out," he wrote, "they will fade little by little, as if of their own accord."[33]

Public schools serve as the public repository for the promise of democracy. We must preserve the *public* in public schools to realize this promise. We must keep the ideals of the American Creed and the American Dream in front of us at all times, lest they become a diminishing and fading reflection in our national rear-view mirror.

NOTES

1. Lasch, C. (1995). *The revolt of the elites and the betrayal of democracy.* New York, NY: W. W. Norton and Company.

2. Gutmann, A. (1999). *Democratic education: with a new preface and epilogue.* Princeton, NJ: Princeton University Press.

3. Ibid.

4. Gutmann, A. (1987). *Democratic education.* Princeton, NJ: Princeton University Press, p. xiii.

5. David Mathews (1996, 1997, 2006).

6. Ravitch, D. (2010). *The death and life of the great American school system: How testing and choice are undermining education.* New York, NY: Basic Books.

7. Tocqueville, p. 547.

8. Food Research & Action Center. "Breakfast for learning." Retrieved March 25, 2011 from http://www.frac.org/pdf/breakfastforlearning.PDF and Montana Office of Public Instruction. "Get Going with Breakfast: How to Start a School Breakfast Program." Retrieved March 25, 2011 from http://www.opi.mt.gov.

9. Severson, K. (2010). "Scandal and a schism rattle Atlanta's schools." *The New York Times,* December 11.

10. National Center for Education Statistics (2009). *Mapping state proficiency standards onto NAEP scales, 2005–2007.* Washington, DC: U.S. Department of Education.

11. Urbina, I. (2010). States lower test standards for a high school diploma. *The New York Times,* January 12.

12. Bonner, L. (2010). "Social promotion hurdle falls." *The News & Observer,* October 7.

13. Drucker, P. F. (1989). *The new realities: In government and politics/In economics and business/In society and world view.* New York, NY: Harper & Row Publishers, p. 245.

14. Campbell, J. (1995). *Understanding John Dewey: Nature and cooperative intelligence.* Peru, IL: Open Count Publishing Co., pp. 215.

15. Dewey, J. (1916). *Democracy and education: An introduction to the philosophy of education.* New York, NY: Macmillan, p. 72.

16. Snauwaert, D. T. (1993). *Democracy, education, and governance: A developmental conception.* Albany, NY: State University of New York.

17. Campbell, J. (1995).

18. Bellah, Robert N., Madsen, Richard, Sullivan, William M., Swidler, Ann, and Tipton, Steven M. *The Good Society.* New York, NY: Vintage, 1991.

19. National Council of the Churches of Christ in the USA, May 2010.

20. Schwartz, H. (2010). *Housing policy is school policy: Economically integrative housing promotes academic success in Montgomery County, Maryland.* A Century Foundation Report. Washington, DC: The Century Foundation.

21. Wu, A. (2010). "Closing the achievement gap in Maryland." *Newsweek,* October 31.

22. Giroux, H. A., and Saltman, K. (2008). Obama's betrayal of public education? Arne Duncan and the corporate model of schooling. *Truthout,* December 17. Retrieved December 19, 2008 from http://www.truthout.org/121708R.

23. Follett, M. P. (1918). *The new state: Group organization the solution of popular government.* University Park, PA: Pennsylvania State University Press.

24. Gastil, J. (1993). *Democracy in small groups: Participation, decision making and communication.* Philadelphia, PA: New Society Publishers.

25. Meier, D. (2003). "The road to trust." *American School Board Journal, 190, 9,* 18–21.

26. Judge Billings Learned Hand.

27. William Arthur Ward.

28. Judge Billings Learned Hand.

29. Barber, B. R. (1993). "America skips school." *Harper's Magazine*, 287, 1, 39–46.

30. National Commission on Excellence in Education, 1983.

31. Giroux, H. A., and Saltman, K. (2008). "Obama's betrayal of public education? Arne Duncan and the corporate model of schooling." *Truthout,* December 17. Retrieved December 19, 2008 from http://www.truthout.org/121708R.

32. Barber (1993), p. 46.

33. Tocqueville, p. 464.

Epilogue

The Future of the *Public* in Crestwich Public Schools

When we first visited Crestwich Public Schools, a school board election had just resulted in the nine-member board of education swearing-in four new members. While this epilogue focuses on Crestwich and its leaders, we believe the challenges and choices we describe are relevant to all school districts and public school leaders. Here's what happened since then.

The four new members, along with an incumbent member now the board chair, comprised a majority committed to reversing the previous board's student assignment policy based on socioeconomic diversity. The new majority began work on a proposal for a zone-based assignment plan that would give greater emphasis to parental choice and neighborhood schools. As details of the proposal emerged, so too did criticism. Not only would there be no base school assignment for students, but critics argued that such an approach would lead to creating schools with greater poverty and increased segregation.

When it came time for the board to vote on whether to proceed with developing a zone-based plan, one newly-elected board member joined with four members from the previous board to halt development of the plan. The new member continued to express support for community-based schools and for the new majority, but expressed disagreement with the zone plan that was being developed. A house divided, deadlocked in a 4-1-4 configuration, the board seemed unable to back up or move forward. How did Crestwich get to where it is today?

Just two generations ago, public schools were a local responsibility. Majority interests within each community tended to prevail, such that schools were segregated by race, wealthier districts provided more funding for schools than did poorer districts and students who were physically, emotionally, or academically different were given a separate and unequal education.[1] Most communities had a dominant religion which permeated the school system. Policy conflicts were diffused by elevating majority private interests above the public interests of public schools.

As public schools became of greater interest to governors, state legislatures, the courts, and even the U.S. Congress, they shifted from being agents of socialization for majority interests in local communities to being agents of socialization for state and national interests.[2] This often put public schools in the middle of cultural and ideological conflicts between the politics of local majorities and the politics of state and national pluralities.

Today schooling takes place at the intersection of the rights of the family and the rights of society.[3] It is the right of parents to choose the educational experiences and influences to which they expose their children. And it is the right of a democratic society to use education as a means of reproducing its core values, beliefs and institutions through a common school experience.[4]

Because public schools serve as the only public institution of socialization in our society, they operate in a sphere of rights, equal opportunity and the secular. Traditional institutions of socialization—family, community, faith—operate in a sphere of the private, the personal, and the sacred. Conflicts over the boundaries between these spheres often play out in public schools.

This conflict is between giving each individual child the chance to achieve his or her dreams versus enabling all children to achieve their dreams. With local political power and normative preferences curtailed by state and federal laws designed to redress economic and equity imbalances, and with local majority privilege subordinated to a broader public interest, a backlash arose in many communities.[5] We need look no further than Crestwich Public Schools.

CRESTWICH AND THE PUBLIC GOOD

Basic public education, philosopher Michael Walzer points out, is coercive.[6] School attendance is compulsory. Parents and students are required to comply with a host of conditions, ranging from dress to test. To make public education possible, school districts must distribute the places of school among the population of children and distribute the population of children among the places of school.

Educational resources—whether in the form of teachers, books, curricula, or learning activities—are distributed according to the nature and needs of students. For example, as future citizens students receive a civic education, as future workers a vocational education, as future athletes a physical education, and so on, for as many different categories as we wish to create.[7] All students receive multiple educational resources, but no student receives all of the available resources. What kinds of educational resources are available to students is important, but so too is access to these resources and their cost and convenience.

Children, on the other hand, are each others' resources—friends, neighbors, rivals—who help and challenge each other in a myriad of ways, and who may form relationships crucial to their adult lives. The content of the curriculum is probably less important than the human environment in which it is taught.[8] Because schools distribute education to students and vice versa, how they distribute each becomes a matter of fairness and justice.

Allocating children and educational resources raise two fundamental questions of distributive justice.[9] First, how should Crestwich leaders distribute the available educational resources of schools to children? Second, how should Crestwich leaders distribute children in accordance with the available educational resources of schools? Merger, integration and magnet programs were three policy approaches adopted by Crestwich in response to the first question. Crestwich adopted district-directed, choice-based and socioeconomic-based assignment in response to the second question.

As we discussed earlier, because policy problems involve both technical and normative issues, they are never solved in any permanent sense. All policy solutions are time-limited because the constellation of values involved shifts over time. This means that really important policy problems reappear over and over again as newer versions of themselves. A good policy solution is both technically feasible and politically acceptable. Based on the most recent school board election, none of these assignment approaches is politically acceptable today.

To move forward, the Crestwich board of education must adopt some method or system for defining the student population of each school. The technical problem is primarily logistical, how to distribute students physically and geographically. The political problem is one of justice, how to distribute students fairly and equitably in terms of available educational opportunity.

Crestwich Leaders have Three Vastly Different Choices

The first choice is to randomly assign children to schools. It satisfies fairness in one sense, in that it treats every student and family the same. But it does little to advance individual opportunity, which will seem unfair to most residents. If adopted, neither it nor its governors would last long. Within relatively short order, the sheer weight of such an unfair and unequal distribution would grind it to a halt.

The second choice is to allow each family to decide which schools their children will attend and for reasons of their own choosing. The district would rely upon parents to act on behalf of their own children. Inevitably, "entrepreneurial ruthlessness and parental indifference"[10] would result along with chaos, social disorder, financial waste, bribery, and perhaps even physical violence. There would be no one to act on behalf of the public as a whole. Unfettered individual freedom will destroy the common good.[11] In due time a call would emerge for the heads of those responsible, and a revolution, or at least an electoral revolt, would likely take place.

The third choice is some form of purposeful student assignment. Proponents of neighborhood schools are not wrong, any more than proponents of diverse schools are wrong. But neither is more right than the other. Crestwich leaders must address both goals. "Schools that purport to be open to all and yet endorse values that are not accepted by all are an affront to the dignity of people who think and live otherwise."[12] This choice would require making the problem and solution the responsibility of the entire Crestwich community, not just the school district. Forging collective action and collective responsibility is the true task of public leaders.

PUBLIC LEADERSHIP CHALLENGES IN CRESTWICH

Crestwich leaders should not seek to make schools the same, but to ensure that all children receive a common education across some degree of variation in neighborhoods and schools. This variation can take the form of racial, ethnic, wealth, cultural, political, religious or even curriculum differences. However, no single difference should dominate any one neighborhood school, or result in less than a common education for any child.

The policy goal should be to preserve the shared educational experience necessary for transmitting common knowledge and values while at the same time allowing for a sufficient range of choice within the educational experience.[13] In seeking to achieve this goal, both current and future board members will face many of the same challenges.

Challenge 1: Educating Students and the Public

To state the obvious, "that the first duty of schools is education, turns out not to be self-evident. There is a strong tendency to equate education with teaching—transmitting skills and knowledge—which it is not."[14] If the first duty of public schools is to educate, then we might ask educate whom and towards what ends.

Crestwich leaders have an opportunity to define public education more broadly and demonstrate that addressing the role that public schools should play in the community and how schools should be populated are as much part of public education as what takes place in classrooms. How students are assigned to schools affects the composition of the classroom, but it also affects the constitution of the community. Leaders can create a true learning community and help to educate citizens by harnessing the passion surrounding student assignment.

Challenge 2: Moving Beyond Majoritarianism

A second leadership challenge involves moving beyond a majoritarian board to a democratic board, one that works to create a school system that is truly responsive—not only to a particular group, a minority, or even to the majority, but to all its members.[15] Since "voting is a good way to take a snapshot of disagreement" but not a very useful way to get people to do something together, we should be talking not about voting but the fostering of "democratic values."[16]

For Crestwich leaders, this means developing a framework for student assignment that is based upon a community-wide conception of the common good instead of claims based solely upon individual or group desires. It means developing a normative framework for student assignment that satisfies multiple values and goals. Such a framework must be one that can be applied equally to everyone, and can be explained and justified in terms that can be understood by everyone. And it means pushing for a solution that achieves a public good that is diverse in its interests and not settling for a solution based on a single interest in which some people win and some people lose.

Achieving such a solution will require genuine leadership. Genuine leaders are moral leaders.[17] They seek the good, and do right things to achieve it. Genuine leaders treat followers, constituents and citizens as ends in themselves, not as objects to be manipulated. They do not betray the common good for purposes of personal aggrandizement. They seek to release human possibilities, not to suppress them.

Challenge 3: Balancing Wholeness and Diversity

Not only in public schools, but throughout American society, communities struggle with balancing wholeness and diversity. Too much wholeness can result in totalitarian attitudes and behaviors. Too much diversity can destroy the wholeness. To prevent the wholeness from smothering diversity, there must be a tradition of pluralism and healthy dissent.[18] And to prevent diversity from destroying the wholeness, there must be a tradition of accommodation and coalition-building. "No leaders...today can doubt that the achievement of wholeness incorporating diversity is one of the transcendent goals of our time."[19]

We cannot be different all by ourselves. This is the paradox of diversity – that it is our membership within a community that makes meaningful diversity possible. Genuine leaders understand that a mutual dependence exists between individuals and groups, and they emphasize the obligations and responsibilities of each to the other. Genuine leaders bring people together, enabling them to recognize both their differences and what they share in common. This was a challenge in the time of the founders, and it is a challenge in contemporary America. It is the great public challenge for Crestwich public schools.

PUBLIC LEADERSHIP CHOICES IN CRESTWICH

Difference (e.g., sides in a campaign and votes in an election) and division (e.g., heated discourse at public meetings and hearings) tell us we have hold of an important public issue, but not what the issue is about, what it means to us, why we care about it so passionately or what we should do about it. To create difference and division in a community requires power. To make a community better requires leadership. The leaders of Crestwich face several leadership choices.

Choice 1: Focus on Commonality or on Difference

Crestwich leaders can perpetuate division in the community by focusing on difference instead of commonality. No doubt some citizens may be satisfied with the current level of difference and divisiveness, and less interested in seeing a common good solution, particularly if they feel their individual interests are being met.

Leaders have an opportunity to transform the concerns and passions of individuals and groups into language that reaches out towards the public place and up towards common ground. When people speak at a public hearing, for example, they rarely speak of what they have in common, or how the common good might be preserved, but rather about how a particular action or proposal "enhances or threatens their individual rights."[20] The language of the self-reliant individual will always be the first language of public life, but it need not be the only language.[21]

Citizens do not learn the language of community or become capable of democratic self-determination by accident.[22] Republicans from Montesquieu to Jefferson to Tocqueville have recognized that the character citizens need to develop for participation in face-to-face self-government can only be learned and acquired through repeated civic experiences.[23] It is the responsibility of all Crestwich leaders to provide citizens with such experiences.

Choice 2: Wait For a Majority or Build Consensus

Some Crestwich leaders favor waiting for the next school board election and hope that a numerical majority emerges that can push through an agenda without having to engage those with different views. Even if this happens, a majority achieved through campaign politics is unlikely to produce a viable solution because neighborhood and diverse schools have been framed as being in conflict with each other. A policy solution that favors just one view, regardless of whose view it favors, will be short-lived.

Newly-elected leaders are often elected because of a pushback against a current public policy solution. When new leaders assume power, they are often less interested in governing than in retribution. The change in power is not nearly as problematic as is the cycle that such changes tend to perpetuate. At what point, Crestwich citizens might ask, do payback and retribution transform themselves into leadership and governance?

Crestwich leaders have another choice available. They can use the current political conflict as an educational opportunity to build consensus across the entire community. But this will require collective leadership to push through to a solution that satisfies the multiple interests of the community. Many leaders will be tempted to consider their task completed when a solution emerges that satisfies their individual interest.

Choice 3: Engage the Community or Just Each Other

Leaders always face the temptation of engaging only each other. Clearly, there are times when that is the only available course of action. But Crestwich leaders have a rare opportunity to engage citizens and each other in meaningful discussion about what they want from public schools and what a community-wide vision of public schools might look like.

In addition to the language of the individual, there is a second language leaders can call upon, one of tradition and commitment anchored in community that most Americans know as well.[24] Crestwich leaders have an opportunity to create public spaces where citizens can talk to each other and make sense of the tensions they feel between their personal and private interests related to public schools and their sense of responsibility and obligation to the larger community and to the public good. If discourse is the soul of democracy, conversation is our grace.

Such a conversation might involve exploring what socioeconomic equality, diversity and segregation mean to citizens. Leaders might ask, "What words, terms, phrases or images come to mind when you hear the terms neighborhood schools and socioeconomic diversity? Which of these are positive, negative or neutral to you?"

Such a conversation might also explore the implications of more or less socioeconomic equality for the Crestwich community. Leaders might ask, "When you think about the long-term welfare of Crestwich, will Crestwich be better off in the future with more neighborhood schools or more socioeconomic diversity than it has today, less, or about the same amount? What consequences do you foresee if neighborhood schools or socioeconomic diversity increase, decrease, or stay about the same?"

Somewhere in Crestwich, in an as yet uncreated public space, there is a common good waiting to be uncovered. The goal of all Crestwich leaders should be help citizens discover this good. "We know the good, wrote the Greek playwright Euripides, "but do not practice it."

PUBLIC LEADERSHIP TEMPTATIONS IN CRESTWICH

Like all temptations, leadership temptations are difficult to resist. They offer us immediate gratification, and only later are the consequences revealed. Crestwich public school leaders face several leadership temptations.

Temptations of leadership include a desire to see others lose and proclaiming others to be wrong so that we can claim to be right. One board member, hopeful that a deliberate and collective approach will allow members to build consensus, said, "Leadership is . . . listening to others, being respectful of others, being inclusive." Another board member disagreed, saying, "Consensus is the lack of leadership. We need leadership, not consensus. Consensus means drawing up a plan that doesn't offend anyone and that usually results in a bad plan."[25]

Another temptation is assuming that others disagree with us whenever they express preference for a value different from the value we prefer. "Right now, those who believe in forced busing and socioeconomic engineering have found a new ally," said one board member.

Temptations also include rejecting difference because it's different, assuming that power is diminished rather than enhanced when we share it with others and playing "win-lose" because we're afraid to believe in "win-win." As one board member proclaimed loudly in a meeting, "There's no such thing as a win-win. Somebody's got to lose!"

Desire for attention, approval or for the public spotlight can become temptations as well. Acting in accord with what others think is just so as to be held in esteem by them is not the same as acting justly. Sometimes, acting justly may require us to forfeit the approval of those whose approval we most crave.[26]

One very common leadership temptation is to treat our fellow citizens as enemies. Several majority members on the board publicly chastised one of their own for voting against the proposed zone-based student assignment plan and for considering a more deliberate approach to student assignment as advocated by the board minority. "We're not a majority," said one board member. "We don't have the fifth vote, and [that member] seems to be on the other side. I don't know where [that member] stands." We make war with enemies, writes democratic scholar Jean Elshtain, "but we do politics, democratic politics, with opponents.[27]

Perhaps the most important temptation of public leadership is to demand responsiveness and accountability from the system we are elected to govern but fail to demand the same from the citizens who elected us. Most of the campaign rhetoric in Crestwich focuses on how the school district should meet the interests of citizens or how it fails to do so. There is little public discussion about how citizens should respond to the goals of public schools or how they should be accountable for the success of their schools. Those who would govern Crestwich public schools cannot invoke the obligations of the school system to citizens without also invoking the obligations of citizens to public schools.

Yielding to temptations of public leadership has consequences. It makes it nearly impossible to create the public space and reach for the higher ground that policy problems require. In addition, every time a governing board finds itself stalemated or undermined by mutual effort, a few more citizens conclude that representative democracy no longer works. They withdraw from public life. And from then on, if they enter the public realm at all, it will be only to protect their own private interests.[28] The public needs public schools, and public schools need a public.

PENTIMENTO

If it seems that the same questions and choices keep appearing, they do. There are no new policy choices, only new contexts within which we make these choices. We wrote earlier that policy problems are like onions; they have layers. Policy choices, on the other hand, are like a pentimento, an underlying image that reappears in a painting that has been painted over. Serve on a governing board long enough and you will see the same public problems and choices reappear, albeit in a slightly different fashion and with slightly different emphases.

Addressing reappearing policy problems is made even more daunting by having the freedom to make these choices. We cannot have freedom in all things at the same time. This is what creates tensions among public values. Somehow, we must find a way to balance what we get and what we give. This is no small leadership challenge. "It's an odd thing about this universe that, though we all disagree with each other, we are all of us always in the right."[29]

The crucial leadership challenge isn't the tensions themselves, but acknowledging and addressing them. Merging districts, assigning students, providing program equity, creating magnet schools and adopting different school calendars are all efforts to solve policy problems. Each creates new policy problems, or at least new versions of the same policy problems. Because the kinds of policy problems we have discussed are unsolvable in any permanent sense, these policy problems give rise to reappearing versions of the same value conflicts.

Take, for example, the report released by the National Commission on Excellence in Education in 1983. While commissions like these often begin with a specific economic-related charge, they provide business and public leaders with an opportunity to discuss the purpose and goals of education. When this happens, leaders often recognize a broader view of public education, one in which room must be made for multiple and competing public values. In this instance, commission members forged a vision of public education in which commitment to academic achievement, equal opportunity and diversity are joined together rather than made separate:

> "We do not believe that a public commitment to excellence and educational reform must be made at the expense of a strong public commitment to the equitable treatment of our diverse population. The twin goals of equity and high-quality schooling have profound and practical meaning for our economy and society, and we cannot permit one to yield to the other either in principle or in practice. To do so would deny young people their chance to learn and live according to their aspirations and abilities. It also would lead to a generalized accommodation to mediocrity in our society on the one hand or the creation of an undemocratic elitism on the other."[30]

Looked at today, it appears very much like a pentimento in the continuing political repainting of Crestwich public schools.

In weighing approaches to distributing students and educational opportunity, Crestwich leaders may attempt to paint over some of the choices made by leaders who preceded them. In both art and policy, this won't work. The essential images of student assignment, dealing with powerful themes of opportunity, fairness, justice and equality will, over time, reveal themselves again and again. For example, a proposal surfaced to use student achievement as an alternative to socioeconomic status in assigning students to schools. Call it what you will, the policy images of the past will forever be visible regardless of how we paint the politics of the present.

WRAPPING UP

We have come to the end of our exploration. We hope it is just the beginning of yours. We believe the leadership lessons and governance principles discussed in this book are relevant and important to every public school, district and community in America. As we have tried to demonstrate through a variety of examples, public education distributes to children not only their future but their present as well, which means that public schools cannot avoid taking on the responsibility of deciding what to distribute, to whom, and how.[31]

This is the key governance responsibility of local boards of education in the 21st century. It is the only real reason why they should exist in a modern, technocratic society. Tasks commonly identified as the governance work of school boards, such as visioning, systems thinking, establishing standards, assessing learning and continuous improvement are really management tasks common to virtually all large and complex organizations.[32] These tasks, while important and useful, can be carried out in a variety of ways by a variety of people.

But management tasks do not involve public values, and therefore they do not conflict with one another. We can identify and agree upon the one best way to carry out each of these tasks and thus avoid having to confront competing goals and values that cannot be reconciled easily with one another. Management tasks do not require elected citizens in the same way that the normative and distributive responsibilities of public schools do.

As citizens, we share a collective responsibility to provide the next generation of Americans with a truly democratic education. To do this requires simple equality—a common educational experience toward a common end. But to provide a democratic education for each child means addressing tensions between public and private, and between present and future.

We must navigate between the rights of the family to use education in the best interests of each individual child versus the right of the community to use education in the best interests of all children. And we must navigate between education for the community we are today versus education for the future to create our community of tomorrow.

In Crestwich, for example, public school officials recently announced that the district had become a majority minority school system. Will Crestwich leaders govern education to benefit the residents of today or will they also govern education with one eye on the community of tomorrow? In a democratic society, how we decide is as important as the decisions we make.

Pentimento policy problems offer public school leaders opportunities to help their communities take one step closer to fulfilling the promise of democracy. In closing, we offer to all citizens and public school leaders a version of the Athenian Oath as it might apply today to public schools:

> *We will fight for the ideals and the sacred things of our schools both alone and with many; we will transmit our schools, not only not less, but greater, better, and more beautiful than they were transmitted to us.*

Long live the public in public schools!

NOTES

1. Hochschild, J. L., and Scovronick, N. (2003). *The American dream and the public schools.* New York, NY: Oxford University Press.
2. Ibid.
3. Levin, H. (1999). "The public-private nexus in education." *American Behavioral Scientist, 43, 1,* September, 124–137.
4. Gutmann (1987).
5. Hochschild and Scovronick (2003).
6. Walzer, M. (1983). *Spheres of justice: A defense of pluralism and equality.* New York, NY: Basic Books.
7. Ibid.
8. Ibid.
9. Rawls, J. (1971). *A theory of justice.* Cambridge, MA: Harvard University Press.
10. Walzer, p. 219.
11. Hardin, G. (1968). "The tragedy of the commons." *Science, 162,* 1243–1248.
12. Callan, E. (1997). *Creating citizens.* Oxford: Clarendon Press, p. 172.
13. Gutmann (1987); Levin (1999).
14. Lasch (1995), p. 160.
15. Etzioni, A. (1993). *The spirit of community: The reinvention of American society.* New York, NY: Touchstone, p. 115.
16. Long-time public official and statesman Harlan Cleveland. Quoted in O'Toole (1993), p. 125.
17. Gardner, J. W. (1990). *On leadership.* New York, NY: The Free Press.
18. Ibid.
19. Ibid, p. x.
20. Kemmis, D. (1990). *Community and the politics of place.* Norman, OK: University of Oklahoma Press, p. 67.

21. Bellah, R. N., Madsen, R., Sullivan, W. M., Swidler, A., and Tipton, S. M. (1985). *Habits of the heart: Individualism and commitment in American life.* Berkeley, CA: University of California Press.

22. Kemmis, 1990.

23. Bellah et al., 1985.

24. Ibid.

25. Hui, T. K. (2010b). "We need a fifth vote, Wake schools bloc says." *The News & Observer,* October 25.

26. Rawls.

27. Elshtain, J. B. (1993). *Democracy on trial.* Concord, ON: Anansi Press.

28. Kemmis.

29. Logan Pearsall Smith.

30. National Commission on Excellence in Education, p. 14.

31. Walzer.

32. Gemberling, K. W., Smith, C. W., and Villani, J. S. (2009). *The key work of school boards guidebook,* 2nd ed. Alexandria, VA: National School Boards Association.

Index

About the Authors

Phil Boyle is co-founder of Leading and Governing Associates, a public purpose consulting practice dedicated to preserving democracy and representative government. He works with elected and appointed public officials and business and community leaders to help them engage their constituents and each other in meaningful governance and public policy conversations.

Del Burns served as Superintendent of the Wake County Public School System, the 18th largest in the country. Prior to becoming superintendent, he taught and served as principal in elementary schools and high schools, served as assistant superintendent for curriculum and instruction, associate superintendent for finance and human resources and deputy superintendent. He is a consultant and director of education services for GMK Associates.

CPSIA information can be obtained at www.ICGtesting.com
Printed in the USA
BVOW071422190112

280919BV00002B/1/P

9 781610 485432